W9-BMP-004

*f*P

DRIVING TO DETROIT

★

An Automotive Odyssey

Lesley Hazleton

THE FREE PRESS

New York London Toronto Sydney Singapore

*f*P

THE FREE PRESS

A Division of Simon & Schuster Inc.

1230 Avenue of the Americas

New York, NY 10020

Copyright © 1998 by Lesley Hazleton

All rights reserved, including the right of reproduction

in whole or in part in any form.

THE FREE PRESS *and colophon are trademarks of Simon & Schuster Inc.*

Designed by Jenny Dossin

Manufactured in the United States of America

1   3   5   7   9   10   8   6   4   2

Library of Congress Cataloging-in-Publication Data

Hazleton, Lesley, 1944–

Driving to Detroit : an automotive odyssey / Lesley Hazleton.

p.   cm.

ISBN 0-684-83987-3

1. United States—Description and travel.   2. Hazleton, Lesley, 1944–   —Journeys—

United States.   3. Automobile travel—Social aspects—United States.

4. Automobiles—Social aspects—United States.   5. United States—Social life and

customs—1971–

I. Title.

E169.04.H397   1998

917.304'929—dc21   98-24778

CIP

Excerpt from "Little Gidding" in FOUR QUARTETS, copyright 1943 by T. S. Eliot and renewed 1971 by Esme Valerie Eliot, reprinted by permission of Harcourt Brace & Company. "Cadillac Ranch" by Bruce Springsteen. Copyright © 1980 by Bruce Springsteen. Reprinted by permission.

For Sybil

We shall not cease from exploration

And the end of all our exploring

Will be to arrive where we started

And know the place for the first time.

T. S. ELIOT, Four Quartets

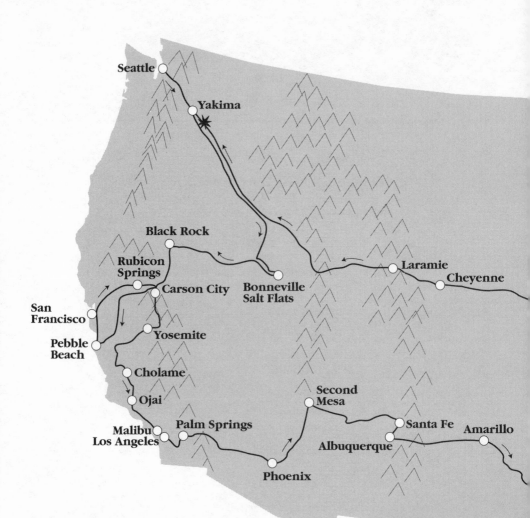

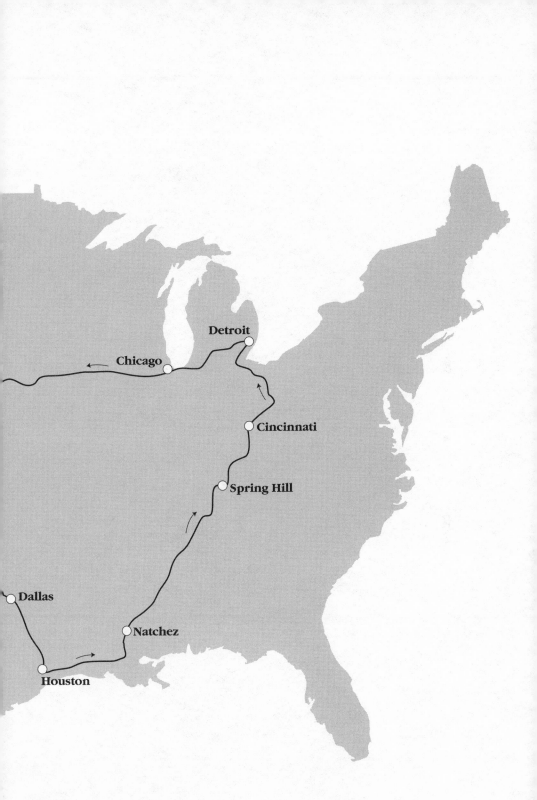

The Route

DRIVING TO DETROIT

Chapter One

It was all Monty Python's fault. I'd been on the road since seven in the morning, and by early evening was still three hours from home. But when I found Terry Gross interviewing the Pythons, one by one, on *Fresh Air*, I knew I could make Seattle that same night. The NPR station somewhere in eastern Washington came in loud and clear, and the program was just what I needed: witty and warm and comfortingly English, a perfect contrast to the winter weather I was driving through.

In the middle of the interview with John Cleese, on the phone from London, Terry asked: "Was your mother really an acrobat?"

There was a pause—you could almost hear Cleese doing a double take—followed by a burst of laughter. It was the only time I've heard him truly laugh. I could make out someone else chortling in the background; so could Terry.

"Who's that?" she asked.

"My shrink," said Cleese. And if she even thought of asking what on earth his shrink was doing there, she forgot it as he confessed that he'd made up that detail about his mother years before out of sheer boredom at having to write yet another of those little press-kit bios. His mother being, in fact, a rather staid English country lady of mild habits and genteel aspirations.

I was fascinated. So deep into Pythonland, you might say, that I paid no attention to the other reality around me, in which the rain I thought I was driving through had already turned to freezing rain, and the plain wet road to a skating rink.

I was in the outside lane, edging past yet another huge semi, when my Ford Expedition began, very slowly, to fishtail. A long, slight, ever-so-gentle sway, really. First to one side, then to the other. I controlled for it—lift off the gas, steer, counter-steer—and for a moment thought I'd managed it. But then I fell behind the semi and got caught in its slipstream. My rear wheels whipped out. I knew what was coming.

I was alone in the car, yet I said the classic last line out loud. The same words uttered by pilots as they go down, and later erased from the published "black box" transcripts:

"Oh, shit."

I said this very slowly and very distinctly, as though it had to register somewhere in the ether, to be placed outside myself as a kind of record that would survive what was about to happen.

The car went into a metallic ballet, pirouetting over the asphalt. I thought the dance had come to a full and very final stop when the concrete median divider appeared right in front of me, and I headed nose-first into it with a resounding thud. But no, the car bounced back onto the ice and began doing pirouettes in the other direction, with me along for the ride like a fairground passenger, until it finally ran out of momentum, stalled, and came to a stop in the center of the roadway.

There was a moment of absolute silence—a very long moment—as I slowly realized that I was alive, and that this fact was entirely due to all those young, good-looking, virile, alert, and superbly skillful truck drivers who had somehow managed to avoid crashing into me as I'd performed in front of them. I was vaguely aware that John Cleese was still talking, but he seemed very far away, and the words all ran into each other as though he were speaking a foreign language. All I could think was that I owed eternal gratitude to the truck drivers, since if they had not been so very young, good-looking, virile, alert, and superbly skillful, I would already be in another kind of eternity.

I was trembling, but this fact didn't quite connect with ideas of shock or fear. A paunchy, gray-haired trucker appeared at the window and asked was I injured. I checked neck, hands, feet, and discovered that thanks to the seat belt and the air bag, I wasn't. Then I checked the car. It had not been so lucky. The front had crushed a foot or so, the steering wheel would only turn to the left, and the radiator was clearly busted. The trucker helped me maneuver off the highway and down a ramp, then disappeared, promising to call the highway patrol. I waited blankly until red and blue lights appeared behind me.

Trooper Ditter really was young and good-looking, and kind too. "Are you all right?" was his first question.

"I would be if I could just stop shaking," I said.

He ushered me out of the freezing rain and into the back of his patrol car. "It's warm in there," he said as he opened the door. I felt protected and cared for.

The first thing Trooper Ditter did was call a tow truck. The second thing he did—"I'm sorry, but I have to ask you a lot of questions"—was begin filling out forms.

When he asked my profession and I said "automotive journalist," he got quite excited.

"That must be great! You mean that's why you've got Michigan plates? Ford just gives you a rig like this to drive around the country? That's the greatest job."

"Yes it is, but I can't believe I was so dumb . . ."

"I bet you've driven every car out there."

"Just about. Oh God, I can't get over the fact that this happened. What a dumb thing to do . . ."

"Ferraris? Lamborghinis? The new Porsche?"

I nodded miserably. "Yes, all of them. How could I do such a dumb thing?"

Poor Trooper Ditter. He'd drawn patrol on the worst evening of the winter, he knew it was going to be a long, long night, and here was someone he could talk cars with. And a woman too! A woman who could normally talk cars for hours on end, though right now the only sentences that would come out of her mouth were ones that included the word "dumb."

I wished I could oblige and start singing the familiar tune of horse-power and handling, but I couldn't. Trooper Ditter was stuck with a bundle of shivering misery.

His report form included a line for "Object Struck." In my case—

State of Washington Police Traffic Collision Report #0029009, dated January 17, 1997—Trooper Ditter wrote "Bridge."

This was both true and untrue. It was the concrete median divider of an overpass on I-82, which stretches north from the Columbia River and through the apple-growing country around Yakima to Ellensberg, where it hooks up with I-90, soars over the Cascades, and then settles down for a straight run in to Seattle.

When the tow truck arrived, it didn't look too promising. In fact it looked as though it would soon be in need of a tow itself. But the freezing rain was pelting down, and reports of more crashes were coming over the radio. Even in my dumbness, I realized I was lucky the truck was here.

Two Mexican men climbed out of the single bench-seat cab. They were from nearby Sunnyside, the kind of small town in southern Washington State where half the greeting cards in the stores are in Spanish, catering to the apple pickers who had come as itinerant workers, and stayed. I could see two young boys inside the cab. "My sons," said the driver proudly. "Six years old and two years old."

The boys stayed in the cab while the driver and his friend, helped by Trooper Ditter, set about hooking up the Expedition. "Where do you want us to take it?" asked the driver.

"The nearest Ford dealer," I said.

"That'll be Yakima," he nodded. "No problem."

The tow truck didn't look as though it could make it as far as Yakima, thirty miles on, even in the best of weather. I'd rather have stayed in the back of Trooper Ditter's cruiser and nursed my misery to sleep. But when the driver said, "Hop in," I did, between the driver and his friend. The six-year-old sat on the friend's lap. I got the two-year-old, who was fast asleep.

Until then I hadn't been able to stop shaking. But there is something about a bundle of sleeping two-year-old that calms you right down. I breathed in the powdery smell of a young child's head, wrapped my arms around him, and felt my limbs relax against his. His presence on my lap was a gift, and I felt an immense gratefulness for it.

I'm not sure how we reached Yakima in that two-wheel-drive truck, over iced-up roads. It must have been a nightmare drive, but I clung dreamily to my bundle of warmth and let the driver and his friend handle it. The child slept on, safe and trusting.

By the time we dropped the truck at the dealer's lot, it was close to nine in the evening, and a long discussion began over which motel to take me to. The driver kept suggesting places; his friend kept nixing them on one account or another.

"Hey, *compadre*, on the way back you have to tell me how come you know so much about the inside of motels," teased the driver. I hoped the six-year-old would be as fast asleep as his brother by then.

They settled finally on the Super Eight. Since I'm generally of the belief that motels with numbers in the name are to be avoided if at all possible, I had my doubts, but these men had been so kind that I was not about to voice them. Besides, I was wrong. The driver's friend knew his motels all right.

The men waited to make sure there was a room for me, helped me in with my bags, and set off for the horrible drive back to Sunnyside. I stood out in the freezing rain waving them off. "Drive carefully," I said. And even as I said it, was surprised at my lack of irony.

Back inside, I asked the desk clerk for the numbers of car rental companies so that I could get home to Seattle the next day. "I'm going there tomorrow morning," said the man who'd checked in ahead of me. "If you like, I can take you."

He went off to make a phone call, and I looked questioningly at the desk clerk. "Oh, you can trust him," she said. "He's the manager of one of the main trucking companies in the West. All his truckers stay here, so he does too. You'll be fine with him."

It was a long drive the next morning—the ice barely melting, the highways only just reopened after being closed through the rest of the night. But Ed, my Good Samaritan, drove well and turned out to be unexpectedly interesting company. Not only was he a trucking executive, but he also had a doctorate in philosophy. And was a preacher, to boot. A charismatic preacher. The kind who lays on hands and heals.

Two more unlikely people to end up involved in transportation would be hard to find: he a philosopher come preacher, and me a former psychologist who at one stage had flirted with the idea of becoming a rabbi. We talked nonstop. About trucking, and about God. About the Middle East, where I'd lived for many years, and about the Midwest, where he'd lived for many years. About medicine and healing, faith and doubt. By the time we pulled up at my place, I felt . . . well, almost healed.

Over the next few weeks, I told the story of my crash again and again, subduing terror by making it familiar. Ed was the perfect figure to appear at the end of the story, related for the most part to staunchly agnostic friends wide-eyed with amusement at such a turn of events. By the time I'd finished, the crash seemed almost the kind you might create if you were finishing off a book about a long cross-country journey. Almost the kind you might want to have if you were listening to the story over the dinner table, with the flames flickering in the wood stove and the wine bottle being passed once more.

And if my listeners were thinking, "What a nice sort of crash to have," they were probably right. No injuries, no other cars involved, helpful truck drivers, a kind cop, and the gift of a two-year-old. What more could you want from a crash?

Nobody asked the hard questions. Neither, for some time, would I.

But then that's the point of such stories. You tell them and retell them to take the sting out of them. It's classic catharsis: the horrified looks when you start, the laughter—uncertain at first, then gaining in confidence—and finally the relief. Not *Hamlet* after all, but *All's Well That Ends Well*.

And if you tell the story well, you lull your audience. Everyone accepts that there's nothing you could have done to avoid that crash. That it really was simply an accident. A matter of chance. Misfortune. A bad break.

Yet for weeks afterward, my classic last words seemed to reverberate in my brain. I'd find myself saying them out loud, trying to get the inflection just right. To re-create the moment. It began to dawn on me that those two words marked my formal entry from one sphere of existence into another. A short song, if you like, of innocence and experience.

The first sphere is the one where Everything Is All Right, where there's good talk on the radio and the car is warm through the miserable weather outside and you're only a few hours from home after a punishing three-day push and you know you're going to make it just fine.

The transition to the second sphere doesn't register for a moment. You sense that it's beginning—that it's already begun. But your adrenaline lags. Your heartbeat takes a moment to catch up. You tell yourself you can handle this, and by the time you know you can't, you're spinning madly out of control.

Like most people who have been in a crash, I was very good at denial. It was a long time until I could finally admit that at the end of five months on the road, and thirteen thousand miles around the country, I had nearly killed myself in freezing rain just three hours' drive from home.

★

It had been midsummer when I'd set out, part of those few weeks when Seattle shucks off its cloud cover and becomes gloriously Mediterranean. That's when my houseboat on Lake Union, just north of downtown, is the ideal place to be.

True, it's really little more than a shack built on a raft, floating on forty feet of water. But ever since the movie *Sleepless in Seattle* was filmed on a rather more solid houseboat one dock over, it has become a most desirable shack. If there's not a true ninety-degree angle anywhere in the house, and if the raft itself lists slightly to one side, so what? It's *my* houseboat—mine and the bank's, that is—and it makes me ridiculously happy.

Friends say it suits me, and they're right. Yet this is curious for someone who has made her living from cars for the past decade. A houseboat dock is an old-fashioned community, far removed from the world of metal, combustion, and grease. Cars are left on land. My neighbors and I walk past each other's open doors, stop in to chat, and swim and kayak together on the lake.

In short, an idyllic existence. Paid for, in my case, by an obsession with automobiles.

My life had a rift going straight down the middle. You could see it clearly in the crazy assortment of magazines that lay around the house. *The New Yorker, Harper's, Atlantic,* and *The New York Review of Books* were all mixed in with *Automotive News, AutoWeek, Car and Driver,* and *Flying* magazine. *Vanity Fair* lay under the latest issue of *Sierra, Outside* on top of *Road and Track.*

It seemed absurd that a card-carrying member of the Sierra Club—a Greenpeace supporter who voted for Ralph Nader in the last presidential election—should have fallen so under the spell of the internal combustion engine as to have abandoned political reporting and been an automotive journalist for the past ten years. Yet as I was aware when I began, this sudden switch in focus on my part was an act of desertion. Almost a repudiation of respectability. Which of course was part of its attraction.

My political and literary friends had been dismayed. How could a writer of repute even dream of entering so disreputable a field? Politics was worthy of serious attention; cars were trivial by comparison. I was wasting time and talent.

I hate to use so hackneyed a word as burn-out for my involvement with the Middle East, but it's an apt one. Sometimes I think every political journalist is a would-be politician with a skin too thin for the real thing. At our keyboards, we get to right the world without having to dirty our fingers with the messy stuff of day-to-day politics. I knew I needed a respite from matters of life and death. Like the fool I am, I thought I could find it in cars.

And for a time, it worked. I felt as if I was riding high on the frothing surf of life instead of being pulled down in its undertow. There was a careless thrill to the ride, and a vast relief at having thrown aside responsibility. Or at least, imagining I had.

I thought at first that I'd become a "car guy" like most of my new-found colleagues. Then I realized I didn't want to be one. Once I'd mastered the details of horsepower and torque, mechanics and technology, I was dismayed by the torrent of clichés in which cars are celebrated—and by the equally fervid torrent in which they're criticized. I wanted to reach deeper. Wanted to journey into the heart, soul, and wallet of the enduring American obsession with the car.

I made forays here and there, flying in and out of story after story over the years, the way journalists do. But the essential story was still missing; there was no continuity. I wanted to see my subject whole, but all I could catch were fragments. And eventually I realized why: If I truly wanted to journey into the passion for cars, I'd need, literally, to drive into it. By its very nature, the journey would have to be a physical one: a journey into America, a road trip intimately bound up with the road itself.

So simple, I thought. Every January, I'd flown from Seattle to the annual bash of hype and glitz that is the Detroit auto show. This year, I'd drive there instead. The long way round. Take a few months, go down the West Coast, through the South, and then up to Detroit. And en route, search out the milestones of automotive obsession.

I'd find people who saw cars as multi-million-dollar vintage art objects, and as custom-made expressions of vibrantly raw sexuality. As machines that can take you as fast as a jet plane on earth, and as the most highly visible consumer status item, clad in sheet metal shinier than gold. As nostalgic memories of youthful pasts, and as the means of escape from everyday life. Sometimes even from life itself.

It seemed a pleasingly elegant idea—a kind of automotive geography of America. Yet even as I planned a rough route, leaving plenty of room for serendipity, I was uncomfortably aware that journeys have a way of creating their own momentum. They take you places and reveal things you never knew you were looking for. Once I put myself on the road, I'd lay myself open to the way experience toys with fine ideas and tosses them into chaos, forcing you deeper and further than you ever wanted.

I wasn't sure if I was ready for this, and as July came to a close, tried not to dwell on it. After all, it was the perfect time for me to make such a trip. I had no professional commitments other than newspaper and magazine columns, which I could write from the road. Back in England, my father was well on the mend after having been severely ill that spring. And Seattle's summer, glorious though it was, would not last much longer. So the second week of August, I paid up all my bills, said goodbye to friends, stopped the newspapers, asked neighbors to pick up my mail. And when I closed the door to my houseboat behind me early one Monday morning, I felt I was closing the door too to my other life, my "real life." All sense of everyday responsibility was being left behind. I was cast loose of my moorings.

There was a fine romance to this: the very American romance of taking to the road. For if the history of the United States is one of settlement, its romance is one of abandoning the settled life.

"Come travel with me!" called Walt Whitman in the nineteenth century.

"The road is life!" yelled Jack Kerouac in the twentieth.

Who was I to resist?

I was beginning the most American of all journeys: cross-country, the whole hog, all the way. And if it was only a couple of years since I'd become the proud possessor of an American passport, so much the better. An immigrant making the journey, even one who had lived here fifteen years until the formality of naturalization, was all the more true to tradition. In more ways than one, I was undertaking a rite of passage.

Not that any of this occupied my mind that first day, as I headed southeast over the Cascades and through the high desert toward Utah and the Bonneville Salt Flats. It was enough to let myself be seduced once more by the hum of the engine, the rolling of the wheels, the almost childlike pleasure of motion.

Within a couple of hours of setting out, I'd slipped easily into the kind of reflectiveness engendered by being on the road. Every detail was somehow heightened in this state, as though my vision had sharpened with my sense of distance. Each hawk wheeling against the blue seemed significant, every play of sunlight on the barren high desert hills. I watched other cars going by, all headed somewhere close. Local traffic, I told myself dismissively. I was in for the long haul, and there was a strange sense of superiority in that. Pointless, but there nonetheless.

A herd of horses galloped over a hillside as I sped past on the highway. They looked free and wild, as though nobody had ever roped or trained or ridden them. They seemed a glimpse of an America that once was. A cowboy country, wide open and lawless. A perfect landscape for the Clint Eastwood image of the cowboy as roamer and drifter, never to be tied down—not by money, not by status, not even by love.

That's the myth of the cowboy, at any rate, built up through an end-less stream of Hollywood westerns. I'd read my Wallace Stegner; I knew how little the myth corresponds to reality. But then myths never do. They have their own rationale, and history's not it. The lone drifter wandering through the vast spaces of the West persists through the end of the twentieth century, with just a stand-in or two. The car becomes the modern equivalent of the horse, and the road is the trail to every-where and nowhere: an American version of the Tao, the path to enlightenment.

Absurdly romantic? Of course, but how else does one start out on a long solo journey? You trust to hope, to a kind of cultivated innocence, and, yes, to the kindness of strangers. Travel alone, and nothing medi-ates between you and the world. This is both terrifying and seductive. It leaves you vulnerable. Places you on the edge. Makes you into a kind of Lone Ranger, a masked stranger on a white horse, which is what I felt like when I stopped in a small town in Idaho and walked into the diner.

The buzz of conversation came to an abrupt halt as the door swung to behind me. All eyes turned my way, checking me out. The questions hung in the air, unspoken but still asked, until I opened my mouth and the mask fell away. They heard the accent, still English after all these years, and then visibly relaxed. A foreigner. *Ça s'explique.*

Outside, my white horse was in fact red, and had wheels instead of legs. But it was a magnificent steed, the kind that drew quiet nods of appreciation from exactly the kind of young men who might otherwise give me trouble, which was partly why I'd chosen it. What I drove would inevitably be part of the journey—what Jonathan Raban astutely called a "narrative vehicle"—and I'd given the matter some thought.

It had to be American: this was an American journey, and my goal was the mecca of American cars. It had to be capable of going off-road, for I knew my own tendency to take off on any road that looks interest-ing, and my dislike for back-tracking if the going gets rough. It had to be comfortable enough to drive for hours at a time, even days at a time if need be. And it had to be big enough for me to stretch out a sleeping bag in the back and get a good night's sleep if I wasn't within reach of a motel.

When Ford offered to loan me the Expedition, a full-size sport-utility based on the F-150 pickup truck, it fit the bill perfectly. Large and imposing, it had four-wheel drive and lots of power. It was also brand new and far too shiny, but these minor disadvantages would quickly mend with time and distance. The dirt would accumulate, and I'd leave it there as a kind of badge of honor. From that very first day, as I headed for Bonneville, I thought of the Expedition as "the truck," and the truck it would remain. Just by looking at it, anyone would be able to tell I was going the distance.

Chapter Two

Nothing had prepared me for the salt.

Cross the border between Nevada and Utah on I-80, go through Wendover, come over the crest of the hill, and the whole of the salt flats is laid out before you—a vast whiteness streaked with black. Not a tree, not a house, not a shrub. *Nada*. Just the Rockies in the distance, and an immense shimmering emptiness between.

I turned off at Exit 4, where a solitary sign for the Bonneville Speedway led me onto a blacktop running by the edge of the salt. A couple of miles on, the road took a sharp curve, and I found myself on a narrow causeway running right out into the salt.

Either side, the flat whiteness was like a huge sheet spread out to dry. The road itself seemed an anomaly, an odd afterthought. Or perhaps humans had been so afraid of the salt they dared not set foot on it, and so laid a thin strip of human industry over this inhuman white waste. And then, after five miles or so, gave up. Because that's where the causeway came to an end. An absolute end.

It had never occurred to me that a road could end as conclusively as this one. Even a dead-end road ends somewhere. It doesn't simply stop in the middle of nowhere, as this one abruptly had: stopped and given up the ghost as if the pavers had run out of asphalt, or decided that the whole idea was a fool's errand and turned back.

I checked my directions, squinting to make out the scribble in my ring-binder notebook: "When road ends, go another mile or two in same direction until berm."

I hadn't thought to question that phrase "when the road ends" when I'd jotted down the directions over the phone. I thought it meant when the asphalt turns into a dirt road. Or at least some kind of marked track. But there was no track. Just salt. Salt in every direction as far as the eye could see.

When a road stops, you stop. I got out, hovered at the edge of the salt, and squinted into the distance. If there was a berm, I couldn't see it. Couldn't even see any tire tracks leading away from the asphalt. All I could see was salt.

I didn't feel lost. Rather, at a loss. This was the place where Malcolm Campbell wowed the world in the Bluebird back in the fifties, driving faster than anyone had thought possible. It was the mecca of all land-speed record challengers. I'd expected at least sheds, an office building, viewing stands—some sign of the presence of so venerable and famed an institution as Bonneville.

But there was nothing. Not so much as an ant. Just an immense solitude.

I stepped gingerly out onto the salt. Bounced up and down to see if it would hold. Stepped out a bit farther, bounced again, and began a little salt dance, hopping and turning with arms spread wide. The surface crackled underfoot, almost like ice-crusted snow. I bent down, dug into it with my finger, and scooped a bit up. It stuck to my skin, sucking moisture out of it. When I wiped my finger on my shirt, crystals stuck to the cotton. And I could smell it now, even in the dry desert air: the familiar sharpness, the faintly acrid tang.

There was nothing to do but trust to my directions, so I took a deep breath and eased the truck out onto the endless whiteness. The surface was firm—as firm as the asphalt had been—and as I gathered confidence and speed, the salt began to take on definition. All around me, it looked like a frozen sea, run up into little riffles every few feet, like water under a light breeze. I seemed to be floating rather than driving. There were none of the usual reference points of driving: no landscape going past, no road being swallowed up under the hood, no landmarks. Just this dream landscape, this eerie emptiness.

Within a couple of minutes, I'd lost sight of the causeway in the rearview mirror. It had been swallowed up by distance. Or by the heat. Or maybe, I thought suddenly, by the salt itself. When I finally saw the berm—no more than a dried mud hump some three feet high rising out of the haze—I was so relieved I didn't even wonder what it was doing here in the middle of the salt.

"Turn left and follow about two miles," my directions said. I followed.

"Berm curves right; follow." I kept following. But now the dream landscape began to transform itself into a nightmare one.

What I'd thought was vast before, now appeared endless, an infinity of whiteness with no horizon. And as I drove on into it, the whiteness welled up in front of me as though it were breathing and growing, gathering force.

"It can't be," I told myself. "It's not really doing that." Yet some more primitive part of me was convinced that beneath the surface, the salt had the power of a great ocean wave welling higher and higher, until finally it would tower over me, break, and engulf me in its shimmering immensity.

I shook my head and the illusion subsided for a moment, only to start rising again. I realized I was holding my breath, as though breathing itself had been rendered redundant, an absurd gesture in the face of such vastness. And still the light shimmered, and the haze hung low, and I could see nothing but salt.

A certain panic began to build inside me. That dreamlike feeling of having stepped into another dimension. The peculiar conviction that what once was, no longer exists, as when someone you love puts on a Halloween mask and you suddenly can't remember their real face any more, need to pull the mask off and reassure yourself that the face you know so well is still there. Everything I came from—the causeway, the interstate, Seattle, home, real life—seemed to have shifted and disappeared, and I had the sudden certainty that even if I were to do a one eighty and drive back as fast as I could, I'd never be able to make my way off the salt.

And then, in the far distance, a vague shape appeared in the haze. It dissolved, then re-formed. I picked up speed. Yes, there was something there, something definite now. Only the clearer it became, the more absurdly fantastic it seemed to be. What I was seeing could have been an encampment out of a Mad Max movie.

It was a huddle of internal combustion. In the center were two large fuel trucks, a long white trailer sprouting a tent along one side, and two shorter trailers. Circled tightly around them were a mix of a dozen or so sport-utilities, pickups, and minivans, as if the survivors of some terrible devastation had hungrily grouped together around the fuel trucks, warding off fear and isolation with the false consolation of gasoline.

I drove up, got out, and saw instantly that things were not going well. There was no hive of activity. A few men in red Chevrolet jumpsuits were hanging around at the edge of the tent. They stared blankly as I walked toward them. No smiles. Not a word.

I had arrived.

★

Inside the tent was The Car. The car Craig Breedlove was convinced he could drive through the sound barrier.

A sleek white cigar of a thing, The Spirit of America was the perfect expression of the old cliché about fast cars—"drives like a missile"—for that was exactly what it looked like: forty-four feet long, the fuselage about three feet high, with huge vertical wings sticking up at the back. Part of the aluminum skin was off, revealing the tubes and valves of a jet engine beneath—a J49 from an F4 Phantom fighter, costing one and a quarter million dollars new, and five thousand dollars surplus. The Spirit of America's engine was surplus.

It is hard to think of a jet engine as a car. True, this one had wheels—a triple wheel in front, and two rear wheels, one under each wing—and a driver's seat was built into the tiny triangular cab stuck on the nose. But it had as much relation to what most people call a car as does the Guggenheim Museum in Bilbao to what most people call a house.

The nakedness of what Breedlove planned to do hit me full force: he was going to pin himself to the front of a jet engine and be propelled to supersonic speed. Like Slim Pickens in *Dr. Strangelove,* hollering and whooping as he rides the bomb to annihilation.

Not that anyone was hollering here, let alone whooping. "He's not going to talk to you. He's not talking to anyone," said one of the crew.

"You tell him I'm here like we agreed on the phone," I persisted.

After a long, silent wait, Breedlove emerged from his trailer. He had a strange gait, almost as though he were walking on air. It was the gait of a dancer, I realized, and it seemed peculiarly at odds with his role as daredevil speed racer.

He looked younger than his age—mid-forties at most. Short and trim in a well-preserved kind of way: pale blue eyes, tank top, running shorts, legs muscled like those of a long-distance runner, full of cords and tendons. His hair was vaguely curly, a peppered mix of dark blond and gray. He must once have been extraordinarily good-looking, but by comparison with the photos I'd seen of him—vaguely noirish, artily dramatic—the reality seemed faded, washed out.

To go after the land-speed record in your twenties is understandable. Nuts, maybe, but put it down to the recklessness and imagined immortality of youth. As any fool can tell you, racing is a game for the young, when the body is so vital, so alive, that it seems impossible that anything could stop it.

But Breedlove was fifty-nine. And he'd already held the land-speed record three times. The last time was twenty-nine years ago. It was broken a couple of months later. And since then, though the record had changed hands a couple of times, it had stayed stubbornly in the same range.

Right now, it stood at 633 mph. Breedlove had not only declared he'd break it, but also upped the ante several notches. Not enough that he'd been the first man to break 400, 500, and 600 mph on land, he now aimed to be the first to break 700 mph, and then go right on through the sound barrier, which on land and at this altitude would be somewhere in the region of 735 mph.

He was surely far more aware of the risks now than when he was young. Was surely conscious of physical frailty, of slower reaction times, decreased stamina, faltering concentration. Yet where most of us become slower but wiser, he seemed determined to be faster and just as unwise.

We shook hands and he smiled limply, never quite looking me in the eye. "I have to work on my bike," he muttered. "Can't get it to start."

There was an oddly lackadaisical inflection to his speech. A sense of merely going though the motions. Maybe it was the heat and the salt-whitened sky. Maybe it was just that he had a cold. Or maybe he just really didn't give a damn.

The blue BMW stood on its kickstand just outside the tent. He scrunched down beside the small boxer engine; I pulled up a crate and sat down on it.

"I suppose you're going to ask why I want to do it," he began warily, working a wrench on a bolt. "Everyone does." He didn't pause for a yes or a no. "The answer is because it's fun, and it's damn interesting. Anything else is just waiting in between. You start out with a blank piece of paper, design a vehicle, find all the components for it, find the facility to build it in and the sponsorship for when you run out of money, and put together a team. Then"—and here for the first time there was a flicker of real life in his face, a kind of wide-eyed boyish look of amazement that he, little Craig Breedlove, should be doing such a thing—"then you go out and drive faster than anyone's ever gone before."

And he gave an oddly flat laugh—not a laugh of despair, but not one of joy either.

He worked his way half under the motorcycle, on his back, spotted something, and swore softly. We began to talk about his family, his voice floating up from under the bike. His mother, he told me, was a chorus girl with ballet training. That explained his walk. His father was a special-effects man in movies, and built the talking car for the old Jerry van Dyke TV series *My Mother the Car*. I wasn't sure quite what that explained, but it did seem to explain something.

In the late fifties, Breedlove worked as a fireman for the city of Costa Mesa, drag-raced on Saturday nights, and poured concrete slabs on his days off. He was twenty-one years old, had three kids, and was struggling to make the house payments. "I was optimistic, and it seemed like I could do anything. I was looking for something I could do to make my mark on the world."

"Why was it so important to make your mark on the world?" I asked, and the answer came back with a simple raw honesty that stunned me.

"I wanted to do something more than just have a job and live a regular life. I felt like if I went on with the fire department, I'd just live my life and die, and nobody would ever know I was here. So I had to do something significant."

That desire lurks in all of us, of course, but most people would be too embarrassed, or too wary—too sophisticated, perhaps—ever to dream of saying it outright. When ambition comes in so purely naked a form, and chooses a goal so patently absurd, there are two options: one is to laugh it down, the other, to watch it unfold in fascination. I had already chosen fascination.

"What's it like to go that kind of speed?" I knew it was a stock question, but I had to ask it. I really wanted to know.

The answer was utterly expected, the same answer any race driver would give: "It's exhilarating. And terrifying at the same time. It's a straight deal—there's no forgiveness for making a mistake." And then he veered into the unexpected: "But you don't have to be very skilled to do it. I don't have one percent of the skill of a Formula One driver. I picked this odd arena because it was the only thing I could do. It works for me."

There was a touching simplicity to this. Whether calculated or not, I wasn't sure. He seemed a modest man, aware of the oddness of his mission, and yet that modesty was somehow unreal. A younger man could pull off this kind of aw-shucks bashfulness, but in a man near sixty, it didn't ring quite true. And yet it made sense that this was simply the one thing Craig Breedlove knew how to do well. Or at least, had known.

He stood up and tried the BMW's starter again. Nothing happened. He winced. It was an odd situation: a man who intended to break the sound barrier, unable to get a motorcycle to start. He stood staring tight-lipped at the bike, as though it were doing this to him on purpose.

I rushed in with another question: "How do you know what will happen when the car goes through the sound barrier?"

He threw the wrench aside and shrugged. "I don't. Nobody does. I think I know what will happen, and I think I can handle it. But this is the point of it all—you're going into uncharted territory."

Let it never be said that I am against the idea of exploring uncharted territory. And God knows there's little enough of it left on this planet. But to shrug it off as uncharted and that's that, seemed to me somewhat cavalier. Foolhardy at best, suicidal at worst. It took all the resources of the American Air Force to break the sound barrier in the air. And several lives until Chuck Yeager succeeded. On the ground, those fearsome shock waves would surely only be compounded. To treat the unknown so carelessly seemed crazily fatalistic. Or childlike.

After all, the sound barrier was part of Breedlove's childhood. He began going for land-speed records the same year Chuck Yeager made history. He broke them in the same decade Tensing and Hillary climbed Everest, which was the last decade there was still the unconquered to be conquered on earth. But now? Now there was something antediluvian about the effort. As antediluvian as the landscape around us.

He banged a fist lightly on the bike's starter button, lips pursed in frustration. "Come on," he said. "I'll give you a guided tour of the car." And turned away from the bike as though he'd already forgotten its existence.

Inside the tent, it was fractionally cooler. A single mechanic was tinkering with some bolts. Breedlove ignored him. Up close to the car, he seemed to relax a little. He shut his eyes a moment, then took a deep, slow breath. "When I want to think," he said, "I climb in and just sit in her." And for the first time, he smiled—really smiled—just thinking of it.

And the moment he said that, I knew I had to get into that seat. I was convinced that if I could sit there, even for just a minute, I'd understand what impelled this man to place such short odds on his life.

The cab was built into the narrow pointed cone attached to the front of the engine. Getting in with any kind of grace would demand the skill of a contortionist. I made do without grace: hoisted myself up, gingerly worked one leg at a time up and over one crossbar and then under another, and lowered myself into the hard plastic seat. This seat had been specially molded to Breedlove's proportions, and though I'm considered slim, his hips were far narrower than mine. I squirmed sideways into it, like an adult trying to seat herself in an infant's highchair.

But finally I was in. And stuck. There was no room to move even a leg or an arm. Straps hung everywhere, and Breedlove showed me how they went—over elbows, wrists, legs, calves, thighs, groin, chest, shoulders, any part of the human anatomy that had the slightest room to jar and break under the stress of giant speed. Control buttons and switches covered every available surface. They filled the side pillars, the ceiling, the panels in front of me. It was like being in the cockpit of a jet fighter, except smaller and tighter.

Breedlove explained each of the controls, but it all became a blur. I was too busy trying to imagine what it would be like with the engine roaring behind me, being propelled through the air: the ground disappearing so fast beneath me I wouldn't even see it; the shuddering so vast I wouldn't be able to tell the difference between ground and sky; the speed so great I'd see nothing but a funneling blur.

I stared ahead, filled with the absolute certainty that this engine was made for the thin air of high altitude, not for the dense, muddied air just inches above the surface of the earth.

I tried to tell myself that what I really wanted to do was drive this thing. For a brief moment, I almost believed it. Never mind that there was no way of "driving" a machine designed to go in a straight line, and nothing more. All you could do, so far as I could make out, was guide it. If you were lucky, you could keep it upright with the wheels in contact with the ground. If you weren't . . .

"Where's the Eject button?" I asked.

"There isn't one."

It occurred to me that Breedlove might as well nail himself to a cross.

"That's it," he said. "Your ass and a hundred gallons of gas."

"That simple, huh?"

"That simple."

★

I can understand the attraction of speed. For a time, I was completely in thrall to it. That was just after I'd begun my life as an automotive journalist, when every automaker who made a fast car was inviting me to drive it on one racetrack or another. Nobody had ever let me behind the wheel of such machines before. And as I learned to handle them, I reveled in a sense of something very pure and clean.

The purity was that of speed. Speed cut away from the danger and recklessness of the shared highway and pared down to a delicious sense of transgression. It was deeply personal, a matter not just of mind but also of body. For the transgression was far more than throwing over the bonds of respectability; driving fast—really fast—is a transgression of the laws of nature.

In a race car, every nerve tells you that you are going faster than the human body was designed for. Acceleration is a sensory intensifier. The effect of the G-force on the body—the pull of acceleration, the pressure of physics against flesh—is massive.

The G-force is essentially dislocation. Being moved out of place. You can find it on a fairground ride, on the roller-coaster or the cyclone, but there it is entirely passive. In a race car, you produce it by your own action. You create it, and you defy it. You deliberately go beyond the boundaries of what is human.

One G is normal gravity, where a 150-pound body weighs precisely that. But at speed, G-force builds. At two G's, you weigh twice as much as normal. At four G's, four times as much. And when you experience it, there is no doubt this force is outside you, and is far stronger than you. It pushes you hard into your seat, pulls you violently to one side or the other in corners, distends the muscles of your face into a ghostly grimace. You are thrown at an unnatural angle to the world.

Hesitate for a moment, and you've had it. The world rushes by in a blur. Your eyes can't keep up. You develop tunnel vision, knowing that things are happening faster than your brain can grasp them. You trust to reflex. The adrenaline pulses through your system: heart races, mouth dries up, eyes open unblinkingly wide, pupils dilate, neck and shoulders strain to keep your head upright and your eyes level with the road.

You lose all sense of time. Split seconds last for minutes; whole minutes rush by in what seems seconds. Distance is only a matter of how far from one corner to another, of judging when to brake, when to turn, when to accelerate out of the corner. And speed? It is no longer an abstract. You are driving in and through it. You have *become* speed, and for as long as you can make it last, it is the only thing in the world.

It's this totality of speed that is so utterly seductive. Like sex, it takes over both body and mind, expanding to the very edges of consciousness and shutting out awareness of all else. Everyday doubts and cares are left behind in the blurred world you're moving through. Whatever the rest of life may be, this is pure. You ride a high, thin line on the outside edge of life, hover on the very edge of death and peer over, then shoot on past it, laughing.

I knew this from driving a mere 175 miles an hour. Formula One drivers go up to 240. I could only try to imagine what 700 miles an hour must be like, and Breedlove had no words for it. But I understood that faraway look in his pale blue eyes. I could see why they never quite made contact. There was only one place he really wanted to be, and that was pinned out on the edge of nothingness. Nothing else had any real meaning for him.

★

The course was barely visible: a smooth, polished strip stretching out from the encampment to the horizon. It was divided into six lanes, apparently by simply drawing a stick in the salt so that the black mud beneath showed through. There were no mileposts, no markers of any kind. Just that strip defined by thin dark lines converging in the flat, featureless distance as though to say, This Way to Infinity.

The team was waiting for a new parachute canister to arrive before doing their first practice run. They'd come all the way up from California only to find that the canister was the wrong size. There were two parachutes on the car, a main one and an auxiliary, and they were Breedlove's only means of braking. The main one was the one whose canister wouldn't fit.

It occurred to me that they should have discovered this before hauling car, trailers, fuel trucks, and crew all the way to the salt desert, but it didn't seem too politic to give voice to this thought. The new canister was due the next morning. Meanwhile there was no reason I couldn't make my own practice run. "Just stay off the left-hand lane," the crew chief told me.

I picked the second lane in from the right. In the distance, a small island of rock floated in the sea of salt. I'd head for that, I decided. I lined up the truck. Put my foot down on the gas. And found myself watching the gauges. There was nothing else to watch.

The needle swung up over a hundred miles an hour. I registered the fact, but didn't feel it. There was none of the excitement that usually comes with going into triple digits. In fact the gauge seemed utterly pointless. It proclaimed speed, yet I had no sensation of it.

I had never imagined that the act of driving could be one of sensory deprivation. But this was the high-speed equivalent of one of those enclosed water tanks used back in the sixties, where you'd float in the warm saline dark and your mind would take self-induced acid trips sparked off by the total lack of external stimulus.

The odometer ticked off the miles. At seven, the course broke up into puddles of dried mud, and the floating island seemed no nearer than it had seven miles back. I stopped and checked my map: it was twenty-eight miles away.

I turned and drove back along the side of the course, the tires scrunching on the crisp unpolished surface. How could there be meaning in speed when there was none in distance? Speed is a function of time and distance, and you have to experience one or the other to get a sense of it. At seven hundred miles an hour, I'd be hurtling along at 342 yards a second. That's more than the length of three football fields a second. And one mile every five seconds. How does the eye even see such speed?

The answer is, it doesn't. Speed is relative. As I cruised back on the salt crust at thirty miles an hour, it felt much the same as had one hundred on the way up. In the lack of anything to hurtle past, speed had become an abstract, reduced to time and distance measures on a laser gun. Some strange kind of Einsteinian inversion seemed to be at work: the faster you went, the less your sense of going fast. These vast white flats made a mockery of the very idea of speed.

They had also made a mockery of Breedlove's plans. He needed eleven miles to make his record attempt: five miles to reach supersonic speed, one measured mile for the record, then five miles to stop. And the course was only seven miles long. There simply wasn't enough room.

This was no longer the same salt as the one where Malcolm Campbell's Bluebird had flown into the history books. The very name Bluebird seemed to resonate now like Rosebud, symbol of a purer time long gone. In the intervening years, the salt had eroded.

Back then, it was up to ten feet deep, as hard and firm as Arctic ice. Now it was just a few inches thick at best, and on parts of the course, barely an inch. Thirty thousand acres, and not eleven consecutive miles of solid salt to be found on them.

Nobody is quite sure why the salt that lay thick and solid for millennia should have eroded so drastically in just a few decades. Some blame the Union Pacific railroad, whose line crosses the flats on a huge dike to the south of the speedway area. Others blame I-80, whose dike was laid down in the sixties, parallel to and slightly north of the railroad line. Yet others blame the salt mines—the potash-mining operation now owned by Reilly Industries, which operates just south of the interstate dike, and has been doing so since 1917. But of course if the idea of human intervention destroying one of the world's great natural wonders is too awful to entertain, there's always climate change to blame. Drier winters don't produce enough runoff water in the spring to flood the flats and allow the salt to precipitate. The fact that a few years of dry winters have happened many times before is conveniently ignored.

Most likely, the construction of I-80 is the immediate culprit. Its timing coincides with the start of major deterioration. Not that the interstate alone would have caused the salt to thin out, but that it turned out to be the tipping point. The salt could withstand the effect of the railroad dike. It could withstand the mining operations. It could shake off a few dry winters. But add in that one factor too many—the interstate dike—and the extra stress tipped the whole ecosystem over into degradation.

In one of those sad, perfect ironies of history, the most famous place in the world for driving cars fast had been destroyed by a highway.

★

Breedlove's fallback place was the Black Rock Desert, a huge dry lake bed in northwestern Nevada, two hundred miles to the west. But he couldn't go there. Not yet, and maybe not at all. A group of five environmental groups had obtained a stay against use of the playa for land-speed racing, and though Breedlove's team had an appeal in, it might take so long to come up for a hearing that the weather would break first, early winter rains turning the hard-packed surface to viscous mud.

Breedlove was grounded. As, for the time being, was I. After the long drive in from Seattle, I wasn't going to leave until I'd seen the car run, if only in practice. I drove back off the salt and checked into a motel in Wendover.

There are two Wendovers, one either side of the state line. The two exist separately in time as well as space, since the state line divides the Pacific Time zone from the Mountain one. I chose to go Mountain on the Utah side, away from the constant pinging of fruit machines in Nevada. But a town divided by both political and temporal geography is inevitably a strange place.

Somewhere around one in the morning, two people ran through the courtyard, feet loud in the nighttime silence. "You fucker, I'll kill you," yelled one of them. He sounded like he meant it. The other said nothing, just kept on running. I heard their panting as they ran past my window, and listened as both gasps and footfalls faded into the night.

Early the next morning, a large paunchy man in his fifties was casting a fishing line over the courtyard swimming pool. He wore a white shirt, business pants, sunglasses, and polished black dress shoes. A can of Coke stood on the concrete beside him. The pool had been drained, and was covered with a blue tarp.

I grabbed some coffee and made for the truck. It looked like it was trying to become a salt sculpture. The stuff was hanging off the fenders in huge gobs, as though I'd spent the day before driving through a Detroit snowstorm. I could practically see the metal corroding before my eyes. Breedlove would have to wait: I headed for the one car wash in town.

It was one of those do-it-yourself kinds where you insert quarters and get measured amounts of soap and water. The kind where you end up washing yourself as thoroughly as the car. It had been some time since I'd last used one, so I made for the instruction sheet on the wall, but half of it had been torn away, and the surviving half was illegible under a layer of graffiti. I asked other drivers there for help, and discovered that I was the only one who spoke English. These were the cleaners and sweepers, maintenance men and kitchen help. They were the night workers, the Mexican immigrants without whom the casinos and motels would grind to a halt. "Sorree," they said sweetly, and used mime to help me figure out the machinery.

The salt clearly loved the underside of the truck. It had adhered and accumulated in more nooks and crannies than I'd thought existed. No matter how hard a spray I used, it would not wash off. Each time I thought I was done, I'd check and find the stuff drying into whiteness again. In frustration I kicked at one of the fenders, and a chunk of salt the size of a cinder block fell to the concrete from somewhere deep under the chassis.

I got down on the concrete, slid under, and took a closer look. Thick salt caked the rubber boots over the joints, the brake lines, the spirals of the MacPherson struts in the wheel wells, the electrical lines inside the bumpers. Oh God, and it wasn't even my car. I began to gouge out great lumps. They fell in my hair and on my face and all around me on the concrete.

An hour and a half later, I was nearly as salt-caked as the truck had been, but at least one of us was clean. I stopped back to the motel to shower and change. The business-clad fisherman was still there, casting his line onto the tarp-covered pool. As before, he seemed neither happy nor unhappy. Just utterly impassive. I shrugged, and headed on out to the salt.

The Spirit of America was out of the tent, and lined up at the beginning of the marked course. A tight knot of people had gathered around it, antlike figures against the flat whiteness. Breedlove was going to make a run.

"Come on," someone said. "Let's drive on out and watch."

"Stay at least three hundred yards away from the course," yelled the crew chief.

"Sure, no problem."

Seven of us piled into one of the team's Chevy Blazers—I wasn't going to volunteer the Expedition and spend another hour and a half cleaning it—and went trundling three miles up the sea-rippled salt. The driver came to a halt right on the edge of the course. Another half-dozen vehicles followed, and pulled up nearby. Nobody said anything about being too close. The crew pulled out walkie-talkies, someone else pulled out an assortment of Cokes and Seven-Ups, and everyone leaned against the vehicles and chatted with studied casualness as the minutes ticked by.

"He's going to hold this one down to three hundred. Just a little practice run."

"But if it feels good, he'll take it higher."

"That what he said?"

"That's what the man said."

"Think he'll make four hundred?"

"Could do, easy."

"He does four hundred today, he could do five hundred tomorrow, be ready to go for the record the day after."

"Yeah, everything goes okay, why not?"

"Wonder what's holding them up."

"Checking that parachute canister again."

"Nah, it's fine. He'll come when he's good and ready."

"That's what it's like, land-speed racing: hurry up and wait."

"And then, vroom!"

We hurried up and waited a good half-hour until a tinny "We're off!" came over the walkie-talkies. Coke and Seven-Up spilled on the salt. We clambered onto the vehicles—roofs, running boards, door sills, trunk lids, anything to gain a bit of height. Some peered through binoculars, others squinted into the white.

"There!"

"Where?"

"There, that cloud."

"What cloud?"

And then in the far distance, you could see it. No wonder it had been so hard to spot at first: the sleek white Spirit of America was now oddly black against the salt, its shape distorted into a bubble. Its size was doubled by its reflection in the shimmering white, and doubled again by the vibration of movement. Strangest of all, there was no sound.

"It's not moving."

"Sure it is. It's still a long way away."

And then it went zooming right past us. One moment it was in the distance to the south; the next, it was gone to the north. We didn't even hear it so much as feel it, the vibration drumming through the air, the familiar roar of a jet engine on its take-off roll, and then . . . *Bap.* Gone. Silence and stillness again.

"Eyeballing it, I'd say that was well over three hundred," one man said.

"Damn close to four," said another.

I wondered how they'd managed to eyeball anything at all. My own eyeballs had seen a sleek white tube emerge from the black bubble, hang in the air before me for the most minutely split second, then dissolve back into a black bubble. It occurred to me that it made no difference if Breedlove was going three, four, or seven hundred miles an hour. If you were watching, all you could register was the fact of speed. There was nothing more to see.

"Oh my God," someone said.

"Oh Christ."

"Jeez."

The black bubble had veered to the left, off the polished surface of the course and into the rough salt. Something was tumbling along behind it, pulling it askew. With excruciating slowness, that something began to expand: the parachute, only half deployed. The bubble skewed around ninety degrees, spraying salt high into the air, and stopped.

We stood frozen, like Lot's wife turned to salt. Nobody said a word. Then the canopy on the driver's compartment edged upward into the thin blue air, and that one small, distant movement broke the spell. We scrambled for the nearest vehicles and went racing up the course.

Breedlove was out of the car by the time we got there. "Parachute malfunction," he muttered. "Get the spare one in, and we'll make another run this afternoon."

He seemed oblivious to the fact that the car was as caked with salt as my truck had been. The stuff was packed tight into the air intakes, under the fenders, everywhere you could see. I knew how much there had to be everywhere you couldn't see. And how hard it would be to get off. There'd be no second run that day.

★

In the evening I sat by my motel-room window and watched the man in the white shirt and black pants casting his line. There was still a can of Coke beside him. I wondered if it was the same one.

From what I'd seen, Breedlove's supersonic goal looked like a fool's quest. Sure he'd be a hero if he succeeded, but he'd be a desperate loner if he failed. And probably a dead one too. Put that way, he stood square in a long line of American romantics, taking things to the extreme. So what if breaking the sound barrier on land was essentially meaningless? When he climbed into the cab of the Spirit of America, he was climbing into his one chance of a place in history.

He'd known fame. The taste of it still lingered on his tongue. The records he'd set when he was in his twenties had changed his life, just as he'd planned. He'd been an international hero, "the fastest man on earth." Yet each time, his record had quickly been broken. The publicity, the respect, the awe in people's eyes when they met him—all gone in a flash of someone else's metal over the salt.

But going supersonic would be his forever. Records could be broken, but nobody else could ever claim to be the one to break the sound barrier on land. This time, the respect and the awe would last. That would be his revenge. Because in his mind, Breedlove was David against Goliath, the little man against all the experts who said it couldn't be done, all the cynics who mocked him.

He had even found his own personal Goliath in the form of Richard Noble, the English entrepreneur who was the current holder of the land-speed record. Noble was also aiming for supersonic speed, and was even now testing his new car in the Jordanian desert, under the aegis of King Hussein.

Noble and Breedlove: the names sounded like the inventions of a third-rate novelist determined to hammer home every inch of stock symbolism. And Breedlove's manager had stepped up to the challenge. He was presenting the race as a classic showdown: *High Noon* at the sound barrier. The cars seemed made to order. Noble's was squat and black, heavy and imposing—a Darth Vader car if there ever was one. Even its name was aggressive: Thrust. Breedlove's smaller, white Spirit of America was an exercise in elegance by comparison.

The whole setup was just too pat, yet something in me resonated to it nevertheless. Noble hadn't designed or built his own car, and he wasn't driving it himself either. He was the money man, with a team of well-paid professionals, the BBC dancing attendance, and big British business behind him. Yet if his car got to the sound barrier first, Richard Noble would be known as the man who did it. Breedlove, on the other hand, had both designed and built his own car, and he'd be the one to drive it too. His scratch team was poorly paid, he was still scrambling for sponsorship, and the only TV interest in sight was from the newly formed SpeedVision cable company, desperate for content.

Noble was in it for the money, Breedlove for love. That was the myth being created. Buy into it, and it was easy to ignore one tiny fly in the ointment, so easy I'd discover it only later: the sound barrier had already been broken on land, and a long time before—back in 1972.

It was in a rocket car, at Edwards Air Force Base, but the driver, a professional drag racer, never entered the record books since he didn't fulfill the land-speed record rules by running twice, once in each direction. He did make the first run, though, and he did break the sound barrier. But even in racing circles, nobody remembers his name. That's how it goes with the kind of history that makes instant headlines. The ink fades, and along with it, memory.

"Bonneville? Fancy your being there," said my father when I called England the next morning to check how he was doing. "That brings back memories. Isn't that where . . . What's his name? Darling," calling to my mother in another room, "what was his name?" Pause. "You know, the one who broke the speed records on the salt flats." Another pause. "No, not here. In America."

"Malcolm Campbell," I said.

"What was that?"

I repeated the name. "Oh yes, I knew I'd remember. They made him a knight, you know: Sir Malcolm Campbell. Now what was the name of the car?"

Chapter Three

"Be all that you can be through Jesus Christ," urged the voice on the radio. The preacher seemed eager for me to improve myself and achieve my potential. I felt my potential was doing quite nicely: I'd left Wendover and the salt flats behind me early that morning, and was making for the champagned headiness of the Pebble Beach *Concours d'Elégance*, down in Monterey, California, where million-dollar cars were considered bargains and the eighteenth hole of the Pebble Beach golf course was as rough as it got.

The preacher's voice echoed tinnily. He had to be broadcasting from his basement, where the cinder-block walls and cement floor played havoc with sound. He'd probably rescued this corner of the rec room from the kids' train sets and his abandoned home-improvement projects, cleaned up the sawdust and the spider webs, and made his voice louder and more powerful than it ever was at home. Or perhaps he wasn't a family man at all, but a misfit loner, holed up in a shack with a radar dish and radio mast out back, trying to save himself by saving the world. An ex-Marine, probably, adopting their recruiting slogan for his quirky combination of old-time religion and new-age psychotherapy. He didn't have the voice of an old man, somewhere in his late thirties or forties, I'd say. Had he already been all that he could be?

I wondered how many hours he broadcast every day. He showed no sign of flagging. He was the only thing on the radio here in northern Nevada, and I suspected he felt an obligation to fill the silence.

I felt obliged to listen to him. I'd determined not to use tapes or the

CD player in the truck, but to let what was on the airwaves be part of wherever I was driving through. If this was God's country, so be it. I let the preacher accompany me for as long as his signal lasted, which turned out to be a good fifty miles, and felt kind of sorry when his voice began to break up into the crackle of distance. I-80 wasn't the same without him.

The interstate is not the best way to see Nevada. It's not the best way to see anywhere. I'd aimed to stay off major highways as much as possible, but if you want to go west from Wendover, you don't have any choice. If I stayed on this road, it would take me straight into San Francisco. I could stop for the night with friends, then head on down to Monterey the next day. That was probably the sensible thing to do, but after four days on the salt flats, I wasn't feeling sensible.

By lunchtime, I'd reached Winnemucca. I turned off the highway, found the town diner, and spread out my maps. There were only three sections of "scenic byway" marked on the state map put out by the Nevada Department of Transportation, and none of them were near here; in fact, one was the Reno ring road. This was odd, since even from the interstate the scenery was stunning: high desert landscape, jagged with granite ridges cooking and cracking in the midday heat. No, I was definitely not ready for the manicured greens of Pebble Beach.

The map showed a dirt road leading almost due west from Winnemucca to Gerlach, at the base of the Black Rock Desert. It went a hundred miles or so straight through the hills, a tempting thin gray line following the hatched line of the Union Pacific railroad. Black Rock: that was where Breedlove intended to make his record attempt once the permits came through. About two minutes was enough to convince myself that it was my reportorial duty to check out the place. Another two minutes revealed that though I could get there by paved road—two or three hours farther down the interstate and then a straight drive north—it was far more in the spirit of the place to take the overland route, even if it would take four times as long.

I filled up on gas for the truck and bottled water for me, and headed for the hills.

The trail was in pretty good shape. Someone had been over it with a bulldozer since the end of the last winter, smoothing out the worst washouts. True, it wasn't made for speed. Fifteen miles an hour seemed about fine, with here and there a cautious first-gear crawl as I picked my way across a gully. Sometimes the trail ran right beside the railbed. Others it veered off into the hills. I preferred the hills.

Twice I saw a herd of antelope off in the distance. But aside from them, and several glimpses of lizards, whatever wildlife roamed these rocks was far too sensible to be out in the afternoon heat. "Mad dogs and Englishmen go out in the midday sun," ran the old Noel Coward song. No mad dogs here, and just one ex-Englishwoman.

My main company was high above me—hawks and golden eagles wheeling against the blue. Late in the day, a pair of eagles took a shine to the gleaming metal of the truck and began circling low overhead as if it were a huge playmate. They flew just ahead of me, huge wings flashing gold as they turned into the lowering sun, becoming black silhouettes as they banked away from it. My desert escorts, mute and beautiful.

I could say that I was suffused with a sense of natural wonder, and this would be true. I was venturing into wild, abandoned country, and the eagles seemed to be welcoming me into their domain. Yet I was driving this trail courtesy of the Union Pacific, which clearly kept it up in order to service the track. And a moment's sober reflection told me it wasn't me who had attracted the eagles, but the gleam of shiny red metal. I could get as naturalist as I wanted, but the fact was that I was out here, in this clean, primeval landscape, thanks to forty thousand dollars worth of machinery that was burning hydrocarbons and spewing their residue into the clean desert air at a four-wheel-drive rate of one gallon every ten miles—and one every five miles when I was down in first or second gear.

It occurred to me that I was surely the only person ever to have driven this trail with high heels and evening dress in the back of her truck, alongside the sleeping bag and food supplies. For a moment I had a horrible flash of being a real-life commercial for the outback-to-opera advertising line for sport-utilities. To see oneself as an ad-man's dream is not a pleasant experience. I pushed aside such thoughts for the moment; there'd be time enough for them to come back and haunt me.

As the sun lowered, I scrambled up a high rock outcropping to watch. I sat shivering with that sudden sense of loss that comes each time the comforting red ball disappears over an open landscape—a primitive feeling that the sun has died for the day, disappeared and left the world to the lonely chill of night. And when the warm colors of sunset faded into the cold, bleak blue that comes just before dark, I knew without a doubt that I was a complete fool. Fifty miles from anywhere by a dirt track on which I'd seen not another living soul, I was placing a lot of trust in the Expedition, and as much again in my own ability to handle the rough spots on the trail. If anything happened, I faced either a long wait or a long walk out. Or I could just sit by the railroad track and wave a red jacket at a train as it came close. This last thought cheered me immensely.

But if a train came through some time in the night, I didn't hear it. Bedded down in the back of the truck, I woke only to the pale whistle of the pre-dawn wind. I saddled up after sunrise, and rode on down the trail, with more eagles riding shotgun high above. A couple of hours later, the whole of the Black Rock Desert spread out below me, a vast four-hundred-square-mile playa, flat, dry, and empty. I was driving the length of it, and it wasn't until midday that I came down the side of a hill toward Gerlach, close up against the eastern rim of the Sierras. It looked like one of the most beautiful towns in creation, with the first trees I'd seen in close on a week.

Gerlach was tiny—population 251, according to my map—but it had a very large diner. "Bruno's Country Club, Motel, Cafe, Casino, and Saloon," said the sign. Bruno had a good sense of humor. I brought my caffeine level up to normal and downed a burger as the waitress filled me in on the local news. It seemed the lawsuit against use of the playa had been initiated to try to prevent the Burning Man event from being held here again.

I'd heard about Burning Man: a kind of new-age, old-hippy pagan festival fueled by drugs, alcohol, and crystals, where body paint and tattoos substituted for clothing, and hard-rock music for the desert silence. The high point of the two-day event was a ritual burning of a forty-foot effigy, with thousands of celebrants dancing around the bonfire, and this detail was what seemed to concern the festival's critics the most: the ancient biblical fear of idol worship.

The general feeling in the diner was far more tolerant than I'd expected. The environment was just being used as an excuse, it seemed. "It's four hundred square miles of flat nothing," declared a grizzle-faced old-timer who was apparently ensconced in his window booth for the day. "Those people down in Reno are darn fools. There's nothing any-one could do in a weekend that would make the blindest bit of differ-ence to that there desert." And as though amazed at having produced so voluminous a sentence, he sank back into contemplation of his beer.

"Those people down in Reno" were a local environmental organiza-tion who'd initiated the appeal against allowing the Burning Man event to be held on federal land—and along with it, any land-speed record attempt. "The desert should be a place of solitude," wrote the woman who drafted the appeal. And as I left the diner and headed for the playa, I sympathized with her.

I also like my solitude. I have no interest in dancing naked around a burning effigy, no matter how good the drugs are. And now that I was away from the single-minded pursuit of speed on the salt flats, I couldn't see much point in that either. But the desert has always been used for strange purposes. From the tribes of Israel wandering in exodus to Wild West stories of hunted desperadoes and desperate miners, it has at-tracted the outcasts of society. Burning Man celebrants and speed-obsessed racers were only the modern variants of the same caste. The desert would survive them.

Especially this desert. Close to the edge, the truck kicked up a vast trail of dust, billowing behind me for a good couple of miles like a giant vapor trail. But as I drove on toward the center, the dust disappeared. The mud had been burned smooth and solid by sun and heat. It barely held the tire tracks of other vehicles that had been here before me. I looked back, and couldn't even see my own. I was driving free and clean. Within a few minutes, Gerlach had disappeared from view in my rearview mirror. There was just me, the truck, and the lake bed, hemmed around by mountains falling almost vertically into the dried mud.

It felt like a vast playground, safely within limits, and I began to play.

I did figures of eights and tight three sixties. Slaloms and quarter-mile dashes. All the things a teenager might do in such a place. But it wasn't until I turned around to head back to Gerlach that I saw another vehicle.

I had no idea where it had come from. I could have sworn it hadn't been there before, but it must have been—this lake bed so big that a single vehicle could be lost from view on it. There it was, smack in the middle of the playa, and so far as I could make out, not moving. I headed toward it; perhaps somebody needed help.

It was a well-traveled Ford Bronco, with its tailgate up. A man and a woman, both in their late twenties, stood under the tailgate. I pulled up nearby. "Are you okay? Do you need a tow?"

"Oh we're fine," said the man, smiling. "We're just letting off rockets."

He said this like it was the most normal thing to do. "Rockets?" I repeated stupidly.

"Yes. Didn't you see the one we just shot off? It was a beauty."

I'd been too busy doing figure eights. "What kind of rockets?" I asked, and then somehow I was out of the truck and under the tailgate with them and he was showing me all the paraphernalia of the amateur experimental rocketrist. I wasn't sure if rocketrist was quite the right word. Rocketeer kept coming to mind, and then, absurdly, Rockette . . .

"We've shot off two already," he was saying, "but we still have one to go. If you like, you can hang around and watch."

I liked. "Harry Cole," he said, offering his hand. "Nancy Cole," she said offering hers. They were from Carson City, Nevada, where he worked as a corrections officer, and they seemed quite sane and pleasant aside from the fact that they were launching rockets in the middle of the desert.

Harry reached into the back of the Bronco and lifted out the last of his three babies, holding it level on two upraised hands like a sacrificial offering. I was suitably impressed. It was white and slim, about three feet high, with big fins around the base—a miniature of a real live NASA rocket. He placed it upright on the ground and I took a step backward. "Don't worry," he said. "It's not armed yet."

I took another step backward.

He explained the workings and the fuel to me as he prepared the rocket for launching. Most of it went over my head, but I made out that it was powered by composite rocket fuel, and that though it cost him only forty dollars to make, it had taken three weeks of his time. It weighed three pounds, he said. "If they weigh over 3.3 pounds, you need a special license from the FAA to launch them. You should see some of the monsters at the rocketry festivals. They go up to ten thousand feet."

"Rocketry festivals?"

"Oh yes. Hundreds of us congregate here certain weekends. It's a good family atmosphere. People bring their kids and set up their lawn-chairs, and everyone cooks out. Plus we can launch rockets here without disturbing anyone. It's a peaceful place for rockets."

I nodded unwillingly, trying to get my mind around the idea of such a thing as a peaceful place for rockets. Maybe my Middle East past had biased me. When you've had rockets shot at you, it's hard to think of them as good clean family fun.

Harry finished with his tinkering, stood back, and offered me the black control box: "Since you're the visitor, would you like the honor?"

It had taken him three weeks to make this thing, and he was offering me the culminating moment. I really didn't want it, but when an honor is offered, it is churlish to refuse. I felt slightly sick as I took the box and Harry explained the controls. They seemed horribly simple: flick a switch to arm the rocket, then press a big red button to launch it.

I took a deep breath and flicked the switch. The little rocket gleamed, whitely menacing, ten yards in front of me. "Do I count down?" I asked.

"If you like."

I started the countdown. "Ten, nine, eight, seven," aloud into the empty desert air, feeling like an absolute fool. "Six, five, four," in full awareness of the sheer absurdity of my standing here doing this. "Three, two," the numbers coming slowly now. "One"—a long pause—"Fire." I made a determined effort to keep my eyes open, and pressed the big red button.

And my God, it was wonderful! That little thing behaved just like a big grown-up rocket. Smoke belched from beneath it in billowing clouds as it shuddered, roared, and then very slowly began to rise into the air. The smoke dissolved, leaving just pure flame spouting between the fins, and the little white rocket gained momentum, gathering speed and height until it reached a point where it seemed to leap off into the sky, leaving me standing there on the ground, head turned up, mouth open, control box hanging by my side, in total awe at what I had wrought.

I know something came out of my mouth. I heard someone say "Ooh" and "Aah" and "Ohmygod" and vaguely realized it had to be me, but suddenly I didn't know who this "me" was. Something had gone click in my brain, and my normal pacifist tree-hugging self had been transformed into a Dr. Strangelove apparition that wanted nothing more than to yell and shriek and yahoo and yeehaw at having unleashed such power.

The rocket hovered at the apex of its arc, then I blinked in surprise as it put out a tiny Day-Glo pink parachute and began to sail slowly back to earth.

"That was three thousand feet," said Harry.

"That was incredible," said I.

Power, I kept thinking. It's all about power, about the use of machines and fuels to gain it, and cover the fact of our real powerlessness. There was the power of a huge engine, all those horses at the touch of a toe or a fingertip. The power of making something belch smoke and fire and then soar up into the sky. The power of being at the controls of a fighter plane, as I once was, taking off in sharp chandelles in pure defiance of both physical and mental gravity. The kind of power that takes over the senses and dulls the thinking part of you that knows its uses.

Harry and Nancy were so—how can I explain this?—so very normal. Nice, good people, a delight to be with, nothing in the slightest bit odd about them. Except for his hobby.

"We do have esoteric interests," he admitted.

"You want to see what I'm into?" said Nancy brightly. Something in her tone told me I really didn't want to know, but she was already moving to the front of the Bronco to show me. She reached in and emerged waving a magazine. "Here," she said, and thrust it into my hand.

I was holding a copy of *Reptiles,* with a glamor cover photo of a boa constrictor.

"You have a boa?" I said very tentatively.

She nodded, with a sweet smile. "A ball python. His name is Sam."

"I hope you don't have kids."

She grinned. "None of my own, but you could say I have twenty of them. I teach third grade at a school in South Lake Tahoe, just over the border from Nevada."

And as she said that, her eyes lit up. "Hey, I have an idea," she said.

"So long as it doesn't involve snakes . . ."

"No, better than that." Her eyes gleamed as the idea took shape. "How would you like to correspond with my third-grade class? Send them postcards from everywhere you go on this journey you're making. Then we can follow you around the country. We can put up a big wall map and pin the postcards to wherever you are. They can learn geography that way, and writing, and journalism, and cars. What do you think?"

"Me as a pedagogical tool?"

"Mmhm!" She was beaming now, full of enthusiasm.

Even as I thought about it, I envied the children she taught. With a teacher as open and innovative as this, they were getting a great head start. I knew that you don't start a correspondence with twenty eight-year-olds unless you intend to continue it. There was a certain obligation involved here. But there was also really no way to say no.

"So long as the kids write me first," I said. "It's up to them to start."

"Done deal." We shook hands on it. "Do you want to be called Ms., Mrs., or Miss Hazleton?"

The sudden formality jarred. "None of the above," I said. "Plain Lesley will do just fine."

"That's great," she said. "We can play a game called 'Where's Lesley now?'"

The idea both disconcerted and delighted me. At the start of a determinedly solo journey, I had managed to pick up twenty long-distance passengers. The middle of a four-hundred-mile dry lake bed was not exactly where I'd expected to be transformed into a pedagogical tool, but now that I'd agreed, it sounded just fine.

We ended up hugging goodbye, and I set off southward down the one paved road out of Gerlach, ready to face both the glitz of Pebble Beach and, after it, the lens of a movie-maker making a television documentary about cars. As I drove past Pyramid Lake and turned onto the interstate toward San Francisco, I kept thinking of that moment when I'd pressed the button—when I'd sent the rocket surging into the air, and briefly, ecstatically, felt its power as my own. With the truck set on cruise control and my driving mind on automatic, the years disappeared, and I was back to that first moment when mechanical power became mine. The moment of realization that I could engage in auto-motion. That I could move myself.

★

"Just put your foot down," he said.

"It *is* down."

"The other one, the right one."

The engine revved crazily. An awful lot of noise for zero movement. "Nothing's happening."

"No, of course not, I told you, you have to lift your left foot at the same time."

"Like this?"

The car jumped a few inches forward, and stalled.

"No, no, not like that." He clutched at the dashboard, as though trying to save the car from whatever damage I was about to inflict on it. "Why don't you listen?"

"I *am* listening."

"You're not. I explained it to you three times already."

"I *am.*"

Always talking in italics to my father. Trying to make him hear me, recognize me as an existence apart from his making. Trying to assert myself as separate from him. My own sixteen-year-old, not girl, not virgin any longer, though he didn't know that. Sexually a woman, in his eyes "always my little girl."

Over thirty years later, he'd say the same thing to me, across eight thousand miles of phone line, as I told him about my plans to drive around the States. Telling him not to worry, I'd be fine, with a breezy assurance that I was far from feeling inside, the dank loneliness of motel-room nights already haunting my imagination.

"But we do worry about you, you know. For us, you'll always be our little girl." The phrase that drove me crazy all through my teens and twenties. That now just made me smile and sigh: just another of those stock family phrases, a kind of familiar tic.

No, he couldn't let go of his little girl. Like most fathers, perhaps. Yet by teaching me to drive, he was giving me the means to drive away from him. Handing his little girl the keys.

"Take it easy, now. Lift your left foot very gently off the clutch, and at the same time put your right foot very gently down on the accelerator."

The car stalled again.

"*Gently*, I said!"

A certain satisfaction in forcing him too into italics. But a far greater sense of frustration. Driving a car seemed a balancing act I'd never be able to muster.

His right hand gripped the dash now, his left the edge of the passenger seat. Nervous about teaching me, and rightly so, but not for the reasons he thought. Not a born teacher, his teaching me was an attempt to retain control, even as he handed it away.

"Try it again, Lesley. *Slowly*."

The knuckles white on hands reddened from constant washing after each patient. He'd already taken the precaution of keeping me out of his own car—the car in which he made his rounds, went out on midnight emergency calls. Instead, he taught me in my mother's car. The second-best car.

His system was simple: he'd buy a new car, always an appropriately sensible sedan with a trunk for his doctor's cases and patient records, drive it for three years, then hand it down to my mother. She never got any choice about what car she drove. Though I know now that a little MG would have suited her just fine.

She was making do at the time with a Triumph Herald, which as I remember it did have a certain style, my father's anxieties about propriety notwithstanding. Or perhaps the style came from the way I drove it, or the places I drove it to. For of course, the moment I got my license, I'd use the car to go meet my boyfriend on secret assignations down by the river, where we'd make love. At the time, the car was the means to sex, and sex was the key to adulthood, all the more delicious because it was forbidden. But now I'm not sure that the car wasn't by far the larger step into adulthood.

And it was my father who sat beside me while I took that first step. Not exactly encouraging me—in fact, restraining himself from screaming at me—but there nonetheless, determined that if his little girl was going to expose herself to the dangers of the road, then it would be, at least initially, under his guidance.

Perhaps, I think now, he was simply a realist. He saw the inevitable bearing down on him, had resigned himself to it, and was merely fighting a symbolic rearguard action.

I hadn't felt so clumsy since I'd been eight years old, "all arms and legs," as my mother kept saying. That was when she began to call me "Legs," a nickname that never struck me as odd until quite recently, when she was visiting me in Seattle, and, old custom reasserting itself, called me Legs in front of a friend. He looked up in benign but sharp amusement: "What was the name of that gangster Thomas Kennedy wrote about?" he asked.

"Of course," I said. "Legs Diamond." An old childhood name suddenly became romantic, almost dangerous.

I tried once more to get legs and arms to work in harmony. Shift into first, lift gently off the clutch, at the same time press gently down on the accelerator . . .

And it happened.

Hemingway's "did the earth move for you?" had nothing on how I felt at the very moment when, under my control, in response to my arms, my legs, the Triumph Herald moved. The whole ton and a half of it went hurtling down the street for a good twenty yards, with me in the driver's seat yelling, "It's moving! Its moving!" So excited by the very fact of what I'd wrought that it didn't even occur to me to steer.

"Change gears!" I vaguely heard my father's voice through my excitement, but the words carried no meaning. "And steer, for God's sake! You're going off the road . . ."

What did I care where I was going? The very fact of automotion suffused the whole of my brain, left no room for such minor considerations as direction. The car hit the edge of the raised sidewalk, made as though to climb it, gave up on the idea, and with a big lurch, stalled.

"Now look what you've done," my father said.

But I was looking, and it was beautiful.

"Why didn't you change up into second gear? What's the use of my trying to teach you to drive if you won't listen to a thing I say?"

His words still came from very far away. The foot or so of space between us had, in those few seconds, opened into a space as vast and wide as I could ever hope to drive. There was the length of all the world's roads between us, all the driving I would ever do. The keys to the car—and I knew this without even having to think it—were the keys to my life.

So far as my father was concerned, he was just teaching me how to drive. Yet unwittingly, or at least so it seems now, he was teaching me far more. It would have been ideal if we had been able to acknowledge this, one of those perfect father-daughter things that exist only in books with sepia- and pastel-tinted photographs and lots of haze, the kind of books presented on Father's Day as though the recipient could ever live up to the glossy, air-brushed images of wishful thinking.

But this was real life, and we stuck to our roles: protective father, rebellious daughter. He kept on talking about what I should and shouldn't be doing, and complaining that I wasn't listening. And he was right. In the three or four seconds between engaging the gear and stalling the engine, I had had the clearest vision, fully formed, of myself hurtling headlong down the road, laughing into the wind, heading into the long distance of my own life.

For the first time, I had experienced power. It wasn't the power of the weak—the manipulative power of tears or the sulky teenage power of stubborn refusal and sullen silence. Nor was it the power to control and manipulate others, a power I would later discover in an inspired few minutes of pure demagoguery here and there—at a political demonstration or a conference or a reading—but which has always made me feel, beyond the exhilaration, somewhat shamed.

No, this was power plain and simple, in it purest form. Brute mechanical power, at my disposal. Literally, at my feet. And even then, I knew with absolute certainty that there was nothing at all plain or simple about it.

Chapter Four

Within a week of leaving Bonneville, I was lolling in the lap of luxury. Specifically, I was lolling in the driver's seat of a pale yellow convertible made years before I was born, waiting for the film crew's camera to start. I lolled because the car demanded it. It brought out something louche in me, cradling me into a decadent slouch. My eyes were half-closed, dreamy as with a dose of morphine.

I rolled down the window so that I could stroke the top of the door. The metal begged to be touched. It had a sensuously chiseled sleekness, like the high cheekbones of a supermodel. I was in love with this car. This car was in love with me.

I was also exhausted. It was getting on for ten at night, and after a full day of filming, all I wanted was to curl up on the plush bench seat and sleep. We'd been on the go since seven in the morning, and had finally made our last stop of the day, the Blackhawk Museum in Danville, just east of San Francisco, four hours behind schedule.

There was a certain unreality to Danville: the moneyed luxury of a place where everything was so very new that its claim to existence felt awkwardly tenuous. Buildings, lawns, even trees were too bright, too manicured, too perfect. There hadn't been time enough to wear down the sharp edges of the shaping human hand and give at least the illusion of permanence. And the contrast with the salt flats, still shimmering in my memory, only strengthened the sense of dislocation.

The museum sat imposingly on top of an artificial hill, the architectural equivalent of a Ferrari or a Lamborghini: too obvious, too eager to stand out. We had the run of the place—the director, cameraman, soundman, production manager, and me—and as we roamed around, our voices echoed, bouncing coldly off the black marble floors. We were, I realized, in a modernistic mausoleum filled with metal ghosts.

Even as I admired the beautiful French cars imprisoned up on the second floor—the Bugattis and Delages and Delahayes and Talbots—I pitied them. Every line of these cars, every swoop and angle, proclaimed that they were made to move, and move fast. Immobile, they'd been rendered into oxymorons. I wanted to rescue them from their enforced immobility, just as when I go to a zoo I want to open up the aviaries and let the birds fly, even though I know they'll die out in the open, unable to fend for themselves.

"Which one do you want, Lesley? Pick any one," urged Ned Judge, the director.

I knew what he meant, but for a moment I suspended disbelief and imagined that he'd buy me any one I wanted and I'd get to drive it off into the star-studded night. A frisson of pure delight went through me, as though I were a movie star being cossetted by her studio head. I felt quite giddy and girlish.

"Any of the French ones," I said, drawn as always to the clean sharp lines, hard-edged even in their swooping elegance. These were the salon cars of the thirties, the time when the rich and titled ordered their cars from coach builders whose names—Saoutchik, Figoni and Falaschi, Guillare, Letourneur and Marchand—were as famed as those of their clients. Fenders bulged and flared, with sweeping tendrils of chrome highlighting their lines. Roofs arched and dived, making metal athletically fluid. These cars were designed to give visual form to the idea of speed, still flagrantly exotic and unabashedly sensuous.

But the air-conditioning system on the second floor was humming too loud for the microphones. I had to make do instead with the most French of the cars downstairs—the pale yellow 1939 Packard convertible. It was the first Hollywood Darrin, according to the placard beside it: French-designed but Hollywood-built, and now valued somewhere in the region of a half million dollars.

I settled in, leaned back, and waited for the camera—"Ready for my close-up, Mr. Preminger"—lazily stroking the door all the while. The unreality of Danville, of the museum, of a half-million-dollar car, plus the exhaustion, all combined to compound my feeling of dreamy languor.

Perhaps Ned saw this. As the camera rolled toward me on a dolly, he crouched beside the cameraman and said: "Who do you think this car was made for, Lesley—a man or a woman?"

"A woman," I said dreamily. "Definitely a woman." The camera was rolling, and as though at its bidding, that woman began to come into being. "She was an actress," I continued, dreamier still. "Not young, not innocent. Old enough to have lived life, to have acquired experience. And taste too. Thirty years old, she was, with long flowing curls, the kind of hair you see in pre-Raphaelite paintings. It fell over her shoulders and trailed over the back of the seat as she drove. Red hair—a deep russet red that caught the sunlight as she moved."

And I tossed my head to let the tresses settle attractively over my shoulders and the back of the seat. The gesture was second nature, born of the memory of what it was like to have long hair.

I needed no prompting now. "She was French," I continued, "and she still had a slight accent." My voice fell into the accent as I spoke. "She was known for having many lovers, men she would pick and love as she pleased. And then leave as she pleased—how you say?—at whim. Because each time, she would tire of them. And when she did, she would leave them standing in the dust as she drove off at a hundred miles an hour to the next adventure that waited for her, tossing her long silk scarf over her shoulder as she went . . ."

And I tossed the silk scarf I was wearing over my shoulder, letting the end of it hang over the windowsill. In my mind, I was already in motion, kicking up dust as I took off into the sunset. For a brief moment, I half wondered if the end of my scarf would get caught in the spokes of the rear wheel, like Isadora Duncan's. But such caution was unworthy of this splendid redhead, and I put it out of mind.

The camera came level with me, and I spoke straight into it. "And this car is as beautiful as the day it was made," I heard myself saying. "And the woman it was made for—is dead."

"Wonderful," Ned breathed, and cut the camera.

"Spooky," said the production manager, shaking herself as though a ghost had just walked over her grave. "Why would she be dead?"

"There is no why," I said with perfect conviction. "She is."

The scene never made the final cut.

★

The best rational explanation I can find for this fugue state is that for the past few days, I'd been surrounded by talk of who had once owned which car. In collector car circles, this is known as "provenance," and it had been one of the main topics of conversation at the Pebble Beach *Concours d'Elégance,* the long weekend that is to the world of vintage cars what Ascot and Saratoga are to the world of horses.

For a rare few days, two hundred of the most elegant and valuable cars in the world—cars with hood ornaments made of Lalique glass, with seats covered in the skins of pythons, with exotic wood dashboards and brass and silver detailing—were gathered together in defiance of rust and time. Painstakingly restored to a state boasted as "better than new," they had been surrendered by their owners to brave the stares of other collectors and the prying eyes of judges, not to speak of the rigors of three days and two nights spent outside a climate-controlled environment, exposed to the salty mists and afternoon sun of the eighteenth green of the famed Pebble Beach golf course.

Certain names kept cropping up as I wandered from the Chrysler hospitality suite to the Mercedes one, greeting friends and acquaintances, and graciously allowing myself to be plied with champagne and chocolate-dipped strawberries and superb Italian food, interlaced with the occasional shot of espresso and perfumed by wafting smoke from the lavish abundance of Cuban cigars. The Aga Khan, Rita Hayworth, Dean Martin, Dolores del Rio, Steve McQueen, Lucille Ball, the Prince of Nepal . . . I didn't know there had *been* a Prince of Nepal.

The names were used to paint an aura of fabulously moneyed glamour around the cars they had once owned. In the casual way the names tripped off modern tongues, you could glimpse the naive faith that some of that glamour would transfer, as though by osmosis, to the doctors and lawyers and businessmen who now owned the cars.

The whole setting of Pebble Beach was designed to boost that faith. On the terraces of the suites in the Lodge, we could sit and watch a fantasy world: hundreds of millionaires picnicking on the grass in white suits and panama hats, cartwheel chapeaux and swirling summer dresses and tulle scarfs and parasols, cravats and ascots and even spats. By the big cypress tree artfully placed in the center of our view, three Turkish-style tents advertised CHAMPAGNE CIGARS MARTINI, and beyond them were the hundreds of millions of dollars worth of cars, row upon row of them parked on the perfect green sod, with the rocky bay and the ocean beyond as backdrop. It all had an English garden-party kind of perfection, as in a Kenneth Branagh/Emma Thompson movie, with everyone being ever so bright and gay.

But it didn't quite work. Despite the costumes and the perfect setting, there was a forced feeling to the gaiety. The glamour, like the cars, was from another era, long before the intrusion of the telephoto lens had reduced the mythic power of glamour to the democratic voyeurism of *Lifestyles of the Rich and Famous.* And its mantle sat uncomfortably on the shoulders of newly prosperous men and women who looked as though they'd be far more comfortable playing golf.

Down on the green, a local television broadcaster was posed in front of a big black Duesenberg, microphone in hand, talking into the camera with a weatherman's earnestness. "Many of these cars are worth millions," he was saying, "cars like this one." He half-turned, cheating to the camera.

"This Duesenberg belongs to late-night talk-show host Jay Leno, a big collector of exotic cars. I don't know if Jay has arrived here yet, but if we can find him for you, we'll ask him . . ."

And his voice trailed off as for the first time, he actually looked at the car. The glazed bonhomie of his face changed suddenly to intense fascination. He forgot about cheating to the camera, and peered in close to the gleaming metal.

"Look! Look at this, folks. Take a close look at the shine on this car.

I don't know if the camera can see it, but I can actually see my reflection in it! Look at that, I can see myself in this car!"

And for a long moment, oblivious to the fact that he was on air, he stood lost in adoration of his own image.

The arrival of the judges put an end to this idyll of self-love. I knew one of them, a former colleague, and tagged along beside him, wondering aloud if the people who bought and restored these cars saw something of their own image in them. "After all," I said, "you could argue that the long, squared shape of a Duesenberg's hood is a perfect reflection of Jay Leno's jaw."

He laughed, and set about setting me right. For the fact was that there was hard cash behind all this staged gaiety. Each of these millionaires wanted more than anything else in the world for his car to win one of the twenty-six "in class" awards, or one of the sixteen "special awards," or even, if the gods and the judges smiled on him, the award for best in the whole show. For months, often years, he'd been on tenterhooks, visiting the professional restorer he'd hired, calling him at all hours, paying bill after bill. Bills he didn't understand. Bills he'd never expected. Bills for things he never imagined could be done to a car. He'd learned to speak the lingo with the restorer, to rejoice with him when he'd found an original part in a Paris junkyard, to agree that twenty coats of paint, each thrice hand-rubbed, were indeed infinitely better than nineteen. The car had damn near ruled his life for all this time, and now was the moment of truth. Now the judges would pore over every nook and cranny, stick their noses under the fenders and down into the innards of the engine, and make the little marks in their notebooks for "authenticity" and "correctness."

Authentic? Correct? His car was both, and more. It was better than new. Rebuilt better than it was the day it came out of the artisan's shop where it was first made. None of those supposedly charming idiosyncrasies of the hand-made car; employ more hands, and you'd get every seam in perfect alignment. Ettore Bugatti himself would weep in awe if he were alive to see it. Only a penny-pinching pedestrian would ever question whether such a car could possibly be described as authentic.

And now, after all the headaches and the bills and the business meetings interrupted by urgent phone calls from the restorer, after the mad pressure of the last few weeks making sure the car would be finished on time for the one *Concours d'Elégance* that really mattered, now was the time for the owner to reap his just reward. A best-in-class award at Pebble Beach would make his car an instant classic; a best-in-show would send it into the multi-million-dollar stratosphere, giving it that final gloss of lasting mystique.

Restoration can take up to five years, and cost ten times as much as the purchase price of the car. And even if the car wins the best-in-show award, it doesn't always pay. Even if it's valued at five million dollars like Ralph Lauren's 1937 Bugatti Atlantique coupe, which won best-in-show here a few years ago.

That was the Bugatti to top all Bugattis, with doors set at an angle, massively bulging fenders, and raised, riveted metallic seams running the length of the car from bumper to bumper. Those nakedly riveted seams were shocking, and the shock itself added to the beauty. The moment I saw them, I knew I would give my eyeteeth to drive that car. Or at least a molar or two.

I'd thought of writing a letter. "Dear Ralph," it would have begun, "please can I drive your Bugatti . . ." But even I had to admit that such an approach lacked persuasiveness, and the letter went unwritten.

Rumor had it that Lauren paid eight and a half million for the restoration, yet nobody seemed to consider this a bad investment. The casual loss of three and a half million dollars was seen as a measure of the same flair and style, the same devotion to originality and beauty, that marked the car. The very idea that anyone could willingly lose that much money on a car was seductive. It would leave this year's award-winning owners heady with the illusion that their wealth had taken them into an almost mythic realm—a kind of metaphysics of money, where all the usual measures and values no longer apply. The theatrical backdrop of Pebble Beach promised to transport them beyond the dreary reality of how they had earned their riches. For this one weekend, they would lead a charmed life.

They wouldn't even go to the evening auctions that have become as much part of the Pebble Beach weekend as the *concours* itself. They were beyond that now. The auctions were too gritty, too redolent of the hard grind of money, even when they were done as subtly and elegantly as the Christie's one on the Sunday evening—a suitably high-toned affair held in a yellow-and-white striped tent on the grounds of the Lodge, with plummy-accented British auctioneers. They certainly would never again go near Christie's naughty rival, the Rick Cole auction, which took place on the Friday and Saturday nights in the Doubletree Hotel and Conference Center in downtown Monterey. Because here, five miles from the rarefied atmosphere of the Lodge and the golf course, the veil of moneyed elegance fell away to reveal, simply, money.

★

The ringmen at Rick Cole's were astounding; I knew instantly that all I wanted was to watch them all night. Nobody seemed to know where the term came from, but the association with the circus was perfect. Though they were dressed up in tuxes with red bow ties and red cummerbunds, evening dress couldn't quite hide the aura of seediness. The jackets were just a shade too tight, or loose, or too shiny. You knew if you looked close you'd see sweat stains on their shirts, soup spills on their cummerbunds.

There were four of them, each with his own sector of the drably painted hotel ballroom, which was packed to capacity so that latecomers stood six deep around the sides and at the back. Pacing up and down the aisles, the ringmen peered along the rows of seats, eyes constantly shifting. Officially, they were there to spot the bids. In fact, they were drumming them up. Raising the ante. Creating the drama people want from an auction.

When a ringman spotted a raised hand in his sector, he'd give out a short, sharp yell, spin round to face the auctioneer on stage, and with arm raised high, punch the air.

"Yes!" he'd yelp, cummerbund rucked high over his waist, white shirt ballooning in the gap, buttons undone. "Yes! Here!" Shouting it out, one arm pointing to the bidder, the other to the auctioneer, like a mad patrolman at a jammed intersection.

It was infectious in a game-show kind of way. "Yes!" I wanted to cry out with him. "Yes, yes, go for it!" And it was all I could do not to raise my own hand and bid, just for the pleasure of pulling another of those orgasmic little yelps out of his pudgy frame.

With each shout, a shiver ran through the audience. A murmur built, spreading from row to row like a wave breaking on shore, gathering force as it goes. The few women giggled with a kind of sexual tension. They snuggled in close to their escorts, eyes wide and shining, mouths open, breathlessly waiting for the next bid, the next yelp and spin and exclamation point, followed, incredibly, by another, and—ohmyGod— yet another, until the final, magnificent, outrageous sum was achieved and the gavel came down, bang.

The audience slumped, stunned, as the car was driven offstage and the next one brought on. The women fanned themselves and rearranged their hair. The men focused studiously on the photocopied sheets that acted as catalogs, penning in notations as the chief auctioneer started the bidding on the next car, the words running together in a singsong chant:

"*One seventy* who'll give me eighty going for one eighty"—a ringman yelped—"*eighty* now I have one eighty looking for ninety who'll give me one ninety looking for ninety"—yelp—"*ninety* two hundred now who'll give me two looking for two . . ."

And now the ringmen leaned in to the delicate part of their work, moving in close on the bidders, mouth to ear, sotto voce, as though they were selling not cars, but sex:

"You've come all the way from New York and you're going to let it go for the sake of five hundred bucks?"

"I know that bidder and I promise you he's not going to go above sixty, so for sixty-one it can be yours."

"Will you be able to live with yourself if you let someone else have this because of a mere thousand dollars?"

And if the bidder shook his head and dropped out, there was a reassuring pat on the upper arm as the ringman sighed and straightened up, as though to say, "That's all right, no hard feelings, I understand." A man-to-man sort of sportsman's pat, buttering him up to bid for the next car.

The ringmen seemed to be working flat out, but at the slightest sign of flagging from either the auctioneer or the audience, they'd suddenly step the pace up another notch, flinging out hackneyed phrases familiar from any used-car salesroom in the country:

"It's red!" one shouted.

"It's the right color!" yelled another.

"Ladies and gentlemen, the opportunity of a lifetime!"

"I can't believe we're going to sell it at this price!"

"Look, ladies and gentlemen, leather seats!"

"It's only money! Let it bring you happiness tonight!"

"*Everybody* can bid!"

"Ten thousand more and it can be yours!"

"Five more and it's yours!"

"One more and it's yours!"

"Think of it—you're *saving* fifty thousand!"

"You've got a million-dollar smile—*spend* some of that money!"

And even the blindingly obvious: "We're selling this car to the highest bidder tonight!"

But none of the bidders looked happy. I could see no million-dollar smiles, even though the higher the final sell figure on a car, the louder and longer the audience applauded. The crowd was happy, as crowds are when there's a good spectacle. They were enjoying the vicarious thrill of watching someone else be seduced into spending enormous amounts of money, rejoicing in the spectacle of a rich man being speedily parted from his wealth.

The rich men looked uncomfortable whenever the crowd broke out into applause. They hunkered down tight-jawed in their seats and tried to smile graciously, but it didn't work. They had read the mood of the crowd correctly, and were already wondering if they hadn't made a huge mistake. It was up to Rick Cole, founder and sole owner of the auction company that bears his name, to assure them that they hadn't. Not for Cole the auctioneer's patter; his job was more subtle. He spent most of the evening squatting down by the chairs of the successful bidders, reassuring them. Making sure they wouldn't renege. Readying them to spend more.

Neat and trim in tux and red bow tie, he had something of the lean and hungry look about him. I watched as he talked to the big money men, his manner all confidentiality, a thin smile visible through his blond goatee. The muscle in his left cheek worked nervously. He might have been good-looking if his eyes would just stay still and stop darting around like there was a contract out on his life. Though come to think of it, there were a few people in the hall who looked as though they might have precisely such a contract.

It was what you might call a mixed audience. Some looked like drug-money types: hair greased back into ponytails, black shirts, bright yellow jackets, and the kind of heft to the torso that seemed to indicate something worn in a shoulder holster. Others had the big-businessman look; they gathered in tight little knots of three or four just in front of the stage, jut-jawed and serious. There was a sprinkling of rich kids, idling long-limbed on two or three chairs at a time as they waited to bid on something more exotic than just another new Mercedes. A lot of small-time dealers were in evidence, along with loners who already had a vintage car or two in their garages and, like the small-timers, were looking to see if there'd be a bargain here. There wouldn't. A few Asian bidders stood either side of the stage; they were not the principals, I was assured, but their representatives, which may be why they looked so tense and why most of them, like Rick Cole, had twitching cheeks. In fact of all these people, the only bidder who seemed to be having a good time was also the only woman I saw enter the fray: a trophy wife in tan, fur, and stiletto heels, South American from her accent, who rewarded her shorter, white-haired escort with a huge hug and multiple squeals of delight when she topped the bidding for a gullwing Mercedes. The two others in their party, bulkily muscled young men with busy eyes and swiveling necks, stood close, as bodyguards should.

"Provenance" was big here. At Christie's, it tends to mean an assurance of authenticity, though even posh Christie's is not above a lavish description of the history of a car, especially if it happened to have been given to Rita Hayworth by the Aga Khan. But here at Rick Cole's, there was no doubt as to what provenance meant. It was a matter of whose backside once rubbed against this leather seat, whose hair oil stained this headrest, whose feet may or may not have rested on this dashboard as she took her pleasure with her lover of the moment. The more famed and glamorous the person, the greater the emphasis on provenance, as though the imprint of a famous backside could last through the years, reach up through the leather, and enter the new buyer, body and soul.

A BMW 507 roadster was once owned by Elvis. A Rolls was part of the Shah of Iran's private collection. A powder-blue Buick was one of Jayne Mansfield's favorite cars. It struck me that all the names were somehow off, slightly dated; if once they'd been the epitome of glamour, now the gloss had faded, much as it had on many of the cars up for sale.

Still, provenance worked, until the very end. That's when a biliously green Lamborghini Countach was driven onto the stage. I'd seen the car a few years before, triple-parked outside the latest nightclub of the moment in Manhattan, with two duty cops standing guard beside it. It looked even worse here in the Doubletree Inn ballroom than it had under the harsh street lights of New York City.

"This car is called 'The Color of Money,'" declared the auctioneer. "Custom-made for billionaire Malcolm Forbes by Lamborghini, it's the only one ever made in this color." I stared. Everyone stared. It was either stare or run screaming from the room.

The car was indeed the color of dollar bills, and this is a color that happens to look atrocious on metal. How could Forbes have done it? It was as though he'd determined to test the limits of bad taste and then expand them. Or indulged in an intriguing exercise in making an inordinately expensive car look astoundingly cheap.

The bidding was desultory, way below the reserve. The auctioneer tried to raise the ante by revealing a few details. "The emblems and interior fittings are all made of 24-carat gold," he announced. To little effect.

"And the dashboard and center console are sprayed with gold dust," he added. "*Real* gold dust."

One of Sam Goldwyn's famed sayings about Hollywood came irresistibly to mind—"Beneath all that fake tinsel, there's *real* tinsel"—and suddenly I was laughing out loud. I was drawing dirty looks from the ringmen, but I couldn't help it. The laughter spread through the hall, either because other people remembered the same line, or simply because laughter is infectious. The bidding ground to a halt.

The auctioneer tried another kind of gold dust instead. "Liz Taylor sat in the passenger seat of this car!" he cried.

No hands moved. Not even for Liz. In the stark face of the Color of Money, cold awareness had settled over the room.

"Princess Di sat in the passenger seat!" he shouted. Still nothing happened.

And in what was clearly a desperate afterthought, his tone already falling off in defeat, he added: "Prince Charles too."

The Forbes Countach was withdrawn. It was every auctioneer's nightmare—a climax that fizzled, the kind of closing note that could only create buyer's regret among the successful bidders. It would be many months yet until I'd be faced with the question of how high the bidding on the Countach would have gone if Diana, Princess of Wales had already stepped into another, ill-fated car on a Parisian summer night.

★

I'd had my fill of glamorous sheet metal and glittering names. The three days of Pebble Beach lingered in my head, creating an added layer of unreality to the artifice of working with a film crew once the *concours* was over. Still, as even their name indicated—Talking Turkey Pictures— Ned Judge and his crew were good company. So when Ned suggested that I stay an extra day and come with them to the Sandia National Laboratories at Livermore, I agreed before I even knew why.

"We're going to look inside an engine," he said.

"As it's running?"

"As it's running."

"Perfect." I needed to come down to earth, and inside an engine was exactly the right place to land: in the down and dirty heart of internal combustion.

I'd stuck my head into plenty of engines during the summer I spent as a mechanic's apprentice in Vermont, soon after I began to write about cars. At first I'd thought of myself as the sorcerer's apprentice: I was very good at sweeping floors. And if I didn't become a mechanic that summer, I did become an experienced apprentice, who could happily spend hours cleaning the gunk off engine parts and getting high off the powerful fumes of the solvents.

But all those engines had been at a standstill; no matter how far I poked my head in, I still couldn't watch them running, not from the inside. And inside was where I wanted to look, like a cardiologist using miniaturized scopes to see inside the human heart.

Like most people, I find it easy to think of an engine in terms of human anatomy. It's tempting to think of the fuel as the lifeblood. Of the valves as the valves of the heart, opening and closing. Of the movement of the pistons inside the cylinders as the heartbeat, pumping blood/fuel through the system. Except that there is one major difference: the human heart is a perpetual-motion machine. Like a Jean Tinguely mobile, it moves forever on its own momentum. Or at least for a lifetime. The blood pumped out is the same blood, refreshed by oxygen, that is pumped in. It's a closed-loop system, eight pints in constant circulation.

The internal combustion engine, however, is an open loop. It consumes its own blood. Fuel is injected in through the valves, gets burned, produces the energy to move the pistons up and down, and is then expelled out the tailpipe in the form of residue—emissions, that is. The same emissions that account for up to two-thirds of urban smog and a quarter of the greenhouse gas carbon dioxide, let alone a number of other gases and particles capable of eating away paint, plastics, rubber, and human lung tissue.

Among these other gases are nitrous oxides. My tongue often slips and calls them noxious oxides, which they are: they interact with sunlight to create the low-lying brown haze that covers so many of our cities. Even the greenest of cities, as I found out after I got my pilot's license. I'd take off from Seattle's Boeing Field on a summer day, fly high into the blue of what seemed to be a clear sky, wave my wings in greeting to the white peaks of Rainier and Adams, Baker and St. Helens, and look back to see a low brown cloud hanging over the city. This wasn't Los Angeles or Mexico City; this was a city whose population included one of the highest concentrations of enviromentalists anywhere in the world, most of whom were down there at that very moment, driving gas-guzzling sport-utilities to and from work. Just like the Ford Expedition I was now driving round the country.

But when the Talking Turkey crew and I piled into the truck the next morning and headed out into the hills beyond San Francisco, the pollution from cars was minor compared to that from forest fires. They'd been burning for days some fifty miles to the east, and though we couldn't smell smoke from this distance, the whole sky was strangely white, like stone-bleached jeans. It gave a suitably ominous feel to the morning, for our destination at Livermore was part of a major national defense research center specializing in new weapons systems.

Dr. Peter Witze, a research engineer untidy even in the tie and tweed jacket he'd put on for the camera, led us through the warren of offices and labs that was the Combustion Research Center, and into a small cinderblock-walled room with pipes hanging from the ceiling and an engine sitting squat on a workbench, surrounded by paraphernalia. Only the banks of computer screens along one wall seemed to distinguish the place from a reasonably well-equipped backyard garage.

No backyard garage would have an engine like this, however. Slowly, I figured out what Peter had done to it. First, he'd blocked off three of the four cylinders, and replaced the crown of the one remaining piston with a glass window. Next, he'd arranged several mirrors much as in a periscope, so that he could look up through the glass window and into the combustion chamber. Then he'd threaded a fiber-optic lead through the spark plug, and set an endoscope into one of the intake ports. Now he could beam a laser into the combustion chamber to make the fuel fluorescent, turn on the night-vision cameras to film everything, and presto—he could see exactly what went on inside an operating engine.

The only question was why.

"What we're doing here," he declared, "is unraveling the last secret of the internal combustion engine: the first thirty seconds after ignition, or what we call 'cold start.' That's when the engine is dirtiest, but nobody's ever understood why, because they couldn't look inside and see what was happening."

When an engine's running clean, there are no flames, no dramatic explosions, just a very low-grade even combustion. What's being burned, in fact, is not so much fuel itself but fuel vapor—the breath of fuel, as it were. But in the first thirty seconds, the metal of the engine is still cold, and so the fuel doesn't vaporize properly. It forms a liquid film, and this film flames up, creating a lot of residue. The residue clogs the engine, which then burns fuel more inefficiently, which clogs the engine further, and so on to breakdown.

In this first half-minute, it seems, is the secret of how long an engine can live, and in what health.

I bent down to the camera viewfinder, aware that my desire to look inside an engine—to *be* inside it so far as my eye was concerned—would have struck me just ten years before as downright weird. "Who cares?" I'd have said. "So long as it works, that's all I need." The idea of watching metal move would have been about as attractive as watching grass grow.

Anyone can watch grass grow, however. Few people had ever been able to do what I was now doing.

I stared at the valves opening and closing with hypnotic regularity, 10.8 times a second. I'd had no idea the eye could see that much. "That's only at 700 rpm, of course," I heard Peter say behind me. "Idle speed. At a normal driving speed of 2,000 or 3,000 rpm, you'd just see a blur."

I ground my face tighter against the rubber gasket of the viewfinder, as though I could somehow climb inside the camera, bounce from mirror to mirror, and find myself standing right where my eye appeared to be, inside the chamber, with the four valves beating in perfect tempo around me.

A surreal sense of transgression crept up on me. I felt half-voyeur, half-intruder. I was looking into a place normally closed to the human eye. A secret place, and I was spying on it.

It was eerily like watching a human heart beating. The longer I watched, the easier it was to forget the mechanics and physics of fuel and combustion, and imagine that this engine had its own life, independent of human beings. Even perhaps its own soul.

Is there such a thing as life to a car? Does a car have a soul? I thought of the fugue state induced the evening before by that pale yellow Packard. Saw Craig Breedlove's beatific smile as he sat pinned to the front of his jet engine. Remembered Stephen King's first novel, *Christine*, about a '58 Plymouth Fury that comes to demonic, vengeful life, taking possession of its owner.

I knew this was absurd. It was a pathetic illusion to see life in metal. Yet I'd done it many times. Driving a sports car at speed, I'd imagined myself riding a pedigree racehorse, found myself talking to it as I would to a horse, calming it even as I urged it on. And walking up and down the lines of welding robots in assembly plants, I'd watched them stretch and poke and straighten and swivel like long-necked metallic birds, each with its own intelligence, nibbling at the metal frames going by on the line like mother swans fussing at their ungainly offspring.

When the television reporter at Pebble Beach had crowed about seeing his own reflection in the Duesenberg, I'd been standing to the side, watching him disdainfully. But wasn't I now doing essentially the same thing? On a different level to be sure: he was admiring the surface, while I was deep in the innards of the machine. But like him, I saw a reflection of the human body.

Even as I watched the beating of the valves, I was aware I'd never be able to take an engine for granted again. Just as someone who's had a heart attack will never take the heart for granted again. The engine's steady regularity pronounced it an entity in itself, a working mechanism so intricate and smooth-running that it filled me with a strange and disturbing mix of gratefulness and awe and even tenderness.

I stood up from the viewfinder and blinked. I'd never thought I could feel tender about an engine.

Ned persuaded me to move aside; the engine was ready for its close-up. I sat down a bit woozily on one of the lab chairs and stared at a bank of computer screens. The two top ones showed live images of the combustion chamber, glowing through the night-vision lens as though it were a real chamber, a vaulted space cut out of rock beneath the surface of the earth, the light greenish and eerie with depth. The two bottom screens showed the fuel burning—blue for even burn, red for flame—against a superimposed graphic of the valve layout.

I watched the fuel injector spraying its measured mite of gasoline over the valves. The spark plug sparking. The valves opening and closing in the familiar yet alien beat, *oompah, oompah, oompah.* The pool fires flashing around the rims of the intake valves, red flames flecked with white, quick and hot and dirty. Like a heart attack.

My hand wandered to my heart. Rested there, feeling the beat. I stared at the upper screens again, the green ones. Like the green monitors beside my father's hospital bed just a few months before. The jagged lines of his heartbeat. The painful sound of his breathing. The tubes snaking in and out of him. The awful weariness in his eyes.

What was it like to be him now, always aware of the working of his heart, always wondering how long it would last? How long until it clogged up again and the muscles flared and contracted and the pain burned through him, red and white flame?

My heart beat faster. Contracted. Squeezed. I pressed down hard on it. Heard Ned calling me. Opened my eyes, only now realizing I'd closed them.

"Stand here," he was saying. "Listen to Peter as he talks while we take a shot over your shoulder."

I stood nodding at Peter as though I understood what he was saying. It was something about experimenting with higher-pressure fuel injection—a finer nozzle, quicker vaporization—but I barely heard his words. Growing ever stronger and all but drowning him out, there was the beat of the engine, the roar of my pulse, the blips of the monitor beeping out the broken rhythm of my father's heart.

And then Peter's voice suddenly came into sharp focus. "It's all a matter of turbulence," he said. "The inside of a flame is pure combustion, a transparent gas, but the outside is turbulent, and therefore unpredictable. If we can find a way to control this turbulence and stop the flames tumbling and flickering, calm them, smooth them out . . ."

"Soothe them," I said out loud.

"Cut," said Ned, and put an arm around my shoulders. "Are you all right? It's only an engine, you know."

"Only an engine," I repeated, and sighed with relief as the world snapped back into its regular perspective.

Chapter Five

The high, pine-studded landscape known as Desolation Wilderness is far too beautiful to deserve such a name. Rimmed by the peaks of the Sierras, snow-capped even in early September, it is made of giant slabs of glacially molded granite smoothed further by wind and melting winter snows, then cracked by pines and manzanita, and finally filled at the lowest points with lakes of mineral-rich black water.

It was a relief to be back in the open again, in jeans and denim shirt instead of silk jacket and high heels. I'd driven the truck up from San Francisco the day before, and together with a dozen other automotive journalists and assorted helpers, made the rendezvous under the hundred-degree sun at Loon Lake, in the hills west of Lake Tahoe. We'd been on the trail just a couple of hours so far and already we were as covered with dust and sweat as cowboys who'd been sleeping out for weeks.

That is, if you could call what we were on a trail at all. A hiker would have to scramble down some of the steep sluices we'd lumbered down. You'd need good boots to get up some of the rock faces we'd mounted, and even then you'd have to run to maintain forward momentum, or find yourself tumbling down. The sweat soaking our clothes was as much from fear as heat. There was no refusing the invitation of the first lake we came to.

I went scrambling over the rocks toward it like a watery version of a moth drawn to flame. A slight pause to steel myself, and I dived in, surfaced gasping at the sudden cold, then headed out to the center. The ripples from my first big splash dissipated, and I swam slowly and precisely so as not to disrupt the newly restored smoothness of the surface. The water felt ineffably deep and mysterious beneath me, demanding stillness. I reached the center, turned, and lay floating on my back, looking up at the great rim of snow mountains around me.

The sun was hot on my face, the water cool on my body. For the first time all morning, I didn't feel like a stranger. Didn't need to keep asking myself, "What am I doing here?" This lake made perfect sense. I waved to the others, beckoning them in. But they just stood on top of a cliff, watching. Twenty of us, yet I was the only one who had leaped into the water.

"You made that water seem so good," said my co-driver, Doug, when I emerged a half-hour later. I'd missed lunch, but he'd saved a sandwich for me, and I bit into it with happy appetite.

"So why didn't you come in and join me?"

He shrugged and looked confused, as though he couldn't figure it out himself. "I didn't come to swim," he said finally. "I came to drive the Rubicon Trail."

"Why can't you do both?"

There was no answer.

★

Sooner or later, if you own a four-wheel-drive vehicle and are one of the three percent of such owners who ever actually take it off a paved road, you hear about the Rubicon Trail. This twenty-six-mile stretch across the high Sierras is the grand-daddy of all dedicated off-road trails, the one against which all others are graded for difficulty, and the only one graded a full ten. And of course it has the perfect name, placing it squarely in the realm of mythic achievement.

"If you can drive the Rubicon, you can drive anything," veterans say. So I had come to cross my Rubicon. The plan was to spend the first day driving the toughest nine-mile section of the trail, from Loon Lake in to Rubicon Springs, camp the night at the springs, then spend the second day driving out. It didn't occur to me then to wonder why it would take a whole day to drive nine miles.

I'd wanted to drive the trail in the Expedition, but when I'd spoken on the phone about it to Mark Smith—the founder of Jeep Jamboree and the by-now-venerable father of off-roading as a sport and a pastime—he'd nixed the idea. "You won't make it in a truck that size," he said. "Too long a wheelbase, too wide a track. You need something a lot more nimble for the Rubicon. We'll put you in a Wrangler."

I felt almost insulted on the part of my truck, and said so. "Put it this way," he said. "Dents and scratches are par for the course on the Rubicon. Sometimes worse. You really want to do that to a brand-new Expedition?"

I accepted his offer.

We'd be roughing it, he'd warned me. But as I'd driven up to Loon Lake, following a dirt road in, the first thing I'd seen was a helicopter perched on top of a large flat rock. Beside it, crates of supplies were lined up, and alongside the crates, wrapped in clear plastic sheeting, was, improbably, an upright piano.

Loon Lake began to seem very aptly named.

The helicopter gave a militarily dramatic touch to the preparations. As did the ten Wranglers lined up at the edge of the lake, modern descendants of the old wartime jeeps. They were buttoned down for business: canvas tops and sides off, doors off, windshields folded flat and latched onto the hoods. If I narrowed my eyes and squinted to make vision hazy, I could almost imagine they were the real thing.

As I parked under a scrawny pine, the helicopter lifted into the air, rotors whumpeting and the piano dangling crazily below it. Dust billowed over the Wranglers and everyone around. When it cleared, I didn't need to squint any more: the dust had mellowed the bright primary colors of the Jeeps. And the piano was on its way to our overnight camp on the Rubicon River.

Mark was easy to spot amid the bustle of preparation: tall and tanned, wearing his Australian bush hat as usual. When he released me from a big bear hug, I confessed I was surprised to see on my map that there really was a Rubicon River. "I always thought it was a name made up just to hype the trail's reputation."

He grinned, still a dab hand at rakish charm in his silver-haired seventies: "Would I do a thing like that?"

Coming from a man who had the Jeep logo tattooed on his right but-tock, and whose malamute dog was named Jeep, that begged the ques-tion. If he'd needed to, he would have.

In fact someone else had done it for him a century ago. The trail was an old one, one of many in the West trodden first by Indians, then by miners and fortune-hunters, then by settlers crossing the mountains for the promised land of California, only to fall into disuse. It had been reclaimed so thoroughly by snow, runoff floods, wind, and thorns that much of it was all but invisible unless you knew it was there. And nobody knew this trail better than Mark. In fact, he owned part of it.

With a group of friends, he'd bought the only section of the trail that was not federal land—the forty acres of Rubicon Springs itself—with the specific intention of ensuring that the whole of it would remain accessible for off-roading. They thought of themselves as the guardians of the trail, and late each spring, when the snow melted, Mark walked it together with his son, Greg, checking to see how the previous winter's twenty feet of snow and the ensuing runoff had altered the landscape, what boulders had moved where, figuring out the angles to make sure a Jeep could get through. Then the two would drive the trail. If they could get through, they reckoned they could get others through. For the past twenty years, they'd succeeded. "Never lost anyone yet," said Mark.

Greg Smith now ran most of the day-to-day operations of Jeep Jam-boree, and as the piano-bearing helicopter headed off to the Springs, he gathered us together for the standard introductory talk. "You'll find out more about off-roading than you ever thought possible," he said, "and more about yourselves than you might ever want to know."

I'd heard practically the same words before, usually in the pits of race-tracks at the beginning of one advanced-driving course or another. They were standard in the car world for any kind of tough driving. A chal-lenge, a gauntlet thrown down, almost a dare. Test your limits, find out what you can do, be all that you can be. I shifted impatiently. I hadn't come to find out more about myself. Besides, I'd had plenty of off-road experience long before the term *off-roading* was even invented. And that was in the Sinai and the Negev, Middle Eastern deserts far harsher than this Sierran one.

I'd spent the better part of 1978 bouncing along wadis and across firing ranges, up mountains and down sand dunes, in old Israeli army jeeps: Willys jeeps, which is an indication of just how ancient they were even then. The name Willys hadn't been on a new jeep since 1963.

They were, to put it mildly, well-used machines. That is, they were very used, but not well. They'd survived legions of young Israeli soldiers behind the wheel, and were designed to do just that by virtue of being testosterone-proof: no frills, no padding. Either you hung on grimly or you emerged black and blue in all the worst places. But the discomfort was worth it. In the year I spent wandering through that desert, jeeps took me deeper into the wilderness than any ordinary car. Where a jeep couldn't reach, I switched to a camel. And where even the camel balked, I climbed on my own two feet, farther than I'd ever imagined I'd dare go.

If anyone had told me then that jeeps would become fashionable, I'd have thought they were dehydrated from the desert sun and suffering from delusions.

I never did have a great head for business.

The utilitarian vehicle par excellence was to become the lifestyle vehicle of choice. Every GI's basic tool would metamorphose into every American businessman's status symbol. With power-adjustable leather bucket seats, pearlized paint, CD players, antilock brakes, remote keyless entry, heated side mirrors, and a wealth of other luxury options, the only black and blue would be in the range of body colors.

It's the old story of the victory of fantasy over reason. In short, the classic marketing story. And the storyteller, to a large extent, was Lee Iacocca.

The military's original call in 1938 was for "a light, maneuverable yet powerful reconnaissance-and-dispatch vehicle capable of carrying weapons and heavy loads." Willys-Overland won the bulk of the wartime contract, and when its "general-purpose vehicle" was introduced into the military in 1941, GIs shortened the name first to "G.P." and then to the affectionate "jeep"—a partial tribute to a small, impish-looking character called Eugene the Jeep from the Popeye comic strip.

If the jeep was as ungainly as Popeye himself, it was also as admirable in what it could do. The normally staid *Scientific American* called it "a clawing, climbing hellion." And what young man, in uniform or out, wouldn't want to tame such a creature, each one Petruchio wrestling his own private shrew?

Willys produced the first civilian Jeep, or CJ, in August 1945, even before the war's end. It registered the name Jeep as a trademark in 1950, and expanded the line with a series of pickups, station wagons, and delivery vans. They sold, but not exactly with the vigor of clawing, climbing hellions. So the Jeep began a kind of automotive sojourn in the wilderness: Willys was bought by Kaiser Industries in 1953, Kaiser Industries in turn was sold to the American Motors Corporation in 1970, and American Motors got eaten up by Chrysler in 1987 when Chrysler's new chairman, Lee Iacocca, realized that if you put four doors on a Jeep Cherokee, you could market it as a "family vehicle." Ghosts of GIs turned in their graves.

In short order, Iacocca turned out a Cherokee that was to an old Willys Jeep what a five-star hotel is to an army barrack. Sales took off. And as other automakers scrambled to catch up, Chrysler began to enforce the trademark, placing the generic "jeep" linguistically off limits. Whoever came up with the clunker "sport-utility vehicle" as an alternative has wisely taken refuge in anonymity, and meanwhile time has at least shortened it to "sport-ute," a word that in all its inelegance seems to express quite well the blunt-nosed brutishness of the genre.

Meanwhile, Chrysler hired a team of anthropologists to define the appeal of the Jeep. The major factor turned out to be a capitalized cultural artifact known as Nature. "The Jeep gives a touch of daring," said the anthropologists' confidential report, "an element of the rugged, individualist outdoorsman or outdoorswoman."

Just a touch, of course.

People wanted to be connected to the wilderness, said the anthropologists. What they meant was that sport-ute owners wanted to consume Nature as well as metal. Or more precisely, their image of nature, which was cropped to exclude the effects of their being there: high emissions, dirty air, and the damage to fragile environments wrought by wide tires carrying heavy loads. It's the fantasy that counts, not the reality. And so, in a stunning reverse take on environmentalism, Jeeps were to be the connection, and the commercials hammered home the point: the lone vehicle atop a mesa, or at the foot of a remote, romantic waterfall.

All this meant that I was uncomfortably aware of a certain absurdity in the Rubicon venture. Especially since most of my trail-mates seemed to be all togged up for the event in brand-new safari jackets and desert boots, along with photographer's vests—those ones with net pockets for pens and film and snakebite serum and God knows what else, and various flaps that are supposed to keep you cool but somehow always make you hotter.

"I feel like I'm about to act out a television commercial," I said to Doug, the managing editor of *Four Wheeler* magazine.

"That's civilization," he replied.

I bit my tongue and made no comment on civilization.

Back in the Middle East, we'd used jeeps to get deep into the desert, but once there, we'd get out and hike. The vehicles were simply the means of getting to our starting point. Besides, nobody but a masochist would want to spend any more time in them than absolutely necessary. Here, the vehicles were both the start and the end point. The driving itself was the main event. The landscape was secondary, present not as beauty or wilderness but simply to provide difficult driving, a technical challenge, and a suitable backdrop for photographs.

The helicopter came back and hovered, blowing another layer of dust over Jeeps and people as Mark's crew hooked up crates to its trailing line. I took refuge on the windward side and watched as the almost entirely male contingent of people strutted and posed, legs spread and arms akimbo, psyching themselves up for the trail. There were journalists here from all the main "car books," as the auto magazines are called in the industry. I knew many of them from various press previews and track events. Some were good company, some not, but they all lived and loved cars and focused on them with the single-mindedness of a preacher closing in on a convert. They were "car guys" in a way I would never be nor want to be, however deep my involvement with cars. And the "guy" thing wasn't just a matter of gender.

There'd been that cover of *AutoWeek* a year or so before. It showed a steep waterfall somewhere in the Arizona desert, the kind of scene that could have been the cover of a nature magazine were it not for the Jeep Wrangler in the middle of the waterfall, vertical, being winched up the fall by a mass of steel ropes. I remembered recoiling as I stared at the photo, wondering what damage the winches and the banging of the vehicle were doing to the fall itself. What marks would be left of this passage? And why on earth would anyone want to do that, when it would have made so much more sense to get out and leave the vehicle behind, either to climb the fall or simply stand under it and let the water pound down on you?

Two of the Wranglers here, I noticed, were equipped with winches. Well, if macho was the name of the game, I could play a female version of it if I had to. Thirteen years in the Middle East equip you well for that. Besides, if things got too Mad Maxish, I could always get out and walk.

★

Mad Max again? I consider myself a peaceable sort of person who'd much prefer a delicately nuanced European-style movie to garish thriller violence. Give me Gerard Depardieu over Mel Gibson any day. But Mad Max keeps inserting himself into my journey. And how not? The images resonate, like shadows on a badly tuned television screen, ghosts of another reality.

There's the post-apocalyptic vision of hot rods cannibalized from parts of other cars, patched together like rusty metallic Lego toys and roaring in marauding packs through the desert outback. And the fierce war for gasoline, in a movie made ten years before the Gulf War, fought out not with high-tech military weapons but in hand-to-hand and car-to-car combat, by crossbow and arrow, by armored fender and scythed wheel.

The combatants in the Mad Max movies had a fierce outlaw pride—something resonant of the old Hell's Angels gangs, when the word *Hog* was still pronounced with two syllables, *haw-ug*, drawn out and threatening. That was before it got restyled into an acronym for Harley Owners' Group. Before Malcolm Forbes started taking Liz Taylor for rides.

Before Harley Davidson began its own tie-in merchandise lines of everything from beer, belt buckles, and handcuffs to lingerie and eau de cologne. A time, in short, when an outlaw still had a strong, solid sense of being beyond the bounds, outside not just legal but also social law. But the marauding gangs of the Mad Max movies could make even a Hell's Angel have nightmares.

I'd seen Mad Max come to life a year or so before, when I'd been exploring the Anza-Borrego desert, east of San Diego and just north of the Mexican border. I felt instantly at home in this no-man's-land where you were warned to be on the lookout for illegal temporary drug stills, or rather for their gun-toting operators. Just fifty miles south of the golf courses and spas of Palm Springs, Anza-Borrego, rimmed in by high mountains, had stubbornly resisted being palm sprung. It was an old-fashioned outlaw kind of desert. Which is why I experienced a flash of *déja vu* when I came across the section of bare land bordering the state park that had been set aside for "all-terrain vehicle recreation."

It was a good linguistic evasion. To call the machines tearing up and down the hillside "cars" in the way most people understand the word would not do them justice. They were giant-tired internal-combustion fantasies, rigged with outlandish exhaust pipes and air intakes so huge and bulbous they looked like they fed on steroids. Favored paint jobs were either Day-Glo hallucinatory or Darth Vader black, though both were challenged by a paint-stripped post-industrial blotched metal drab. And these vehicles seemed to have sprouted organs—pipes at all sorts of odd angles, bare machinery where there'd normally be sheet metal, extrusions of aluminum where you expected a door or a window. They had huge grates for grilles, giant fenders, knives fixed Boadicea-style on giant wheels, and of course skull-and-crossbones pennants flying on masts.

Every driver here was a road warrior, with a Gibson-Schwarzenegger-Stallone movie playing in his head. Heavily inked tattoos made brawny arms seem brawnier. Old metal helmets and faded bandannas tied around foreheads spoke the Hollywood image of the crazed Vietnam vet. "Don't mess with me, buster." "Make my day." "I'll be back."

And yet there was something extraordinarily innocent about the vision. It didn't take much to adjust the ages of the drivers mentally, see them as eight-year-old boys playing on a dusty hill, back to the sandbox except with more power and a lot more noise. And because they were tearing up this one dedicated part of the terrain, they weren't tearing up the land inside the state park, which they would certainly otherwise have been doing. Besides—and this was the point—their four-wheeled games were designed to be played in front of each other. The vehicles to be seen, the drivers' control admired, their performance judged by others. The desert itelf was incidental.

As a one-time desert rat, I should have been disgusted by all this. But there was a joyful defiance to it that attracted me. Made me sit and watch, accept a beer when it was offered, get talking until I realized that beneath the macho exteriors, these seeming delinquents really were just regular guys. And perhaps we got on so well because, despite my better self, I have an abiding fondness for Mad Max. Though "fond" may not be quite the right word in this context.

The first Mad Max movie I'd seen was *Road Warrior,* and if none of the others would make nearly as much impression on me, it didn't matter. I saw it in New York City, a setting as physically and culturally removed as could be from the south Australian desert where the movie was filmed. Or so it seemed at first.

It was a dull fall afternoon, years before I moved to the gentler clime of Seattle, and I was in a fit of deep misery. Nothing was going right in my life. I made for the movie house without even caring what was on. Anything would do so long as it took me out of myself for an hour or two.

The theater was almost empty, the movie due to start in a few minutes. But no sooner had I settled in on an aisle seat than three teenagers walked in, moseyed on down the aisle in that tough street gait that was a well-practiced cross between a movie gunslinger and Muhammad Ali, and deliberately sat in the seats right behind me. I tensed, as I was meant to. They were talking loud and they were talking tough, clearly for my benefit. I tensed more, they saw it, and upped the ante. I knew what game they were playing: Get the white bitch to move.

But I was damned if I was going to move. The sensible thing to do becomes the last thing you're willing to do when you're in a bad enough mood. I sat still, determined not to give them even the satisfaction of looking round. The muscles in my neck got tighter and tighter. I knew I was being as dumb as they were; I suppose I was determined to prove myself dumber. And then the lights dimmed, and the movie began.

The opening scene was one of highly stylized violence—a surreal exaggeration of what would later come to be called road rage. Blood flowed like the paint it was, cars went somersaulting into the kind of photogenic flames that local television newscasts could only lust after, and a few minutes later, Mel was standing alone, astride the center line of the long straight strip of asphalt leading off into the desert horizon, the only sign of injuries that would have killed a normal mortal being a nasty limp.

I perked up. In my misery, this was exactly what I needed: catharsis. And suddenly the hyper-style of it all struck me as brilliantly absurd. I began to laugh, expecting that in the row behind me, the laughter would be louder still.

But it wasn't. At first there was just a strangled titter or two, more an attempt at laughter than the real thing. Then a subdued "Oh, man." And then no sound at all. Just an uneasy silence.

I felt my neck muscles ease as the tension shifted to the row behind me. I longed to turn so that I could see the looks on their faces, but that would completely blow my newly achieved cool. I leaned back, spread my right arm over the back of the seat next to me, and crossed one leg with the ankle high on the other, macho style. Behind me, I heard the teenagers shift uneasily in their seats. A few minutes later, the blood began to flow again on-screen. Again I sat there laughing out loud at it. Only this time, something else happened.

Even as I was laughing, I heard the three teens stand up behind me. Heard them shuffle out of the row of seats. Listened as they walked up the aisle—"oh man," one muttered, "oh man"—and found seats well to the back of the theater, as far away as possible from the madwoman who found this kind of violence funny.

I sat there grinning broadly through the next reel or two of the movie, immensely satisfied by my small victory. It wasn't until the movie was over that I turned and looked for the boys. They were gone. And that's when it occurred to me that maybe they were saner than I was. Was there really something of Mad Max in me?

★

Greg Smith was finishing up his briefing. "Now," he said, "you're going to have three generations of Smiths working with you today. This is my daughter, Sadie." He grinned. "I'll be riding with her in the lead Jeep. She'll be driving."

I hadn't noticed Sadie before. I don't think any of the journalists had. She was so shy she'd avoided all the initial greetings. And so young— just short of seventeen. A slim five foot four, her very fragility seemed to announce that she was far too delicate for this sort of thing. Let alone to lead a cavalcade of drivers who thought they'd done it all. She gave a sort of half-smile and without a word, slipped away from her father's side and back to the vehicles.

The men around me went quiet. Sadie driving the lead Jeep was the kind of challenge no amount of machismo could meet. I could practically feel the testosterone level going down. It reached ground level a few minutes later when Greg asked Sadie to demonstrate how to start the Jeep without using the clutch. She climbed up into the driver's seat, casually leaned back, stuck her legs out over the side and crossed them— see, no feet—and switched on the ignition. The vehicle lurched, then settled down to a gentle crawl. Sadie just sat there looking past us into the distance, that faint half-smile on her face, the picture of nonchalance.

And boy, could she drive a Jeep. She took off in the lead, Doug and I in second place, the others strung out in a line behind us. Within a few minutes, we were watching open-mouthed as ahead of us, her Jeep seemed to have the grace and agility of a mountain goat. Even while our eyes told us that this trail was passable, reason told us otherwise. If I hadn't just seen Sadie drive up what looked like a vertical slab of rock and disappear from view, I'd have sworn it couldn't be done. In fact, I think I *did* swear it couldn't be done. I certainly swore, at any rate.

On rock, there were no tracks to follow, not unless I was to get out and start acting like the tracker in *Butch Cassidy and the Sundance Kid.* Sadie was definitely the Sundance Kid. She didn't need a Butch Cassidy. And though I could make a good stab at tracking in sand or snow, I had no idea how anyone ever managed to track on rock. So I made do with a rough guess as to where her wheels had gone, gave the Jeep a little gas, and held my breath as it climbed up the rock face, expecting it to start sliding back at any moment.

Halfway up, what I'd thought was the top turned out to be only a slight leveling before it went up again, even steeper. "I think she's disappeared into thin air," I rambled out loud as the Jeep, incredibly, kept on creeping up the rock face. "I think she's just gone up over the top and taken off, evaporated. I think we're going to get up there, if there is an up there, and find no sign of her, nothing at all, just us, stuck on top of a huge rock with no way to get down . . ."

Doug said nothing. He was probably thinking exactly the same thing. I glanced over and saw his face grim and white. I sympathized. I knew from past experience how much riskier such driving looks when you're in the passenger seat instead of behind the wheel. I was scared enough; he had to be terrified.

But sure enough, when we came over the top a couple of minutes later, there was Sadie, waiting. Her eyes watched us in the rearview mirror, calm and confident. Was there a hint of a smile in them? We didn't have time to find out. No sooner had we heaved into view than she took off, and again we were two urban adults haring after a slip of a girl who clearly considered this wilderness merely an extension of her own back yard in Georgetown, at the western end of the trail.

"I begin to see what they mean when they talk about the Rubicon," I said.

"How so?" said Doug.

"It's tough," I said.

He glanced down the steep drop beside him and managed a strangled "Mm-hm" of agreement.

But we learned. In low gear with four-wheel drive engaged, we let the Jeep creep over boulders and through streams, up intimidating inclines and down again, figuring out where to place our wheels with the mathematical precision of a professional pool player lining up a bank shot.

After a while I began to gain confidence. It seemed I had the Rubicon down pat. And then the going got worse. We'd arrived at a short, steep, boulder strewn sluice that was clearly treacherous. In fact it wasn't merely boulder strewn. All it *was* was boulders. It cut such a narrow path through the rock that surely no vehicle could get through. Yet Sadie's Jeep was down at the bottom, and she was leaning against the hood, patiently waiting. I stopped and took a good look to either side, figuring there had to be another way down. There wasn't.

Doug got out, scrambled down to stand beside Sadie, and unsheathed his camera. "All yours," he said.

I balked. "I'm not going down there," I declared.

Greg Smith ambled over to the bottom of the sluice. "Piece of cake," he yelled up, grinning.

"You eat the cake. I'm staying right here."

"Just follow my directions. I'll point to where to put the wheels." And he positioned himself right in the middle of the sluice, some thirty yards below me.

"But it's so steep I can't see over the hood."

"That's okay. Just keep it in first gear and let it creep down."

"It'll slide."

"It won't. I promise you. Just keep your eyes on me."

To say this was an exercise in trust is a gross understatement. I certainly trusted Greg, but at the same time I was totally convinced that he was a fool to place any trust at all in me under these circumstances. One slip of my foot and I'd have him crushed beneath a ton and a half of metal.

"Move," I begged him. "Please."

No dice. He just stood there, waving me on.

"You're out of your mind," I shouted.

He grinned beatifically as though I'd just paid him the highest possible compliment. It wasn't a lunatic grin, despite what I'd just said. It was the grin of a happy, confident man, a man in his element. If you didn't know he was recently and painfully divorced, you'd think his life was perfect. And right now, it was. Oddly enough, there was no place he'd rather be than at this very spot on the trail, waving on a woman who was convinced that what he knew was possible was in fact impossible, and was giving voice to her conviction by calling him names.

In the end there was nothing to do but laugh, and start moving. If Greg trusted me to follow his directions, then the least I could do was return his trust.

I eased the Jeep over the top of the sluice, and as it began to tip down, put my foot hard on the brake, all the while staring at Greg. His arms were folded. "Which way?" I yelled.

"Just keep on coming," he said. "You're doing fine."

The next thing I knew, I was standing on the brake, literally. The Jeep and I were vertical.

I braced myself against the back of the seat, as though so slight a shift in my weight would stop me tipping over my own nose and falling head over heels, or rather hood over bumper, down to the bottom.

"Are we having fun yet?" said Greg.

One oath after another tumbled through my mind, but at that precise moment, I was too petrified to answer.

"Turn the wheel slightly," he said, pointing to my left. I turned it and felt my front left tire move up onto a rock. "Straight on down now. Keep coming. Keep your eyes on me." As though, with the trail invisible under the expanse of the hood, there was anything else to keep my eyes on. I kept them glued on him. And felt the left rear wheel spin on air.

"Don't worry, you've got three wheels left."

"Great," I managed. "Maybe you want me to drive on two."

"You're going to do that in just a moment. Take it a little to your right now."

"I'm going to do *what?*"

"A little to the right, okay?"

There was nothing to do but follow his directions. A little to the right. I could do that. The left rear wheel found contact with something solid, but just then the front one went up on top of a boulder and the whole vehicle groaned, lurched, and leaned crazily to the right. I knew it was about to tip. Knew it would smash me against the rock wall of this sluice. Knew I'd be trapped and they'd have to haul the Jeep off me and helicopter me out to the nearest hospital—where was the nearest hospital, anyway?—and I should never have come on this crazy trail in the first place, what on earth was I trying to prove . . .

"Left," Greg was yelling, and I steered to the left and heard the wheels scrabbling for purchase and the skidplate under the engine grating against rock. He wasn't joking when he said I'd be driving on just two wheels. The front left and the rear right, it seemed, but there wasn't time to figure it out, because then somehow the Jeep wasn't leaning any more and all four wheels seemed to have found some piece of rock to cling to and I could feel my way down the boulders as though the tires were the skin of my fingers, and Greg was just a few yards in front of me as I watched him move slowly, very slowly, to the side. My front wheels gently bumped down onto what seemed like the smoothest, most level surface in the world, and for a moment it felt like I was balancing there, standing practically nose-down to the ground, until I let the rear wheels slide down the last boulder a few inches at a time and the Jeep began to come level and I felt the last gentle bump as the rear too came down to earth and I'd made it . . .

"I made it!" I heard Doug's camera click, knew he'd caught the look of sheer astonishment and pure, naked relief on my face.

"Piece of cake," Greg declared, so confidently that for a moment I almost believed him.

"Great shots," said Doug. "Thanks."

I was speechless.

I pulled the Jeep a bit farther up the trail and then walked back to watch as the next one came groaning slowly down the sluice, the driver tight-lipped and silent at the wheel. I could still feel that sweet rush of free-floating pleasure that comes after you've overcome terror to do something you were convinced you couldn't. I imagine heroin users must feel something similar.

★

After lunch, I handed over the wheel to Doug and became a passenger. Sort of. Cooled and invigorated by my swim in the lake, I spent more of the afternoon outside the Jeep than in it. I roamed over the rocks, leaped the manzanita-filled cracks, climbed the hills, and when I got hot, dove into another lake. There was never any danger of my losing contact with the little convoy of Jeeps. They were traveling at one mile an hour.

Sure, they went faster than that in the easier sections, but every time the going got tight, as in that sluice, an odd little traffic jam occurred, the Jeeps stacking up one behind the other on the narrow trail as they waited for everyone to get through. Sometimes it was just a few minutes' wait, sometimes far longer, especially if someone managed to get firmly wedged on top of a boulder with all the wheels off the ground—"high-centered," they called it—and no way to move without being towed off.

Yet there was something very peaceable about one mile an hour. Forget speed, forget time. Get hung up on power, and you'd get hung up on a boulder. Just the gentlest pressure on the gas pedal here and there was enough for even the steepest climbs.

This meant it was quiet. No engines were being gunned, and because we were out of range of any radio station, no music was blaring. There was just the occasional groan of brakes or grating of a skidplate against rock, and as the day went on and everyone became more skilled, not even that.

I perched on top of a hill and watched as the convoy crept along the trail below me, voices floating up through the clear air: "A little to the left." "Easy now." "Give her a touch of gas."

I watched one man in particular, one of the Smiths' helpers, who was riding with the sole journalist who had never been off-roading before, the old hand paired up with the greenhorn. He spent most of the time standing upright on the passenger side, one foot wedged up on the dashboard as he held onto the roll bar, scouting the trail ahead and giving directions this way or that. As they went by, he glanced up and saw me, took off his hat and waved it. "It doesn't get any better than this!" he yelled.

Was he aware that he was quoting an advertising line for beer? I hadn't seen the ad for some time, but I remembered it clearly: four guys around a campfire on a mountaintop, sun setting, the beer being handed around, cans being raised in mutual salute: "Guys, it doesn't get any better than this."

He brandished his hat like a cowboy rounding up cattle. Or a rodeo rider on a bucking bronco, perhaps. Or—of course!—a wrangler. That's what he was in his mind, riding that Jeep Wrangler down the trail, living out his own private Wild West fantasy.

So foolish, I thought. Even the Jeeps looked foolish—ungainly, lumbering beasts. It would take them nine hours to drive what could be walked in three. So why drive them at all? A rhetorical question in this context. They were all being serious car guys, while I had reverted to my old persona of wild nature girl. Which in its way was just as foolish a fantasy as being an old-time wrangler.

It was nearly dark by the time we made it to Rubicon Springs, a small valley set deep in a cleft of the High Sierras. A pianist in a striped silk vest and top hat was playing honky-tonk on the upright piano, set in the middle of a meadow. The scent of fresh barbecue hung in the air as beers were passed around. A generator hummed, powering lights strung up over the open-air bar and kitchen. That helicopter had ferried a whole encampment in here to greet the line of dust-caked wranglers, with tents all ready for us, complete with cots and sleeping bags. This was roughing it in luxury.

Yet as we ate and drank and chatted, I felt oddly ungracious and unappreciative. The man with the wrangler fantasy clapped me on the back, raised his beer can, and said "What do you think? It doesn't get any better than this, hey?" and immediately wandered off to do the same to someone else, relieving me of any need to answer. Which was just as well, because by then I was tired and might have tactlessly told the truth.

I woke in the middle of the night and climbed out of my tent. The sky was almost solidly white with stars. The generator had been turned off, and it was so quiet I could hear the hum of absolute silence. I stood by the line of parked Jeeps and breathed deep—clear mountain air, and then, like the aftertaste of a wine too young to be drunk, the familiar acrid scent of motor oil.

Chapter Six

"Historic hotel" announced the red neon sign. "Bistro," said a smaller blue one beneath it.

It was the bistro sign that attracted me. The thought of good food after three days of potato chips, hot dogs, and Seven-Up was appealing. I'd already noticed an espresso sign in a cafe as I drove into Carson City, Nevada, and taken it as a good omen. Seattleites tend to look at the world through caffeinated eyes: when coffee comes with an Italian accent, we assume, in our provincial way, that we have approached civilization.

Besides, the Saint Charles Hotel would be a pleasant respite. I looked up at the decorative ironwork of the veranda running around three sides of the second floor, making the red-brick cube look almost fanciful. The rooms would probably be heavy on the Laura Ashley, and I'd certainly be in for a night in a brass bed with a sagging mattress and a bathroom down the corridor. But I needed a respite from modernity. I'd come off the Rubicon Trail the night before into a gambling hotel on the Nevada side of Lake Tahoe, and the way I felt then I hadn't come out of the Desolation Wilderness, but into it.

There is a peculiar sadness in coming out of the wild and back into "civilization," especially when civilization comes with quite the vengeance of formica and chrome, mirrored walls and flashing strobe lights, and piped music punctuated by the nonstop pinging of fruit machines. The hotel was a self-contained enclave built right on the state line to lure Californian money into Nevadan coffers, a modern high-rise built in defiance of the lake and the mountains. The moment you were in the door, you lost all contact with the outside. No windows, no natural light. It was clearly intended to be a welcome oasis of urbanity; in me, it induced an immense sense of loss.

Like all gambling hotels, this one was built around the machines and the tables. You had to thread your way through them to check in or to get to the elevators or even to the bathrooms. Eyes and ears were assaulted. Everything was pinging and clanging and crashing and blaring. Shiny primal colors flashed on and off, jostling and shouldering each other for attention—"Look at me!" "No. Me, me!"—while the machines chattered away in a choral litany: Give me your quarters, your nickels, your dimes, your tattered dollar notes, your hard-earned fivers . . .

People played the machines with grim concentration. There was a sudden peal of electronic bells as one disgorged a vast flood of coins, and the player, a woman in her sixties with tightly permed gray hair atop a bright pink sweat suit and white sneakers, methodically scooped them up into a white plastic bucket. Her grimness didn't break for so much as a glimmer of a smile at her fortune. The payoff was business as usual.

Most of my fellow Rubicon travelers, having emerged from the trail too late to make their flights back home, fueled themselves with whiskey and made for the gaming tables. I sought refuge in sleep, spent the next morning holed up in my room, working the phone and my laptop, and then around lunchtime, packed up the truck and set off the long way round to Carson City. I'd been meaning to head south more or less in a line to Los Angeles, but going anywhere in a straight line was becoming less and less attractive. Besides, the very name Carson City made me curious. It was one of those names that Hollywood made familiar even if you grew up the other side of the world, as I did. Names like Laramie and Cheyenne and Abilene, redolent of dust-covered cowboys and sharply dressed gamblers, tattered gold-miners and golden-hearted whores. The Saint Charles was straight out of that world.

I remembered that Harry and Nancy Cole lived in Carson City, and wondered should I call them. They'd be long back from letting off rockets at Black Rock; she'd be well into the school year by now. But I knew if I did call, they'd invite me over, and I needed some solitude. Besides, I wanted to leave the initiative with her third-graders. I hoped they'd write; I'd been picking up picture postcards ever since Black Rock, ready to start sending them off.

Since I was the only guest on the whole parlor floor of the hotel, one floor above street level, I had the run of the place. I found my way onto the veranda, settled into a big white wicker chair with my legs up on a matching stool, and leaned back expansively. There was a splendid view of the dome of the state capitol just across the road, and beyond it, the mountains, streaked with snow even in late summer. This veranda, I realized, was why I'd stopped here. So as I could sit just like this, legs lazily crossed, head back, feeling like I owned the town. Give me a leather vest, a shoulder holster, a cigar, and a tumbler of whiskey, and I'd be ready to take on every cardsharp in the West.

The fantasy was ready-made. By the stairwell of the hotel, a windowless cubby-hole of a room had been set aside as a sparsely furnished mini-museum. About four feet wide by ten feet long, it contained a rickety wooden cot laid with an old blanket and a buffalo-skin throw. A cracked chamberpot poked out from beneath the cot, alongside a dusty pair of boots. In the far corner, an almost dainty wooden table held a kerosene lamp, while a shelf displayed an odd assortment of what today would be called toiletries, including the inevitable straight razor. Hung from nails on the walls were a saddle, a hat, a gunbelt, and a well-worn and well-oiled leather coat. The worldly good and belongings, in short, of a nineteenth-century guest of this hotel, perhaps even Kit Carson himself.

I felt almost guilty as I looked from item to item, as though I were about to search the room and steal something from it. There was an odd sense of voyeurism, a feeling that the man whose room this was might come back any moment and be none too pleased at finding an interloper poking around among his things. And a sadness at the knowledge that even if all these things had once belonged to one man, he never would be back.

Kit Carson did indeed sleep here, a plaque in the corridor assured me. If not in that room, at least in this hotel. But then Kit Carson did a lot of sleeping within a hundred-mile radius of Carson City, if all the claims are to be believed, along with the host of other mountain men and prospectors and trappers who opened up the West, following the old Indian trails.

My room, by comparison to Kit's, was luxury. I was glad to see it had gone easy on the Laura Ashley. The new owner, halfway through renovating the place, had more restraint than I'd given him credit for. And the mattress didn't sag, though the bedstead was brass. By the time I discovered that the bistro was closed—"only open three days a week after Labor Day," said the owner—it didn't matter.

As darkness gathered and the traffic below the veranda slacked off, it was easy to imagine that my horse was tied up to the railing on the street in front of the hotel, instead of my Expedition parked round the back. Ah yes, the Expedition. I heaved myself out of wicker comfort and went down to unload what I'd need for the night. I was about to close up the truck when I heard a woman's voice on the road back of the hotel. At least I thought it was a woman's voice; I couldn't be sure at first, it was groaning so low with pain.

"You can't leave me," she was shouting. "You can't. What have I done to make you leave me?"

I looked around the back of the truck. In the streetlight, she seemed to be in her early thirties, perhaps late twenties. Disheveled, in a faded cotton housecoat and tatty bedroom slippers.

She was dragging a girl of about five behind her, tugging at the child as though she were nothing more than a sack of potatoes to be hauled along the pavement. The girl, like her mother, had long, blond hair, except hers was curled into ringlets with grease and grime. She was crying, a mewling mix of fear and bewilderment and sheer exhaustion, but any sound she made was all but drowned out by her mother.

Walking ahead of them, some thirty yards down the sidewalk, was a man carrying a large plastic laundry basket on his shoulder. I could see shoes in it, and shirts, a jumble of cassette tapes, and what looked like a toolbox—all he owned in this world, probably. He kept right on walking, as though nothing was happening behind him.

"I haven't done anything wrong," the mother cried, her voice echoing up and down the empty back road. "You can't leave me. What'll I do? You can't do this to me. Come back." The voice going ever deeper into agony. The voice an animal might have if it could plead for its life.

But he didn't hesitate, just kept on putting one foot steadily in front of the other, under his laundry-basket burden. A nondescript kind of man, average height and build, sandy-haired, blue jeans and work shoes and plaid shirt. Not the kind of man you'd have thought capable of evincing such desperate passion.

"Just come home," she pleaded. "Everything will be all right. I won't do anything. Really I won't. Just come home. Don't leave. Come back."

I stood frozen, as horrified by my own desire to just look and listen as by what I was seeing and hearing. What was she talking about? What would she not do? Lash out at him with the fury of nails? Attack him with a kitchen knife?

The pain in her voice made me want to rush out and do something myself, though I had no idea what. Grab him and make him listen? Release the girl from her mother's grasp? Make everything better with a wave of my fairy godmother's wand? Yes, and get a fist in my face for my trouble.

A patrol car turned up, probably called by a home-owner angry at having his television time disturbed. The trooper got out and began talking to both the man and the woman in a low, calm voice. I couldn't hear what he was saying, just that professional, reassuring tone, the kind that says, "Let's all go down to the station and work this out." And sure enough, first the girl, then the woman, then the man, and finally, and with some difficulty, the laundry basket disappeared into the patrol car. The engine started, and it went off up the street, leaving behind a silence echoing with pain.

I closed the truck and climbed slowly back up the stairs, carrying what I'd need for the night and thinking of that woman. Did she know her cause was already lost, or did she have some naive faith in the existence of the ultimate payoff, the final happily-ever-after of the romance novel? I wondered if there'd been any payoff at some earlier time. There must have been, surely. I hoped it had brought her more pleasure than the flood of fruit-machine quarters to the woman in the bright pink sweats, but somehow I doubted it.

★

I slept restlessly, haunted by the image of that little girl's face. Got up early, waited for the espresso cafe to open, and ordered a triple for the road. The woman behind the counter did a worried double take. "It's okay," I said. "I'm from Seattle."

"Ah," she replied, as though I'd just explained everything. "You staying in town?"

"Just stopped for the night. I'm heading for Yosemite."

She nodded and pursed her lips slightly. I understood that just about every stranger who came through town was heading for Yosemite. But if so, they certainly weren't heading there at this time on a weekday morning. Route 395 turned into a narrow two-lane blacktop some ten miles out of town, and as I wound through deep aspen-filled gorges, I had it all to myself. There was a chill in the air, but I drove with the window open, ambling along at forty miles an hour. As the sun gained height, shadow gave way to light, indistinct gray to a landscape tinted with the deep golden patina of an Old Master painting. I lost the public radio station I'd been tuned to—"Morning Edition" fading into a forest of crackles—and switched off the radio.

Early morning driving is a particular pleasure, one not to be diluted by radio talk or even music. Of course only someone who never drives a commute could say something like that; the few times I've roused myself at dawn to drive out of New York or Seattle on the highways, I've been amazed to see that they're almost as packed as they are a couple of hours later. But away from the big urban centers, it's easy to imagine that the statisticians—the ones who say that the roads are thirty-five percent more crowded now than they were ten years ago, and that the number of cars is growing faster than the population of people who drive them—have been popping the wrong pills. Route 395 was every ad-man's dream, the kind of road producers of television commercials seek out when they want to play on the old romantic idea of motoring as freedom. You see them all the time: shots of a car driving off into the sunset—sunset is so photogenic—on a beautiful, curving, astonishingly empty road. Cruel and ironic counterpoints to urban and suburban fact.

That urban world was here too, in the casinos: the world of noise and hustle, of traffic jams, cars cutting in, drivers giving the finger, potholes rattling the axles, snails in the fast lane, speeders in the slow lane, smog, rain, ice, snow, horns blaring, sirens blaring, radios blaring, voices blaring . . . But step outside into the mountain air, drive a few miles, and the ad-man's idyll becomes reality.

As I climbed steadily higher along the east side of the Sierras, I could feel anticipation building—that odd tension in the chest, almost a sweet taste in the mouth, definitely a gleam in the eye: I was finally going to see Yosemite.

I'd tried before, back in the early spring of 1983, when I spent a few weeks wandering round this part of the West in an old camper truck with a friend from Big Sur. But that was a big El Niño year, and storm after storm was blowing in from the Pacific, causing late-season blizzards in the Sierras. The road in to Yosemite was closed, the pass unpassable. We headed east instead, and spent a week exploring the canyons leading down to Death Valley.

I'd long lost touch with him. The last I heard he was living with a woman who studied wolves somewhere in the wilds of British Columbia, running with the wolves way before it became fashionable. But Yosemite had remained in my mind as unattainable, and therefore all the more alluring.

Yet the closer I got, the more I was aware of a certain sense of trepidation. It was almost too ridiculous that I was on the verge of driving into Yosemite, as though the turnoff would be marked by a sign saying "Casablanca, this way." It wasn't just the exoticism of four syllables that placed the two together in my mind. It was the role of the lens. The myth-making power of the camera.

With Casablanca, it was a movie; with Yosemite, still photographs. But both places had been predetermined through the lens, and that was what was bothering me. The camera doesn't just record image; it defines it. So much so that as I came down the hill overlooking the depredation that is still called Mono Lake, most of its water long since drained off to feed the city of tawdry angels three hundred and fifty miles to the southwest, the word that came to mind was a title: *Chinatown*, Roman Polanski's 1974 movie about the battle for California water rights in the thirties. And the specific image, the inevitable first association for anyone who has seen that movie, was Polanski himself nicking the tip of Jack Nicholson's nose with a knife.

To be driving toward the highest pass over the Sierras and thinking of Jack Nicholson's nose has a certain absurdity to it. The modern mind is a problematic traveler. We arrive with a vast load of preconceptions, of associations from movies and books, radio and documentaries, magazines and newspapers. When a place is famous, we know it before we even lay eyes on it. And we go there then to . . . what? Confirm what we already know? Or try to forget it?

Ansel Adams's dramatic black-and-white photos of Yosemite are engraved so large into the national consciousness—indeed, the world consciousness—that it is just about impossible to even say the word *Yosemite* without seeing one of his images of it. His genius is unfair to the average eye. We're all photographers now, equipped with cameras that at a press of a button can do what only a skilled professional could do fifty years ago. We forget that Adams waited for days and weeks on end for the right light, and spent further days and weeks in the darkroom, using his technology to enhance reality, heightening the contrast between black and white to reflect the luminous quality the mind's eye saw and remembered.

The reality of color, I feared, could only be faded by comparison to Adams's artistry. What I would see would be merely a pale reflection of those famed photographic prints.

The approach from the east, on State Route 120, added to my sense of foreboding. It was a steep, ant-like ascent between looming mountainsides—towering slabs of bare rock hidden by their own height from the early morning sun. Everything was in deep shadow, and that together with the jagged nakedness of the rock created a sense of almost industrial gloom. This was the Tioga Road, built over a hundred years before as a miners' trail and paved and modernized in the early sixties.

A century ago, places like Yosemite were to be mined for profit, and this road still held the echo, somehow, of prospectors cursing while they tried to catch their breath and their mules slipped and slithered and finally balked at the steep prospect before them.

As I turned and twisted upward, the road seemed to have only a tenuous hold on the edge of the rock, as though at any moment the mountains could shift and the road come tumbling down. It wasn't that unlikely. The whole splendid formation of the Sierras was incredibly young in geologic terms. Even, for someone who'd lived in the Middle East, in historical terms. These rocks were only ten thousand years old; I had stood on excavated pavements and door lintels in Jerusalem that were close on four thousand years old. And some of the volcanoes in the Sierran range only put the final touches to their formation a mere two and a half thousand years ago. If Christ had been born on this side of the world instead of the other, he'd have seen mountains as new as mountains can possibly be.

I was still mired in such calculations when I came over the pass at ten thousand feet. And then, just beyond, the world suddenly burst open. I came out between narrow rock walls into a high, heady landscape that was all the more stunning for being so unheralded. All sense of trepidation evaporated. I had driven not into Ansel Adams's Yosemite, but into another one altogether.

Tuolumne Meadows, it was called. A vast alpine scene of mossy meadows, fast-running streams, small tumbling waterfalls, and rock pools. Snow-tipped mountain peaks stood sentinel around the meadows, grandly distant yet somehow intimately close at the same time.

I stopped, got out, let mind and feet wander. The air was so clear it seemed to ring with that pure, high note, white with snow and blue with sky, that is perfect silence. I followed one trail, then another. Played mountain goat, leaping and running over the rocks, arms spread wide, laughter bubbling up inside me. Sat listening to the water running so clear it seemed I could see every crystal of mineral in it, hear every drop as it rushed on down to the famed valley far below.

I lost all sense of time. Who can tell how much time passes when the mind seems to rise out of itself and the body is light and agile with the sheer pleasure of movement? All I know is that after an hour or two, or maybe three, I began to hear the cars.

I'd forgotten about cars. For a while, they'd had no existence. But sound carries well at ten thousand feet. Even here, I wasn't going to be allowed to forget.

And now I remembered how early it had been when I'd set out that morning. The rest of the world had since woken, breakfasted, and gotten moving. I climbed up an outcropping and looked toward the road. There were only a few cars as yet, but they were going fast, apparently making for the valley, their drivers so blinded by Ansel Adams images that they had neither time nor eyes for this high meadowscape.

"Someone should get that road out of here," I thought. "Someone should tear it up and let me be here in peace."

And then realized who I sounded like: the woman in Reno who'd filed suit against land-speed racing on the Black Rock Desert. "The desert should be a place of solitude," she'd written. I'd never met her, but surely only someone full of the self-righteous purity of the young and ostentatiously healthy could have written such a thing. Someone suffused with the pure selfishness of the search for spiritual uplift in the kind of natural surroundings always capitalized as Nature or Wilderness—a specific space "out there" that must be preserved because it's good for the mind, a kind of medical aid: Nature as the great healer, even if not covered by Blue Cross and Blue Shield.

In fact I agreed with her. Solitude in the desert, or anywhere else untamed, was what I too sought. But then I'd have to fight with her whenever I wanted to walk out into the desert. Only one person can be solitary at a time.

Okay, so at least take the people out of the cars.

Edward Abbey's splendidly bawdy riff on tourists in *Desert Solitaire* came to mind. "What can I tell them?" it begins. "Sealed in their metallic shells like mollusks on wheels, how can I pry the people free? The auto as tin can, the park ranger as opener. Look here, I want to say, for god's sake folks get out of them there machines, take off those fucking sunglasses and unpeal both eyeballs, look around . . ."

I had a copy of the book in the back of the truck. It was the first book

I'd reached for when I packed for this journey, a well-thumbed, well-marked copy whose contents had remained alive and vital despite my having taught it five years in a row when I'd been an English professor a decade before—before I began to write about cars and became far too disreputable for any university. Not that I expected to read it again while I was on the road; I simply wanted its presence, as I wanted Kerouac's *On the Road*, the *Portable Graham Greene*, Jorge Luis Borges' *Labyrinths*, and the handful of other sentimental favorites that made me feel that so long as they were with me, I was at home anywhere in the world.

Abbey died a few years back, but that didn't stop me arguing with him. He would have enjoyed a good argument. Especially here in Yosemite.

"What about democracy at work, Ed? The national heritage and all that? You and I might like to get down and dirty in the moss and see God in granite peaks, but who's to say that's the only way to see beauty? What's wrong with a quick drive-by and a few snapshots?"

"That heap of metal you call a truck has seduced you into laziness, Hazleton," he shot back. "Burn the damn thing. Or drop the environmental pose and vote Republican next time, for God's sake."

I stalked off huffily and left him to sulk by the stream. I was hungry, and had left my breakfast—bread, cheese, and fruit—in the truck. By the time I got back there, the sun was high in the sky. Breakfast had become lunch. And the traffic had become a fairly steady stream.

It looked like the Park Service's task was becoming just about impossible. Keep the national parks pristine but accessible? That's an oxymoron of a mandate.

Specifically, the Park Service was enjoined by Congress back in 1916 both to administer the parks and to "provide for the enjoyment of same in such manner and by such means as will leave them unimpaired for the enjoyment of future generations." Nice language, as Abbey had pointed out in his book. Nice, contradictory language, leaving unresolved the conflict between those who wanted to develop the parks and those who wanted to keep them just the way they were. It left the way open for what Abbey called "industrial tourism," which consisted of "the indolent millions born on wheels and suckled on gasoline, who expect and demand paved highways to lead them in comfort, ease, and safety into every nook and corner of the national parks."

"Go, Ed!" I'd thought on first reading that. "Right on the nail." But now, as I climbed back into the truck and joined the stream of traffic, I noticed that most of the big RVs seemed to hold retired couples.

They looked happy, and why not? They paid taxes just as I did. Part of their taxes went to maintain the national parks. Didn't they have a right to see this park in their own way? Who was I to say there was only one way to travel?

Since I was moving along at a mere twenty miles an hour, still entranced by the meadows, I pulled over from time to time to let them pass. For a while I felt a self-congratulatory glow of good-citizenly tolerance. It wasn't as though they were towing their RVs across the meadows. And if they were content to view everything from a distance, what was wrong with that? Not my way of doing things, but if everyone took my way, the meadows would be teeming with people.

Then an RV began to turn out of a rest stop, paused as the driver saw me coming along, and at the last moment cut in right in front of me. I slammed on the brakes. "Godammit . . ." And saw that the thing was towing a Jeep Cherokee. And that in response to the sudden acceleration, the Cherokee was swaying alarmingly on its hook.

I wanted to scream. I wanted to speed on past. Specifically, I wanted to speed on past and scream: "What's the matter with a Geo Metro?"

A touch of road rage in Yosemite? Abbey seemed to have caught up with me. I could hear him cackling in the back seat. "Want a stick of dynamite?" he offered. I was tempted to tell him where to stick it.

Of course Abbey had the good sense to die just before the sport-utility rage hit the United States. That is, just before automakers discovered that people would pay more, a lot more, for a metal box slapped on top of a truck chassis that offered a rugged image and a driver's seat high off the ground. When Abbey gave up the ghost, Detroit was just discovering that for all the lip-service, Americans really didn't give a damn about fuel economy. And that for all the talk about informed consumers, they were quite happy to fork over thirty percent in pure profit for a sport-ute.

With that cultivated jaundiced eye of his, Ed could probably have predicted what still amazed me: that the more geegaws the automakers stuck onto these things—the more leather and CD players and built-in compasses and Bose speakers—the more people would want to buy them. So what if only three percent of the drivers ever took their metal monsters off-road? They could still fantasize about being wildmen and wolf-running women even as they made the daily trip to the market, or dropped the kids off at school, or used the size and weight of their utes to terrorize the roads.

Or drove a paved road through a designated wilderness replete with road signs, campgrounds, scenic viewpoints, and visitor centers.

I pulled the Expedition into the scenic viewpoint at Olmstead Point, as much to create a good safe distance between myself and the RV with its swaying Jeep as to see the view down over the valley. Other cars had stopped too. People were lined up along the stone retaining wall edging the parking area, taking photographs. A few actually looked at the Park Service sign that explained where they were; most didn't bother. They seemed to be attached to their vehicles by some invisible umbilical cord: none strayed more than some ten yards from them. They were traveling through Wilderness—the capitalized kind—and they were there simply to record the fact that they were there. That is, to take photographs, drive on to the next scenic viewpoint, and take more photographs.

Every now and then, a kid would try to make a break for it, touched no doubt by the subversive influence of Abbey's presence in the back of my truck. There'd be a quick dodge through the line of lens-focused adults, a dash a few yards down a dirt trail below the retaining wall, and then a wail of maternal alarm—"Tiffany!" or "Jason!" or "Melissa!"—followed by a barrage of threats and fear.

"Get back here right now!"

"Don't you know how dangerous that is?"

"Didn't I tell you never to set foot off the road?"

"Get back in the car this instant!"

"I don't know why we even brought you with us."

"Just you wait 'til we get home . . ."

A slap, tears, the slam of a car door, and another child's curiosity was kept firmly in bounds.

A Chevy Blazer with a caravan in tow drew in and disgorged its family of occupants. They left all the doors open and the engine running, though with that rig they certainly weren't going to make a quick getaway. The door-open chime kept going in percussive accompaniment to the family: the mother shouting at the father, the father at the mother, the children at anyone who'd listen:

"Can't you shut the kids up?"

"They're your kids too, you know."

"I didn't ask to come here."

"Right, like you had nothing to do with it."

"Where's the damn pacifier?"

"How the hell should I know?"

"Goddammit you had it last."

"I did not."

"You did."

"I'm hungry."

"I want to pee."

"I want to watch TV."

"I want some ice cream."

Ping, ping, ping, ping, ping, ping, ping . . .

I wished for some giant hand to sweep down and pick them up, car, caravan, and all, and dump them somewhere in the middle of Los Angeles.

"Try the middle of the ocean," said Ed.

"Oceans can be polluted too, you know," I retorted. That kept him quiet for a while.

I sought refuge back on the road. It was fifty-five miles from the meadows down to Yosemite valley, and I still had forty to go. I planned to spend the night there, and wander around by foot the whole of the next day. But ten miles short of my mark, the traffic began to pile up. It slowed, then crawled, then practically stopped.

I was in a traffic jam in Yosemite, the road ahead a solid, immobile line of buses, RVs, sport-utes, fifth-wheelers, all manner of traffic far too cumbersome for the narrow winding roads leading into the valley.

Abbey couldn't resist. "Pity you didn't bring a camper to tow," he taunted. "In this rig you'd have fit right in."

"That's below the belt," I said.

"Best place to be," he replied with a leer.

"Cut it out, Ed."

"You asked for it. Besides, if you think this is bad, try it in midsummer."

I didn't even want to imagine that. I idled along, trying instead to imagine this place before Ansel Adams, when you could hike or ride in—on a horse, not in a car—and see Yosemite fresh, not mediated through famous eyes. When what you experienced was awe, not frustration. When the last thing you'd carry was a camera.

But something about stalled traffic stymies the imagination. As do large numbers of people. By the time I'd crawled to Inspiration Point, all I could inspire was exhaust fumes. And farther on, so many cars and people were parked in front of El Capitan that the great rock face seemed smaller than I'd expected, diminished by this massive swarm of lens-clicking worshippers.

The familiar beginnings of a kind of panic began to build inside me. It couldn't be, I thought, but I knew it was: here, in Yosemite Valley, I was on the verge of claustrophobia. I wanted to turn the truck and head in the other direction as quickly as I could, but I was in a one-way system, forced to keep crawling all the way up to Yosemite Village, which turned out to be nothing more than a campground so packed it felt like a refugee camp.

Forget the waterfalls. Forget Glacier Point. Forget the very idea of a peaceful day hiking the valley. There was only one place I wanted to be, and that was Out of Here. I took the first turn I could find and made my bid for freedom, as though once outside the park boundary, I could begin to breathe again.

"They've got to limit access somehow," I kept thinking. "Ban trailers. Cut way back on overnight permits."

"Go the whole hog," Abbey shouted in my ear. "Ban cars! You know they're going to have to do it sooner or later. Might as well be now."

I pulled up at the park exit to pay the five-dollar fee. "Did you enjoy your visit?" asked the ranger at the booth.

"The meadows are stunning," I answered. "The valley . . ." I hesitated, then added sheepishly: "Too many people. I fled."

She gave a grim smile. "I know what you mean," she said. And I could have sworn that right then she too heard Abbey's final "harrumph" as he got out of the truck, slammed the door, and stalked off, a lost prophet in search of wilderness.

Chapter Seven

It's a good thing I was looking for Cholame, or I'd never have realized it was there. On my map, it looked to be about halfway between Yosemite and Los Angeles, which is to say it was in the middle of nowhere. This was not the California of international repute—neither the glories of the Sierras nor the glitz of the coast—but the tough, dry, hilly grazing land that leads down to *Grapes of Wrath* and Cesar Chávez country, where migrants work bent in the fields of the San Joaquin valley until sunset, their rusted pickups parked haphazardly along the roadside.

I spent a long and satisfying morning entirely on four-digit roads, the kind of roads that are unnumbered on state maps, their lines printed in a gray so pale it looks like it might fade into the paper at any moment. Narrow strips of asphalt, barely ten feet wide, they wind from one tiny township to the next, ten or twenty miles away. A township hereabouts might be just two houses, one either side of a T-junction. Or even no house at all, at least so far as I could see.

The creekbeds were dry except for an occasional shallow greenish scum, and the grass on the dry rolling hills had withered to deep gold. The whole landscape was waiting for the first rains. Even the black cattle huddled under the occasional stand of scrub oak seemed to be waiting for moisture. They'd move on down to the road as I trundled on by, apparently mistaking the sound of my engine for that of the farmer coming with feed, and making me feel like a major event in these parts.

There were easier ways to get where I was going, but I wasn't interested. I wanted the most backward of the back roads, and went out of my way to stay on them, curving way west so that I'd come south through Coalinga. I'd driven through here one morning in that early spring of 1983, when the whole valley had been an almost obscenely luscious green after so much rain, and horses lay on their sides in the pastures, bellies swollen from overfeeding. Vultures hovered overhead, waiting for death. It would come with a vengeance just a week later, in the form of a Richter 6.5.

There'd been a cafe not far outside town with hunting trophies on the wood plank walls, evaporated milk on the bar to pour straight from the tin into your coffee, and the shabbiest pool table I had ever laid cue on. At dawn, it had been full of Hispanic cowboys in ten-gallon hats, faded bandannas, and stacked-heel boots to make them taller. But I couldn't find the cafe again; either the slow change of economics or the sudden one of the earthquake had closed it down. I kept on going south, guided by the sun rather than my map. The radio picked up one Latin music station after another, the music absurdly happy, full of a lusher, more vibrant life. By the time I emerged onto Route 46, about twenty-five miles east of Paso Robles, it was early afternoon.

"Cholame, population 65," said a sign.

Wherever those sixty-five people were, they were very well hidden. There was no small cluster of buildings, no store, just the occasional semi taking the sole east-west route through this part of California that could accommodate heavy trucks. The only building I could see was the Jack Ranch Cafe, whose rundown wooden frame shivered and trembled in the slipstreams of the trucks, as though it might collapse in on itself at any moment.

Maybe I'd been given a bum steer. This didn't seem to be the place I wanted. But if the cafe didn't look at all promising, it did at least offer the prospect of a hamburger. I'd been hungry ever since Coalinga, and if you're hungry enough, even the worst hamburger can taste pretty good.

Two semis were parked in the shade of a large tree off to the side of the cafe. I drew up alongside, searching for a bit of shade left over for the Expedition. Only when I nosed around behind the big trucks did I see that there was a kind of sculpture built around the trunk of the tree:

two curved, overlapping four-foot-high walls of what looked like brushed aluminum, flecked with shreds of sunlight coming through the branches. And at the foot of the silvery walls, a plaque.

I'd found the right place after all.

The plaque was titled "Tribute to a Young Man." In more modest versions, I'd seen hundreds like it all over the United States, homespun roadside memorials to young lives cut violently short. A makeshift white cross, a browned and dried bunch of flowers, a hand-lettered sign: pathetic but touching attempts to rescue sons and daughters from the anonymity of traffic casualty statistics. But this memorial was neither modest nor homespun. In this place, it was jarringly professional.

"His name was James Byron Dean," the inscription began. I'd never known his middle name was Byron. How perfect. "He died just before sundown on September 30, 1955, when his Porsche collided with another car at a fork in the road not nine hundred yards east of this tree, long known as the Tree of Heaven. He was twenty-four years old."

The implied idea of James Dean in heaven struck me as thoroughly odd, since he lived his life as though he had no intention of going anywhere but hell. This plaque might suit a saint. It was tailored to the romantic idea of youth as innocence, and there was something in its use of the tree that reminded me of the John Keats poem about the basil pot, the one where the beautiful Isabella's lover is murdered by her brothers. In a weird combination of the gruesome and the romantic, Isabella finds the body, cuts off the head, takes it home, and puts it in a gardening pot. Then she plants basil over it, and waters the basil with her tears. The basil flowers profusely. Love lives on in fragrant foliage.

Jimmy Dean would have sneered at the idea.

A smaller plaque declared that both plaques and sculpture had been erected in 1977 by a Japanese fan called Seita Ohnishi. He had evidently given the tree a suitably romantic name while he was about it. And fudged a detail or two. There was no mention of how fast Dean had been going. Nor of the name painted on his car: "Little Bastard." Too earthy for a legend, perhaps. And though it's true that Dean crashed at 5:59 p.m. on that day, he didn't die on the spot; he suffered severe internal injuries, and died in the ambulance on the way to the hospital in Paso Robles.

The Spot. That was where I wanted to be. That was why I'd come here. To stand on The Spot where Jimmy Dean died. Forget ambulances and fussy details of time. Despite what I knew, it was fixed in my mind that James Dean died here, in Cholame. Sort of.

I was disappointed. Aside from the memorial and the ramshackle cafe, there didn't seem to be any "here" here. Why erect a memorial if it wasn't on the right spot? Why wasn't it nine hundred yards east?

I ambled over to the cafe. The screen door banged to behind me, torn screens flapping. I stood with the light behind me, squinting into the dark. The lone stranger riding into town again. Only there was no town here. I'd expected at least the truck drivers, but the cafe was empty. Even the bar was empty.

Over to one side, a concrete-floored room—a former garage with the wall knocked through—served as the showplace for what a crudely lettered sign advertised as "James Dean Memorabilia." I wandered round the oddly sparse collection of photos, posters, tin trays, and plaster plaques, all in the kind of bright, primary colors that make Ted Turner's colorized movies look subtle and restrained. The kind of colors, that is, usually reserved for portraits and sculptures of saints. There was a rack of T-shirts, but only two designs, both featuring garish pictures of guitars with the words ROCK AND ROLL in large letters and "James Dean" in small ones; a handful of pens with a wraparound photo of Dean on them—the same pens I'd found some months before in a variety store in Seattle, where they were half the price they were here; and a rack of postcards in fake sepia tint showing bedroom-eyed Jimmy doing his come-hither stance long before Calvin Klein stole the idea and put it on bus-stop advertisements all over Manhattan.

There was a scuzzy, half-hearted feel to the room, as though the owners of the cafe would much rather ignore the whole James Dean business. I could understand that; it must be strange to make your living on someone else's death. Or perhaps they were born-again Christians and just didn't approve of Dean.

I picked out a few postcards—how would I explain Jimmy Dean to the third-grade kids?—went back into the cafe proper, and knocked on the glass counter. "Hello?"

"Coming," replied a weary voice from somewhere out back.

She looked tired, as though the place had been jam packed until just a moment before I walked in and the last thing she could face now was yet another customer. She was in her forties perhaps, but something in her face said that she had looked this tired ever since she was a girl.

"Can I get something to eat?"

"It's a cafe, isn't it?"

I ordered a burger and she called back the order. That accounted for at least two of Cholame's population of sixty-five. As she poured me some coffee, I asked why the memorial was here and not up the road where the crash actually happened.

"He couldn't get the land there," she said. "That Chinaman million-aire. Or Japanese. Whatever." She sniffed derisively. "County wouldn't give it to him."

"So why here?"

"Got permission to use this land from the Hearst family." She spilled the coffee and made a desultory dab at wiping it up. "You heard of them?"

"As in the newspapers?"

She gave me a suspicious look, as if to say, "If you know so much, how come you're asking questions?" I was glad I hadn't said, "As in *Citizen Kane*."

"Yeah," she replied. "Them. They own a lot of the land around here. They let him use it, and that out there is what he did."

I wasn't sure if she objected on the grounds of dislike for modern sculpture, or for Ohnishi's ethnic origin, or for Dean himself. A change of subject seemed in order.

"What kind of tree is that?"

She shrugged. "It's called the Tree of Heaven," she said in a mono-tone, clearly bored with my questions.

"Yes, but what species of tree is it?"

She stared at me like she would at an idiot. "It's a Tree of Heaven tree," she said flatly.

I returned the shrug, and gave up. It had to be a kind of gum tree, I thought, the name merely a fanciful homage invented by a besotted fan.

But later I'd look it up in the *Sunset Western Garden Book,* the bible of every gardener west of the Rockies and the major reference for my own floating garden back home.

"*Ailanthus altissima,* tree of heaven," said Sunset. "Deciduous. Native to China. Planted in the 1800s in California's gold country, where it now runs wild. Fast growth to 50 feet. Leaves 1–3 feet long are divided into 13–25 leaflets 3–5 inches long. Inconspicuous greenish flowers are usually followed by handsome clusters of red-brown, winged seed pods in late summer and fall; great for dried arrangements. Often condemned as a weed tree because it suckers profusely and self-seeds, it must be praised for its ability to create beauty and shade under adverse conditions—aridity, hot winds, extreme air pollution, and every type of difficult soil."

Jimmy would have liked that little detail "suckers profusely and self-seeds." For my part, I liked the bit about the difficult soil.

★

I wasn't sure exactly what had drawn me to Cholame. I liked James Dean well enough, to be sure. Like many women, I have a certain weakness for good-looking young men with "Trouble" writ large on their foreheads. And I was attracted by the pose of the rebel—the sulk, the pout, the clear and imminent danger. Rough trade.

But this is a lie. I knew what had drawn me here. How not, when I had hesitated for so long over whether to take the last of the books I'd thrown into the back of the truck before leaving home? It was a book I'd read twice and hoped I'd never read again. A book that aroused an immense ambivalence in me, inspiring revulsion and admiration in equal degrees. Even as I held it in my hand, trying to decide whether to take it or leave it behind, I was aware that its very presence in the back of the truck might be taunting the gods, an act of hubris for which I would somehow be punished. Yet there was a truth in this novel that I couldn't ignore. I knew I wouldn't open it, but that didn't matter. Its physical presence in the truck would somehow keep me honest. I took a deep breath and threw J. G. Ballard's *Crash* in with the other books.

The first time I read it, on a plane from New York to Chicago, I couldn't stand to take the book with me when I left. I stuffed it deep into the seat pocket in front of me. Only when I'd left the airport did I remember that the plane was going on elsewhere with the same crew. I had a vivid image of the next person to be assigned that seat reaching into the pocket just after takeoff. I hoped whoever it was, was not superstitious.

I read the novel again a few years later at the urging of a student friend. It had become a cult classic by then, especially among the more avant-garde crowd of art and philosophy students, the ones who were experimenting with heroin and multiple piercings. It wasn't hard to see why. The high level of transgressive myth-making in *Crash* would make it irresistible.

A second reading gave me more appreciation of the book as a work of art. It also confirmed my reaction to the first reading. This was truly the most obscene thing I'd ever read.

I don't mean that it was pornographic in the usual sense—the pounding repetition of sexual mechanics to the point where what is endlessly fascinating becomes terminally boring. Though that too was part of the book. No, the true obscenity was the way Ballard took an innocuous, everyday activity, driving, and made it the focus of twisted sexual obsession. "A new sexuality born from a perverse technology," he called it, where flesh would have intercourse not just with other flesh mangled by metal, even to the point of necrophilia, but with metal itself.

Ballard's starting point was the way most people slow down to ogle a crash. The worse the crash, and the greater the likelihood of severe injury or dead bodies, the slower they go. It had often occurred to me that there was a certain titillation in this—that people were "dying to see what had happened." I'd look at their faces as they slowed down and stared, open-mouthed and bright-eyed with fascination, searching for the gruesome details. There was a certain drooling, slavering element to this fascination, tongues all but hanging out at the thought of seeing something forbidden, so very private and intimate a thing as death laid out in the open for all to see. I had seen this, but never quite mustered the guts to call it arousal.

This ogling of death strikes me as all the stranger since my own impulse is to drive by as fast as I can. Get away from the reminder of what can happen. Protect my own illusion of immortality, or at least the remaining shreds of it. When you've seen too much death, illusion becomes very fragile.

I saw a lot of it in the years I spent in the Middle East. Reporting from Jerusalem, I went to too many funerals, most of them for young men. Any temptation to romanticize, let alone philosophize, was curtailed by the awful grittiness of the details: the ghastly moaning of the widow, the bewilderment of the children, the huddle of survivors shivering around an open grave. Standing there by that hole in the ground, you faced the absolute irrevocability of death. It stood across your path like a giant brick wall, immovable, bleakly unresponsive. You could bang your head against that wall for all eternity, and it would not give an inch.

In Israel, Jewish funerals are Orthodox funerals, held within twenty-four hours after death, when the survivors are still in shock. The body is never on view; there is no illusion of the dear departed drifting into sleep like an actor in full stage makeup, cushioned in silk, at rest in the coffin. For military funerals, simple, rough-hewn pine coffins are used, and they serve a horribly practical purpose: the body might be mangled out of human shape, or only part of it might have been recovered. Sometimes I'd wonder if we were burying just an arm or a leg, or even a skull.

But at least with a coffin, ropes were used to gently lower it into the ground. In regular Israeli funerals, there were no ropes, because there was no coffin. Just a shroud over the body, and an awful thud as the body was tipped into the grave and fell six feet down.

That thud reaches inside you, through your ears into your heart, your stomach, your memory. Something at the very core of you goes weak, starts turning, loosed from its moorings in the casual reality of life. A cry of pain wrenches out of you—a subdued whimper for friends and extended family; a low, animal moan for husbands, wives, and lovers.

It has no reverberation, this thud, yet the terrible flat finality of it stays with you the rest of your life. It leaves no room for denial.

And neither did Ballard. Starting from that vicarious thrill of voyeurism, he leaped over the rationalizations, the false sanctimony of "there but for the grace of God go I," and took the fascination with violent death to its extreme—a sexualization of twisted metal and mangled bodies, shattered glass and brain-spattered dashboards.

The revulsion *Crash* inspired was evidence of its power and of the uncomfortable truth that gives it that power. It haunts with its vision of a society so bound up in the car that its images enter our most private fantasies, searching for the ultimate union of flesh and metal. Its sexuality threatens our sense of sanity and normalcy, which is what the art-school crowd mean when they rave about *Crash* as "radical" and "transgressive," and what director David Cronenberg missed when he dared make a movie of it, failing so utterly that he rendered savagely cerebral hard-core satire into something more like soft-core bedroom farce.

Ballard stripped away romance to lay bare its pitted bones—the mechanics of the adoration of cars. As his characters cruise the streets, first searching for crashes and then creating them, the reader is faced with the prospect of people being devoured by their own desire for machines. Is the car the Golem, turning on its maker? Or is it some modern version of the vampire legend, where the bite on the neck leads to the orgasmic swoon? The car as techno-vampire, sucking the blood of youth and beauty.

And youth and beauty, Ballard knew, are an essential part of it. His characters are as obsessed with stardom as they are with cars, and the combination of the two creates a joint eroticism taken to the limit as they re-enact famous crashes like James Dean's, killing others in the process, and even themselves.

Inevitably, after Princess Diana was killed, Ballard's novel would come to the fore again. "By bringing together two erotic fetishes—the Automobile and the Star—in an act of sexual violence (a car crash)," wrote Salman Rushdie in *The New Yorker*, Ballard "created an effect so shocking as to be thought obscene. The death of Diana is just such an obscenity . . . a cocktail of death and desire even more powerful than the one in Ballard's book."

Rushdie, still under a dead ayatollah's death sentence for the crime of being possessed of an imagination, was not fooled by illusion. By linking Diana's death with *Crash*, he must have hoped to shock his readers out of illusion too. But where words had condemned him, they were useless in the face of the blinding force of star power.

Anyone who watched as mourners flocked to the entrance to that Parisian tunnel, eager to be as close as possible to The Spot, had to be uncomfortably aware, however dimly, of the vampirish quality of the adoration. The same thing that made them devour her image in life, also provided the frisson of standing where she died and imagining her death, running through what they knew of the crash again and again. Who even needed the photographers' shots of her as she lay dying? The minds of those who adored her provided them ready-made.

Meanwhile here I was, in Cholame, doing the same thing.

★

The pivotal figure in James Dean's death is not really Dean at all, nor even his car, but a young man called Donald Turnipseed who was driving the car that Dean swerved to avoid.

Donald Turnipseed: the name straight out of central casting. The hayseed chewing on a blade of grass as he lumbered on out into the movie star's path. In fact he was a college student, but fact has nothing to do with myth. Turnipseed had his moment in history, playing an accidental role as the *deus ex machina*, the god in the machinery.

For a moment, a blink of an eye, Turnipseed was graced by his encounter with fame. Like a deer caught in the headlights, he was frozen in place—we have just that one mental snapshot of him, in that one moment and that one place—and then was swallowed up again by the darkness of oblivion, to live out an ordinary life.

But what would have happened if Turnipseed had stopped before starting his engine that afternoon to scratch at a mosquito bite or blow his nose? Or had dropped his keys and fumbled on the ground to pick them up? Or paused to light a cigarette? Anything that would have meant a delay of even a second or two.

Or maybe that's exactly what happened: Turnipseed did one of these things—scratched or blew or fumbled or lit up—and that's what made him arrive at The Spot just a few seconds later than he otherwise might have, at the precise moment when James Dean came speeding over the rise, saw him turning onto the main road, swerved, and crashed.

So, Donald Turnipseed blew his nose. Or didn't. And we then have to imagine James Dean alive. Instead of Jett Rink in *Giant,* his last movie role, we have to imagine him in his sixties, gone to booze like Jack Kerouac or to drugs like Elvis Presley. Beer-fattened, puffy-faced, hair gray and thinning, the flesh that made him now betraying him.

But no, the very idea is anathema. The cult of James Dean depends on his youth. By the grace of speed and danger, he remains young, the *puer aeternus,* eternal boy. A sexualized Peter Pan. He had to die young. And if so, it had to be in a car. And not just any car.

The car is an essential part of the cult. To die young while driving a Hyundai is not conducive to romance. Imagine Isadora Duncan with her long silk scarf wrapped around the rear wheel spokes of a Buick. As they say in Hollywood, it doesn't play. The car had to be something expensive and exotic, though a Rolls Royce Corniche does betray a certain lapse in her myth-making ability. It's just a tad too obvious; a Bugatti would have served better.

Jimmy Dean made no such mistake. The little bastard was a Porsche Spyder, with its racing number, 31, painted on the hood. A two-seater convertible. The perfect car in which to act out Dean's famed manifesto: "Live fast, die young, and leave a beautiful corpse."

Except for that little detail about the beautiful corpse.

Whoever would have taken Dean for an ironist? Yet he must have known that the only beautiful corpses are in fairy tales, vampire stories, and the undertaker's studio. The terrifying brutality of blood turning black in the sun, of tendon and muscle ripped and shredded, of scattered shards of bone and globules of brain—none of this makes for beauty, though it certainly makes for a corpse.

We deal with violence by romanticizing it. A natural reaction for a culture raised on the version of death delivered in Hollywood westerns, where a bullet either kills a man instantly or finds a relatively innocuous home in the soft muscle of his shoulder, providing an opportunity for the golden-hearted whore to nurse the hero back to amazingly limber health.

Even in war movies, romance steals the show, painting everything with the glowing brush of blood and guts and glory. The sick surrreality of being under fire is transformed into heroics, panic into decisiveness. Perhaps the sickest transformation of all is the reaction of many, including myself, under fire, a kind of defensive illusion: "It's just like being in a movie." We force our senses into the numbness of the passive moviegoer, as though that way the bullets and shells will have as little effect on real flesh and blood as they do in the safe darkness of the theater.

And no matter how hard you try later to convey what it was really like, you are brought up sharp against that movie-fueled romantic aura. You see a look of respectful awe come over the listener, as though by having been *there*—a mythical realm on the brink of death from which you have returned to tell the tale—you have achieved some measure of the heroic. Even though at the time it was far more likely that it was all you could do not to foul your pants.

A crude detail? Of course, and deliberately so. But the truth of it doesn't get through. That strange alchemy by which the ugliness of war is transformed into heroics is at work here in Cholame too: the car crash is transformed into romance. People lose the use of their senses; they become deaf and blind, unable to see the mangled mess of flesh or hear the haunting, inhuman, animal-like cry of someone in mortal pain.

Romance makes undertakers of us all. We beautify the bodies, paint on the makeup, hide the stomach-turning damage. By the time we have finished, the person we knew and loved as much for human faults as virtues has been dolled up into some ghastly simulacrum of a plaster saint.

To romanticize death becomes the ultimate pornography.

★

Nine hundred yards east of the Jack Ranch Cafe, I found The Spot. The one place in America that is essential to anyone in search of the romance of death and cars.

At least I assumed it was The Spot. There was no marker, no plaque. Just a narrow dirt road joining Route 46, paved for the fifty yards or so before the junction. I drove up and down, consulted my map. There was no other turning. This had to be it. The precise spot where Donald Turnipseed steered his car onto the main road just as James Dean came speeding over the rise to his right.

The Spot was right by Cholame Creek, which at this time of year—the same month as Dean's crash—was nothing more than a dry ditch. Traffic whizzed past, kicking up dust. Across the road, the landscape fell away to desert hills, barren and forlorn.

I walked up along the side road, turned, and saw the four elongated white letters painted on the asphalt just before the junction: STOP. The white was wearing away. Everything would wear away in this dusty landscape.

A light wind had come up. I could hear it soughing through the barbed-wire fences, whispering over the empty hills. A semi would come past and drown it out, then the wind would take over again, blowing the dust of the semi's tracks in swirls over the four white letters on the ground.

A grain of dust lodged in my eye and I circled away from the wind, blinking, then back into it again, scanning the landscape in the vague belief that there was something more I should be seeing here. Something that evaded me.

What did I expect? Bloodstains? Shards of broken glass? To see the scene of the collision play itself out in my imagination as I stood there? Feel the soul of James Dean rising up out of the ground to possess me?

I wanted to be able to say that I shivered in the summer heat. But I didn't. That a cloud passed over the sun as I wheeled in slow circles, though the sky was clear. That my mind achieved some small epiphany, not earth-shattering, but relevant, at least to me. But there was none. And this perhaps was the essence of it. There was nothing here. No sign, no omen, no epiphany. Just the sad, mundane fact that once upon a time, a long time ago, a collision took place, a man was killed, and no sign of it remained.

Chapter Eight

I kept to the back roads all the way down to Ojai, in the hills some twenty miles inland from Santa Barbara. There I stopped a while to see some old friends. George and Liz and their wild-boy sons, Dash and Tristan, had moved down from Seattle a few months before when George got a screen-writing fellowship at the American Film Institute. "Read Aristotle's *Poetics* and you've learned just about everything you need to know about screen-writing," he used to say, which may be why he got the fellowship in the first place.

The prospect of spending a few days in such company was like the sight of an oasis after weeks of slogging through the desert. Their small stone cottage set up against the hills, among sycamores and ancient oaks, seemed a dusty equivalent of my houseboat in Seattle, half shack, half paradise. "Lesley's here!" yelled Dash as I drew up, and instantly, I was home.

We sat up late under the ramada, flagstones beneath bare feet, a trellis of vines above us, no lights, good wine. Houdini the kitten chased after the occasional peacock that came strutting through the yard, hidden plumage the sole consolation for its ungainliness. He hitched a ride on the big birds' backs whenever he could, undeterred by being flipped head over tail each time he was shaken off.

And we talked. The kind of talk I love with old friends, roaming from one subject to another, finding the points of conflict and excitement and agreement, butting in with commentary, egging each other on. We talked movies and writing, George's habitual intensity making everything seem immensely relevant. We talked AIDS and the work Liz was doing coordinating AIDS outreach programs throughout the greater Los Angeles area. We talked cars and the 1982 XJ6 George had just bought, and he told the story of his first engine fire, a badge of honor for anyone owning an old Jaguar. We talked about George's father, who had died the year before, sending his son into a tailspin from which he was just recovering. We talked about where I'd been and where I was going and why. We talked American politics and we talked Middle East politics. We talked problems and pleasures, puzzles and paradoxes, and when we got up in the morning we started all over again.

All five of us went hiking, the three adults taking turns carrying four-year-old Tristan on our shoulders after the first mile or two. It was a beautiful canyon, with water still in the stream even at the very end of summer, golden eagles wheeling high above us, and not another human soul. "There's another canyon we used to go to all the time, even more beautiful," said Liz, "but there was a story on it in the last issue of the Sierra Club magazine. Now it's full of hikers."

Near the top of the canyon, we sat down for a bite to eat beneath a huge oak spreading over the stream. The boys trailed their arms in the water, swearing they could see fish. Munching on trail mix, I puzzled out loud at the question that had been haunting me all through the Sierras: Is being in such idyllic places a privilege or a right? Or is it neither, but simply a matter of exploration—that very human desire to go farther, see what's over the next hill or round the next bend, stretch the muscles of body and vision and mind?

"They're talking about putting a cable car down the side of the Grand Canyon," George said moodily. "The Grand Canyon! Don't they see that what makes the canyon grand is its remoteness? Make it accessible, and they'll turn it into just another Disneyland ride."

Questions piled up on each other, each one answered by yet another question. Can nothing be considered beyond our reach any longer? Have we lost humility? Is the very idea of wilderness an insult to a technology-driven culture? Does anyone have a right to go anywhere, even if the "anywhere" in question has to be radically altered to allow such access? Where does democracy end and respect for wilderness begin? Is it a God-given right—or at least a federally given right—to go anywhere and take bad snapshots of great photographs, as at Yosemite? Or is it inevitable that a consumer society should create a wilderness consumerism based on bragging rights: the "been there, done that" of adventure-travel one-upmanship?

We talked about the ultimate "been there, done that" in the form of socialite Sandy Pitman's joining Seattle climber Scott Fischer's ill-fated expedition to Everest so that she could finally claim to have scaled the highest summits on every continent.

George had been rock climbing with Fischer. "Your instinct is to hug the rock," he said, "but the secret is it only works if you move your body out away from the rock, so that you have room to maneuver." And with a touch of wonder, he added: "You have to override instinct in order to stay alive."

Could life, after all, be counter-intuitive? I thought of how you handle a spin in the air, pushing the stick forward to keep the nose of the plane down when every instinct in you screams to pull it up. You have to know that if you do pull it up, you'll turn the spin into the aptly named graveyard spiral. With rock as with sky, knowledge—and faith in that knowledge—is what keeps you alive. And as in some paradoxical Zen koan or Sufi mystery, the instinct for self-preservation can be fatal.

That night again we sat up late, talking and drinking and gazing at the stars. A couple of coyotes howled in the arroyo below the house. "Stay longer," George urged, and I suddenly felt an almost physical dread of the long road to come. I'd had no idea how lonesome the Lone Ranger could get until I was among friends again, known and welcomed.

A deliciously incongruous image of the Lone Ranger reading Walt Whitman drifted into my mind. "Hiyo Silver, away!" was not what I needed right now. Whitman's determined romanticism was.

"However sweet these laid-up stores, however convenient this dwelling, we cannot remain here," he wrote. "However shelter'd this port and however calm these waters we must not anchor here."

And so the following Monday, I gathered up my courage, weighed anchor, left the shelter of friends, and went on down to Los Angeles—

a ninety-minute drive according to George and over a two-hour one by the clock in my truck. But as I drove away from that small stone cottage I felt very small and lonely, like a child leaving home. The last thing I'd done before I left was pick a sprig of rosemary from the dusty bush by George and Liz's front door, and now I placed it on the dashboard in front of me. My first talisman of the road.

★

The surf came in so loud on Malibu Beach that I couldn't sleep with the windows open. The hotel room's sliding doors opened onto a balcony right over the ocean, and I'd instantly had a vision of myself lulled to sleep that night by the Pacific. But there was nothing pacific about it. Every few minutes, four huge waves came in one after the other and broke with a gigantic crack right beneath my window, ten thousand miles of open water pounding against the wall of the Californian shore. A chastened romantic, I got up and closed the doors.

On the landing near my room was a blown-up black-and-white photo of Malibu. To judge from the cars, it was taken in the forties: just a huddle of beach houses by the sand, a single gas station and cafe on the other side of the blacktop road, and that was it. It made me long to have been here back then, in Raymond Chandler days. But then everything about Los Angeles spoke Raymond Chandler to me.

Reading him was how I knew the city. Each time I drive its freeways, the names on the signs are familiar, and even after countless visits, I still get a thrill when I find myself on Sunset or Wilshire, Mulholland or Laurel Canyon. These are names I knew long before I had any idea what they referred to—names more romantic in my Chandlerized imagination than in reality. We know Los Angeles through its fictions.

I thought of British architectural critic Reyner Banham's deep affection for the city's residential landscape as reflected in old detective movies: "Where would the private eyes of the forties have been without laurel shrubberies to lurk in, sweeping front drives to turn the car in, terraces from which to observe the garden below, massive Spanish Colonial Revival doors on which to knock, and tiled Spanish Colonial Revival interiors for the knocking to echo in, and the bars of Spanish Colonial

Revival windows to hold onto, or rambling split-level ranch house plans in which to lose the opposition, and random rubble fireplace walls to pin suspects against, and gigantic dream bedrooms from which the sun may be seen rising in heart-breaking picture-postcard splendor over the Hollywood Hills . . . and the essential swimming pool for the bodies."

I took comfort from that old photograph of Malibu because it was familiar. It came from a time when Los Angeles was somehow manageable, before it overwhelmed itself with sheer size and sprawl. And that comfort was necessary: I was scared of the city. Anyone who can spend days meandering on four-digit roads from Yosemite to Ojai is by definition not ready for Los Angeles.

Within a half-hour of leaving Ojai, I'd found myself forced into slow-moving traffic and the gathering pall of smog. "So many cars," I thought, feeling like the country hick coming to the big city. Suddenly my truck was the filthiest thing around. Car-conscious Angelenos wash their cars lovingly. They wax them and polish them and detail them with Q-Tips. Apply separate waxes and polishes to the tires, the rims, the dashboard, the bumpers, the chrome. Clean their cars by breaking them down into their component parts. I have never understood why anyone would want to clean and polish a tire, and know I never will.

This was the city famed for the hottest and coolest cars in the world. The city where people bought flashy, expensive metal to impress valet parking attendants at the best restaurants. Where people knew the subtle differences between a sixty-four-and-a-half Mustang and a sixty-five Mustang, or between a Z1 Corvette and the ordinary, regular, cheaper kind, their eyes attuned to the tiniest cues of badge and wheel designs. They could tell a Bose sound system from a Sony one just by the sound of it as it bounced past on the freeway.

I was convinced of all this, even though I knew plenty of people in Los Angeles who knew nothing about cars except that they needed them to get from home to work and back again. A sculptor, a rabbi, a political scientist, a psychologist—normal people who faded into invisibility in my mind as the conviction grew that I could spend a month here and still only scratch the surface of the most intense car culture in the world. I was lost before I'd begun.

Still, I had one thing going for me: I love driving around the city. I realize this makes me somewhat perverse, but I am enchanted by the mix of scuzz and glitz. Palms and tall Italian cypresses stand elegantly over tawdry street scenes, buildings are painted orange and pink and blue and green, even if the paint is flaking, and the full sun makes everything startlingly, preternaturally bright.

But most of all I love driving the freeways. Where others complain of jams and fumes, I am constantly amazed that the freeway system works so well. Give me a big unwieldy folding street map, direct me to the nearest freeway, and I become the intrepid explorer, making her way through the maze of confusion. I chart my progress from exit sign to exit sign, following the map's network of thick red lines superimposed on the street grid like a diagram of major blood vessels, lifelines of the city.

The freeways bisect the city every which way, so many times that in a way there is no city left, but a conglomeration of separate cities linked by concrete ribbons. At the Malibu Beach Inn, I felt as though I were camping on the fringes of this conglomeration, hoping perhaps to look in from the outside and see the place whole. The ocean gave me a firm sense of place; I was out on the edge, with all of Los Angeles pressing in on my back. A few miles down the Pacific Coast Highway and I could turn left onto the Santa Monica Freeway and enter the system, just another four-wheeled metallic ant doing its bit to whiten the air.

For the air was white, and it wasn't from forest fires. It was from pool fires in millions of combustion chambers, tons of carbon dioxide and nitrous oxides and other tailpipe fumes trapped by the surrounding mountains and combining with fog and sun to muddy the air and confound the eyes with haze. Way over the other side of the city, halfway to San Bernardino, the South Coast Air Quality Management District had spearheaded the move to clean up the city's air, drafting the most stringent emissions laws in the world. There were far fewer days of smog now than just ten years earlier, fewer days when people were warned to stay indoors if possible. But there were also more cars. Thirty-five percent more cars, to be precise. As they say in England, what you gain on the roundabouts, you lose on the swings. Managing air quality is difficult when vehicles like my Expedition get thirteen miles to the gallon in city driving. And when the price of gas plummets by a third the moment you cross the city line. In Los Angeles, gas is far cheaper than Evian water; it has to be, for the city has to feed the machine that makes it a city. Starve the millions of cars, and Malibu would still be a small huddle of beach shacks instead of the star-studded suburb it has become.

There are too many ways to see Los Angeles and its roads. Urban nightmare is the most obvious one. The more artistically inclined, like Reyner Banham, might see it as environmental sculpture on a massive scale. For the anthropologically oriented, there's the simple wonder of where all these people are going all the time. For the technically minded, there's the superb engineering achievement of sweeping freeway interchanges. For residents, there's the driving to the constant patter on the radio of freeway conditions and air quality levels. All these ways overlap and jostle uncomfortably. That's the essence of this place. There is no way to see the city as a whole. There is no narrative to the city.

I made forays into Los Angeles. I was a scout checking things out. Taking refuge back at my camp above the beach each night. Knowing that I'd never find all there was to be found here. That everything I did was bound to feel fragmented, disjointed—the feel of the city itself for any but those who know it well enough to pick out its multiple heartbeats against the white noise of traffic.

I realize now why people collect snapshots. It's to defend themselves against reality. The camera acts as a blind, as something to hide behind. Looking through the lens, you see a discrete portion of the landscape, isolating it from the whole so that it makes visual sense. In Los Angeles, then, I became a tourist, collecting picture postcards of me in the big city.

★

Picture Postcard Number One shows me driving a five-million-dollar car.

It's a Delahaye 165, designed by Figoni and Falaschi, and one of only two ever built. The first was made for the Paris auto show in 1938; this one was made a year later for the New York World's Fair.

The sleek, huge-nosed convertible is the deep, glowing red of dying embers. Its two seats are hand-stitched in white leather with red piping. The deep fenders arch sensuously, the lower edges scalloped over white-walled tires. The elegant, flaring length of the hood and the sides are detailed with elongated chrome teardrops so that even at rest, air seems to be streaming over the metal as in a wind tunnel. The car is so beautiful that I completely forget how much it is worth.

Perhaps this is one definition of beauty: it makes you forget money. Yet in the end, you can't. Certainly I can suggest a car's beauty by saying that it makes me forget its value, but that depends on knowing the value in the first place. It wouldn't work if this was merely a five-thousand-dollar car. It has to be five million.

I found the car and its custodian, Mike Shnaer, the man who restored it, in the unlikely neighborhood of Van Nuys, just off Saticoy in the San Fernando Valley. Since my street map ended a few blocks south, I had to keep stopping to ask directions. I did this many times; in this area, the whole city seems to have gone back to its Hispanic origins, and in local doughnut shops and gas stations, hardly anyone spoke enough English to give me directions even if they'd known where the street was, which they didn't.

I could see why not when I eventually found it: a narrow back street that you'd never know was there unless you had business with one of the small workshops that lined it. One of them provided cars for the movies; its trailer truck bore the motto, "We put the motion in your pictures," and today it was loaded with two cars stripped down to industrial drab, with rust stains specially added. They were the kind of cars you see in backyards all through the poorer parts of rural America, weeds growing up through the floorboards, home only to mongrel dogs. The kind of cars that have to be specially provided in Los Angeles, where even a stripper becomes a work of art.

The outside of Mike Shnaer's workshop betrayed no sign of the riches within. A scruffy bougainvillea vine clung to the brickwork beside the big garage door, but aside from that small concession to esthetics, there was no hint that here was to be found the kind of master craftsman that Roland Barthes was thinking of when he equated cars to

Gothic cathedrals, "the supreme creation of an era, conceived with passion by unknown artists."

Mike is one of the handful of the world's top restorers of vintage cars, one of the quiet men behind the giant champagne bottles and outsize trophies of Pebble Beach and the other classy *Concours d'Elégance.* The one, in short, who does the actual work. Who lovingly deconstructs and then reconstructs a car.

In his forties, with thinning sandy hair, he looks more the archeologist he nearly became—he has a degree in anthropology and archeology from UCLA—than a vintage car restorer. Or maybe, as he'd point out, the two are not so dissimilar, for isn't what he does a form of archeology? Or does the presence of an engine preclude the possibility of seeing a car as a piece of art?

We used lunch as an excuse for me to drive the Delahaye—a short but splendid drive from the workshop to a Greek diner at Van Nuys airport, where we sat at an outside table, watching the occasional taildragger lift off to achieve the grace it so badly lacked on the ground.

Every reconstructed car has a story, and as we ate—hamburgers with lemon and herbs, and Greek salad on the side—Mike told me the story of the Delahaye. It was found in a barn near Fresno. Or rather, the hulk of it was found. It had no seats, no dashboard, no engine; nothing, basically, but the frame. Rebuilding it would mean searching literally the world over—South Africa, Japan, Germany, France—to track down drawings and blueprints and manuals. Mike brought in over two hundred craftsmen to work on separate parts, from master carpenters to chrome workers; unearthed the original engine block, which was in Munich; found the sister car in London and took more than a thousand photographs of it; used five different machine shops to cast and forge the pistons and the crankshaft and the camshaft and all the other moving parts; consulted with hot-rodders on the materials to use for the tail lights; decided on where to use modern technology to brace structural weaknesses in the original design; had long discussions with the owners on the use of urethanes instead of lacquers for the paint.

And then after six years came the day when he ran the engine for the first time—not the first time in the car's new incarnation, but the first time ever; since the 165 had been built as a show car, the engine had never been used. Mike called the owners in the middle of a business conference, started the car up, and held the receiver to the engine compartment so that they could hear the music of twelve cylinders all the way back to the East Coast. That day, he had given life to the machine.

I liked this man. Liked his quiet passion, his calm commitment to his craft, his acceptance of its costs written on his right hand in the form of a row of stitches between his thumb and forefinger; he'd cranked an engine, and the crank had flown loose and come back at him. An old-fashioned injury. He truly was the unknown artisan, the man who applies art and knowledge, experience and time, sweat and tears, who slices open his hands and burns his fingers and puts his back out, and all for hire, all for someone else's car. Often even for a car that may never be driven.

That hurts. He told me about an MG-TC somewhere in Texas displayed inside a glass cage in front of the owner's house. To ensure the car's absolute preservation, all air has been pumped out of the cage; the car exists, literally, in a vacuum.

"Imagine," Mike said in soft amazement, "nobody gets to hear it or even touch it, let alone drive it. I know the MG is extreme, but a lot of these owners will just put the car in a climate-controlled garage and leave it there. They'll see it as an investment, or as a status item, or as an art object, but they'll never experience it as a whole." He shook his head sadly. "It seems such a waste."

★

In Picture Postcard Number Two, I'm standing staring at a house in the expensive enclave of Tolucca Lake, just north of the Universal City movie studios.

Coming here was a kind of sentimental journey. I knew that Amelia Earhart had lived in North Hollywood for the last couple of years of her life, cutting a fine figure as she commuted each day to nearby Burbank aerodrome in her 1936 Cord Phaeton, a long-nosed droptop with deeply etched, angular lines. I had half a novel about Earhart stashed away in a drawer at home, written so that I could transpose everything I felt about flying onto her, and I suppose I felt I owed it to that couple of hundred of manuscript pages to check out where she'd lived. A bit of Chandler-esque detective work seemed called for. Otherwise known as casing the joint.

I had the street name but not the house number, though I did know it was right by the Tolucca Lake golf course. According to my map, that had now become the "Lakeside Golf Club of Hollywood (private)." The Los Angeles River ran just south of it, and turned out to be merely a concrete culvert with a muddy stream at the very bottom. Still, it seemed to establish a clear demarcation line between the tourist-laden precincts of Universal City and the exclusive residential area to the north.

Finding Valley Spring Road the other side of the golf course was harder than I'd expected. Maps seem to go vague when real-estate prices rise, and here, as you might expect when there's a real, live lake in the middle of residential Los Angeles, they were very high indeed, even though the houses were quite modestly sized compared to Beverly Hills. I realized a little too late that driving the carefully shaded streets of Tolucca Lake in a dust-covered truck is a good way to feel conspicuous, especially if you're crawling along and very obviously checking things out. It wasn't a walled-off enclave, but the walls were there nonetheless, invisible, and I was uncomfortably aware that a private patrol car was likely to pull up at any moment and inquiries be made about my intentions. But I reached Valley Spring Road unmolested, drove slowly to the point where it dead-ended beside the golf course, parked on the street, and got out.

It looked like the right house. One of the first here, I'd guess, built in maybe the late twenties in a mixed Bauhaus-Mediterranean style, and now all but hidden from the road by greenery. I did a mental run-through of photos I'd seen of Amelia "at home." Yes, it could well be this house. On the other hand, it could just as well be three or four others.

I stood there wondering whether it even mattered whether this was "the" house. But if it was, I'd certainly like to see inside. The only way to do that seemed to be to walk on up to the front door, knock, and if someone answered, come on with the usual star-struck tourist's line:

"I'm sorry to disturb you, but I was wondering if this was the house where . . ."

Maybe they'd invite me in. "Look around. Take your time. Would you like a drink? Would you like to stay to dinner?" More likely they'd slam the door in my face. Likelier still, a Mexican maid would answer and stare at me in incomprehension as I tried to explain what I was doing on the doorstep.

I was still standing there, immobilized by indecision, when a man came out of the house opposite and opened up his garage. He had the kind of silver-haired good looks I knew I should recognize but didn't. But I did recognize the lovely vintage roadster he backed down the driveway.

"An XK120!" I said as he drew level with me. "The most beautiful Jaguar ever made. You're a lucky man."

I meant it, and he knew it. He beamed in delight. "Isn't she a beauty?" And looked up at me with interest: "Where's that accent from?"

We started chatting, and I explained my mission. "Not many people know about that," he said, "but you've got the right house all right. Nice old place, isn't it? My house wasn't even here when that was built. Hardly any houses were. It was all orange orchards in those days. Must have smelled beautiful in the spring, when all the blossoms were out."

"What do you think would happen if I walked up and knocked at the door?"

"Nothing at all, I'm afraid. They're away. Pity—I could have taken you over there and introduced you."

"I don't think you're supposed to tell me they're away. Security and all that."

He laughed. "Anyone who knows a 120 when they see one is fine in my book. Sorry I couldn't be of more help with Ms. Earhart." He gunned the engine—"Finish that novel!" he shouted—and drove off up the road, leaving me breathing the aroma of exhaust and wondering which old movie it was I knew his face from.

★

Picture Postcard Number Three is one of those cards with several small pictures squished together around a central cameo shot of a smog-induced technicolor ocean-view sunset.

The top right-hand corner shows me down in Long Beach, admiring the low-rider custom cars that seem to congregate here in higher density than anywhere else in the world. It's hard to decide if more work has gone into the car bodies, smoothed and buffed and polished and chromed, or into the human bodies that drive them, equally smoothed and buffed and polished, and even chromed if you take the personal hardware into account. Custom cars played a major role in a brat-pack movie remake of *Romeo and Juliet*—the one with Leonardo DiCaprio as Romeo—which transposed the lovers' story from the nobility of Verona to the street gangs of southern California. So did custom guns, stretched and chrome-plated into pieces of expensive street art. The cars in Long Beach looked like they came right out of the movie. I didn't hang around to find out if the guns did too.

In the bottom right-hand corner, I'm in a warehouse up in Glendale, and the place is full of T-shirts: Nascar T-shirts and Indycar T-shirts, checkered-flag and racing-helmet and flaming-exhaust T-shirts, Pennzoil and Quaker State and Shell T-shirts, Honda and Ford and Ferrari T-shirts, dirt-racing T-shirts and motorcycle T-shirts and demolition-derby T-shirts—T-shirts printed with every conceivable illustration, logo, decal, and design to do with racing, and every one in luridly technicolor combinations. Dozens upon dozens of rows of fully stacked shelves reach twelve feet high, their contents arrayed in sizes to fit anyone from an infant to an obese giant, and the place is buzzing. I keep having to dodge forklift trucks racing up and down the aisles. "You must be the middleman for every T-shirt in every race meet in the country," I say to the owner. He smiles modestly: "No, just every race meet in the West."

The top left-hand corner of this card shows me in Mazda's American design studios in Torrance, eyeing two early fifties cars stashed away in a side corridor: a Saab 92, with the friendly bulbousness of the Morris Minor my father once had, and a Mercedes 190 roadster. "Just curiosities," says Mazda design chief Tom Matano dismissively when I ask about them, but his tone is too hurried and too casual. I don't need to be an industrial spy to figure that he's planning to follow up his design of the Miata—the car that reintroduced Americans to the delights of open-top driving—with something wonderfully retro. In fact I've been urging it on him all along. "Think curves, Tom," I've been saying. "Think bulbous fenders. Think Fiesta Ware colors." He'd laughed uneasily. "Have you been going through my sketchbook?" he said.

In the bottom left-hand corner, I'm in the Petersen Automotive Museum on Wilshire, near Fairfax, watching a man and his six-year-old son in the exhibit of automotive Los Angeles through the decades. They're standing in front of an old gas pump. The father is entranced. The child eyes the floor, clearly bored; there's not even any ice cream in the place. "Look, son, you had to pump this handle here up and down to get the gas out . . ." The child obediently raises his head to look, but his eyes are half-closed. I follow them upstairs, where there's an old Indy car you can climb into. The man climbs into it, grinning from ear to ear. His son waits patiently for his father to stop playing.

★

Picture Postcard Number Four has me in the showroom of Beverly Hills Motoring Accessories, on Robertson just south of Wilshire, the tackier end of the famed zip code. The items on sale here include $300 cans of car wax, burlwood steering wheels for $2,000, and "sheared sheepskin mouton floor mats" for $935, as well as 24-carat gold license-plate frames, "pre-washed and pre-softened 100% cotton diapers" for polishing a car, and "a car cover so valuable it comes with its own insurance policy." Recaro driving seats start at $520 and go up into the thousands, while a Recaro office chair engineered with electric controls, heat, lumbar support, and a 15-hour battery life is offered at a mere $3,395. One day I expect to open up their catalog when it arrives in the mail and find it advertising an entirely gold-plated car.

The sales manager, a twenty-three-year-old with lank blond hair and the kind of preternaturally seen-it-all look to his eyes that makes you realize how quickly you can get jaded in Los Angeles, came out to greet me. "See anything you like?" he said.

"I've heard of babying a car," I replied, "but diapers? Who buys diapers to wax a car?"

"The rich and the shameless," he said, deadpan.

The store was far smaller than I'd imagined, and I said so. He smiled knowingly: "You haven't seen the workshop yet." And he led me back past the showroom and into the real heart of Beverly Hills Motoring Accessories—the place that had achieved the seemingly impossible task of making the Chevy Suburban chic.

The very idea of anything named after the dreaded un-cool of suburbia becoming the peacock vehicle for macho movie stars and gangsta rappers is surely the stuff of satire. It outdoes even the fantasy in *Get Shorty* where John Travolta's gangster, late for a meeting with a movie producer and condemned to accept the only vehicle still available at the rental-car counter, shows up in a black Oldsmobile Silhouette and coolly declares it "the Cadillac of minivans." The movie producer rushes out to buy one the same day. But as in *Get Shorty*'s version of Hollywood, so too in the real one: the Suburban's elevation to hip desirability has played without the least hint of irony.

Irony has never been the strong point of Los Angeles. This urban megalopolis is where America's mechanical mule, the farmer's pickup truck, was first adopted by trust-fund surfers as a flashy leisure vehicle. Its asphalt precincts were the original stage-setting for the transformation of the rugged off-road sport-utility into a commuter car. So perhaps only Los Angeles could have led the way in taking the backyard stripped-to-the-waist working-class ethos of hot-rodders and customizers, and transferring it to the climate-controlled high-tech workshop I now saw.

I climbed up into a monstrous Suburban that had been stripped of all factory emblems and side moldings "to achieve a monochromatic look." A sleek aluminum grill had replaced the factory one and an additional spoiler had been added in front, making the vehicle look like a massive battering ram. Add to that the special high-gloss black paint job—five layers of the stuff hand-rubbed over a base metallic—and the tinted windows and windshield, and what you had was the kind of thing designed to inspire pure terror in the heart of any driver careless enough to glance in the rearview mirror and see it suddenly filled with this Darth Vader apparition.

Inside was all pale-ivory perforated leather and glowing burlwood. The climate and radio controls were in brushed aluminum; the dashboard gauges matched the color of the leather. The electronics included a Sony Trinitron television, a seventeen-speaker sound system with four amplifiers and subwoofers, a VCR and video game system, a fax machine, two laptop PCs with Internet access, built-in front and rear radar and laser detectors, a GPS satellite navigation system, and a linked security tracking system. Not to mention the burlwood-covered phone.

"Do I really want to know what's been done to the mechanicals?" I said.

The sales manager obliged. I saw giant Brembo race-quality brakes. A dual exhaust specially tuned for a deep, throaty roar. The reinforced suspension. And under the hood, the gleaming metal of a twin-screw supercharger.

"Who on earth would want to supercharge a Suburban?" I almost asked, but checked myself in time. I already knew the answer: the rich and the shameless, of course.

Instead, I asked: "If I wanted all this done to my Expedition, how much would it cost?"

The sales manager eyed my truck with merely the slightest hint of disdain for its crust of dirt. "Everything on this particular Suburban?"

"Minus the television and the VCR and the video games," I conceded.

"Plus the Sportino aluminum wheels?"

Definitely the Sportino aluminum wheels, which looked worthy of Boadicea's war chariot.

He narrowed his eyes in a creditable imitation of someone making precise calculations. "I think we could get you out of here for somewhere just under a hundred," he said finally.

I knew it was a stupid question, but I had to ask it just to be sure: "You mean a hundred thousand?"

The nod he gave was so cool as to be almost imperceptible.

On the way out through the store, I bought one of the few things I could afford: a cassette called "Highway Rockin'." Anticipating "Mustang Sally" and "Hot Rod Lincoln," I inserted the tape into the truck's stereo as I turned onto Wilshire and got Meat Loaf's "Paradise by the Dashboard Light," the Allman Brothers' "One Way Out," and Joe Cocker's "High Time We Went." The music made the late-afternoon haze all the more glaring, even through my sunglasses.

★

Picture Postcard Number Five is dark. It shows the gloom of a multistory long-term parking garage at LAX, and you can just make out my figure standing by the side of the Expedition. I seem to be hesitating as though I've forgotten if I'm about to get into the truck or walk away from it. There's a wheeled carry-on case beside me, one of those all the airline crew use, except mine bears a faded red and gold Harley-Davidson sticker so that nobody else will walk off with it by mistake.

In fact I'd just locked the truck, but somehow couldn't bring myself to walk away from it yet. I was suffering from a syndrome known as Los Angeles overload. Too many images had piled up inside my head. Too much ritz and glitz and contrast and contradiction. Far more than one paradox too many. I needed time to sort everything out. Or maybe I was just blaming the city for what had been building in me in any case. I'd been on the road for weeks; I longed to stay put for a few days and catch up with myself. And I wanted to do it somewhere safe and familiar. Walt Whitman would have been mightily disappointed in me; the Lone Ranger's patrician mouth would have twisted into a condescending smile of pity.

But leaving the truck was harder than I'd reckoned on. Spend too much time in a heap of metal and you start to feel very protective of it. I'd spent the last fifteen minutes driving in circles to find the perfect spot: the end of a row, under good light, in full view of everyone passing. I wanted the truck to be safe. And I wanted the large parts of me inside it to be safe too: laptop, books, clothes, all packed away and hidden from any but the most insistent eye.

As I finally turned away, I was even tempted to talk to the truck. "You take care of yourself," perhaps. Or a reassuring, "I'll be back." But Rambo had preempted that line.

In the end I said nothing. Just heaved a sigh and walked off, trailing my carry-on behind me. I looked back a few times, then rounded a corner, put my head down, and forged my way to the ticket counter, where I cashed in a bunch of frequent-flyer miles and booked myself on the evening flight home.

Chapter Nine

Rain!

It was pouring. Seattle living up to its reputation in glorious abundance. Clouds billowing in from the Pacific. Water cascading over the Cascade Range. Puddles splashing, passing cars throwing up spray, and the moisture soft and gentling after the harsh dryness of Los Angeles.

I'd sat on the starboard side of the plane, watching the line of volcanos that form the spine of the West Coast: Shasta, Crater Lake, Three Sisters, Jefferson. . . . But the clouds began to gather as we crossed over Oregon, and any hope of seeing the last of the sunset paint the cone of Mount Hood was gone. Saint Helens and Adams were hidden in both cloud and darkness, and by the time I knew we had to be passing Mount Rainier, there was only the memory of it rising high above the rest of the Cascades in perfect symmetry, like a child's drawing of a mountain.

At Sea-Tac airport, it was easy to tell the difference between Seattleites and tourists as we waited for the shuttle into town; tourists looked disappointed, Seattleites delighted.

"How long's it been raining?" I asked the shuttle driver.

"All day," he said with a tone of satisfied doom. "And all day tomorrow too, is the forecast." There's a strong Lutheran streak in Seattle that is satisfied only when things look dark, which might be what attracted so many Lutherans here in the first place.

From the elevated highway that fronts downtown, taking a long lazy loop around Elliott Bay and monopolizing a perfect view of Puget Sound, I could see the lights of the ferries disappearing into the mist just a couple of hundred yards out. There was no perfect view this evening, but what did I care? I breathed deep in pleasure. It was the first rain I'd seen in weeks. And I remembered this pleasure in unaccustomed moisture from the years I lived in Jerusalem, where the first rain comes at the very end of the long, dry summer, falling onto cracked, baked ground in which even the hardiest thorns have browned and withered. That first rain is like no other: huge raindrops sound as though they've been pitched out of the sky, bouncing up off the hard earth like glass marbles. And though this Seattle rain was a gentler, mistier creature, I had that same sense of regeneration, of moisture rehydrating a world thirsty with waiting.

It was strange, I reflected, that someone who once spent so much time in the deserts of the Middle East should be so happy living in this watery climate. Once the sound of home was the chorus of crickets and the wind rustling through the dry needles of the pines outside my window; now it was the sound of water falling on water, rain on the lake pattering me to sleep.

The shuttle dropped me off at the top of the dock. The sound of my carry-on's wheels rolling along the wood planking was enough to tell my neighbors I was home. I ate a late supper with Ann and Gene, who live three houseboats up from me, caught up on the news and the gossip, and slept that night cradled by the subliminal rocking of the raft. There was the simple, sweet luxury of sleeping in my own bed again, and the strange yet familiar waking to mist and rain, the world covered over with cloud.

I explored my own house the way I would a four-star resort hotel suite, delighting in its details—the paintings and prints on the walls, the way the light played off the water onto the wooden ceiling, the Tuscan rosemary on my small garden raft flowering luscious dark blue in the October rain. The light was a soothing gray after the blinding white of Los Angeles, gentling my eyes. The plants had been watered, and now my life needed watering too—some attention to the realities of bills to be paid, articles to be written, friends to catch up with before I set off on the next leg of my journey. Yet I couldn't slip the awareness that I was home only temporarily. My carry-on lay open on the floor, only half unpacked, as though I were about to take off again at any moment. Which I was. And this awareness created a surreal feeling that home was not quite home, but more of a vacation.

Of course there are those who say that living on a houseboat is a permanent vacation, and they have a point. It could be said that anyone who lives on a raft can make only the most tenuous claim to permanence, as I found out when I bought the place and was informed by banks and insurance companies that my house was classified as a mobile home. Which could be why I was so attracted to it in the first place. But the sense of home is as a permanent place, an anchor, and even as I rejoiced in being here, I felt that I had somehow slipped my moorings.

After the Expedition, my own run-of-the-mill sensible sedan felt very small and low to the ground. I drove up Queen Anne Hill on the usual round of errands. "You been away? Haven't seen you in a while," said the barrista at my favorite espresso stand. "You're so tanned. Have you been on vacation?" asked an acquaintance I met on line at the Thriftway checkout counter. "Overdue once more," intoned the library clerk when I guiltily handed over the books I'd forgotten to return before I left. The Lone Ranger had gone into major fadeout; I was known again.

I drove back home, stuffed the groceries into the fridge, and turned, heavy-hearted, to the huge pile of mail. Gene had taken it out of my mailbox every day and heaped it on my dining table, stacking the magazines neatly alongside an anarchic mound of bills, letters, press releases, postcards, and junk mail.

It was all very well for Walt Whitman to make grand declarations— "Let the paper remain on the desk unwritten, and the book on the shelf unopened!" he wrote, "Let the tools remain in the workshop! let the money remain unearned!"—but all those exclamation marks were a dead giveaway. He was trying to persuade himself as much as anyone else, because sooner or later, everything that's left behind demands its due.

I began triage on the pile of paper, picking out the choice items first. There was a bulky envelope from Talking Turkey Pictures; I opened it to find a short film Ned had made on Edward Abbey. I slipped the tape into the VCR, and was delighted to see that Abbey looked exactly as I'd imagined—a kind of cross between Abe Lincoln and an old-time mountain man. The film followed him as he drove a rattling rustbucket through Arches National Monument, where he'd been a ranger back when it took a day's hard travel to get there instead of an easy half-hour drive over paved road. It ended with him musing on how the place would finally become itself again "when I'm gone, you're gone, and everything we built has faded away"—at which his own image faded out of the picture, leaving just the landscape.

It was the perfect elegy for the man, and it gave me the energy to turn from the sublime to the ridiculous and get back to work on the mail, imagining Abbey's ghost laughing at me as I did. The pile consisted mostly of brown, white, and gray nine-by-twelve-inch envelopes containing press releases, news-sheets, clippings, financial statements. Just opening them all would take hours. I flipped through them desultorily: Chrysler, Ford, Human Rights Watch, BMW, GMC, Northstar Bank, Toyota, Land Rover, PEN American Center, Goodyear, Sierra Club, Motor Press Association, Honda . . . I was on the point of leaving them all for a far-off "another day" when suddenly there was one with the words "Sierra House Elementary School, South Lake Tahoe, California" scrawled large in the upper left-hand corner.

I tore it open. Out spilled a mass of letters hand-blocked in children's writing on lined notepaper, all with drawings at the bottom of the page or on the flip side. Cars drove under rainbows and smiley-faced suns. They hovered in mid-air and dwarfed houses and gardens. Some of them looked more like yachts than cars; others more like rockets. One futuristic bubble could have been a prize-winning style exercise from the Pasadena Institute of Design, the hotbed of automotive design training. Clear personalities shone through the drawings, and even clearer ones through the laboriously penned words.

> Dear Lesley, Hi, I am Alberto and my Dad likes to work on cars and I like to write about cars and our Dodge Ram a lot because it's big and tall and big, I think it is nine feet.

At the bottom was a drawing of him in a very large red pickup truck, waving hello.

Dear Lesley, I love cars. When I grow up I want to work on cars. I like Hot Wheels, especilly number 70 Chevey roadster wheels with Goodyear tires. I also like Lamborginies. I run my toy cars on my chris cross crash. It is fun. Sinsely Danny.

Perhaps as proof of his sincerity, he'd filled up the bottom of the page with a drawing of a drag car in full flame and smoke.

Dear Lesley. I have lots of pets. I have four cats, three dogs, two birds, one guinea pig, and three fish tanks. I have one sister.

This was from Kristen, and I wondered if she was aware of the relative rankings of importance in this list of possessions. She'd also drawn a car: a big purple convertible, with herself and her teacher waving in the front seat.

Dear Lesley, how are you? I am fine. I like to play cars. I like to write storys just like you. I write funny storys. Some scary storys too. Niles.

Martin had written two letters. He'd filled up a whole page, so had written another, separate letter on a second. He was bursting with questions:

Where are you on your trip? Will you go to the White House? Will you go to Arizona and New Mexico and Texas? I want you to teach us about cars. What kinds of cars do you have? How did you learn about cars? What is your favorite car?

Some of the letters needed close deciphering. Half the kids in the class were immigrants, and Nancy was letting them write phonetically for the time being, knowing that enthusiasm for writing was more important at this stage than grammar or spelling.

Dear Mrs Lesley. Mi Mom goes to LA and wen we go to pleyses we go en ei car and wen we go to Mexico we go wit are family en are own miniven and samwan gous en ei car or ei truc. Love Bianca.

Her drawing showed what looked like a limo with a palm tree growing out of the trunk. I stared at that palm tree, remembering how miraculous the world could seem from the back seat of a car when you were eight years old and on a long trip.

★

"Watch," my father said, "we're going to drive up into that cloud."

"We're going to go inside a cloud?"

It seemed impossible. My imagination couldn't stretch to the idea. Clouds were solid things, way up there in the sky. Born in the mountainless south of England, I had never seen a cloud envelop peaks. Come to that, I'd never seen peaks.

But these were the Alps, and we were on the St. Gotthard Pass, hairpinning our way up the high divide between Switzerland and Italy. My father teased my brother and me in the back seat—and my mother too—by leaning out the window and admiring the view: a giddyingly steep precipice at every turn. I'd been hanging on for dear life, terrified, until he said we were going to drive into the cloud.

I wriggled down in the back seat, the better to stare up at the grayness above us. What would happen when we entered the cloud? We'd be able to see nothing at all, that seemed clear. Since you couldn't see inside a cloud from the outside, you clearly couldn't see inside a cloud from the inside either. Eight-year-olds are nothing if not determinedly logical.

"But what about the mountain?" I asked.

"The top of the mountain's inside the cloud too."

And I lay there, staring upward, already wrestling with the old philosophical question of how you could be sure that something existed if you could not see it.

Those summer car trips to Europe were as magical and strange as that entry into the cloud. The other side of the English Channel was still known in England as "the Continent," a place where everything was foreign and oddly alluring, where they spoke other languages and ate other food and drove on the wrong side of the road. For my parents to put two young children into the back seat of a right-hand-drive car and venture abroad was an act of either extraordinary foolhardiness or bold adventurousness. Back then, in the fifties, the English just didn't do such things.

I hadn't slept at all the night before we left. It seemed inconceivable that I could actually be doing this. Going abroad. Venturing into a vast unknown. None of my schoolfriends had been farther than the English coast, where earlier vacations had left me with memories of shivering on rocky beaches, of bee stings and dirty postcards I couldn't understand and the smell of wet woolen cardigans slowly turning to mold.

It wasn't imagining what might happen on this vacation that kept me awake; it was the inability to imagine anything at all. My parents must have spent weeks planning the trip, but they probably did it when my brother and I were already in bed. I had no knowledge of it. So far as I was concerned, we'd be driving into a vast unknown.

We'd take five such trips in all—to France, Italy, Switzerland, Belgium, and Denmark—and they set off something in me that I was not even aware of at the time. They opened up the world for me. It became large and warm and full of light. There was the light of fireworks over the Venice Lido, filling the sky and lasting, it seemed, for hours. Of the water of the Arno reflected, rippling, on the painted ceiling of a riverside *pensione* in Florence. Of sun flickering like a strobe through the rows of poplars lining the straight roads of northern France. Of the blueness of the Mediterranean, so clear that I could stand in it up to my neck, look down, and see my feet broken up by the ripples into gold-rimmed lozenges of green and blue. Of glistening snow-capped mountains, impossibly white against the deep blue sky. Of copper roofs shining green and gold in Brussels. Of the multicolored frivolity of the Tivoli Gardens at night. Of the warm red of the wine diluted with water we were allowed to drink with our evening meal, like French children.

In England, the sky seemed an eternal pale gray, and everything was drained of light. The car brought me into the careless warmth of sunshine, of bare brown limbs rolling in fine Mediterranean sand instead of bruised feet stumbling over the harsh pebbles of the English coast. It brought ease with the casual way European adults had of tousling a child's head, of allowing a child to run wild and laugh instead of continually being shushed and told don't-do-that. In Europe, children could eat out late at night with their parents, and then go with them to the movies and fall blissfully asleep in the comfort of a dark filled with adults.

And in Europe you could drive—just keep on going for as long as you wanted. To a child born and raised on England's island, it was amazing that you could simply drive from one country into another. Each border was a further adventure into the unknown. This was years before the European Union, years even before its precursor, the Common Market, and the borders were John Le Carré arrangements of barriers and checks, full of stern-faced policemen and customs agents who scrutinized these strange passports—wonderful word even then, "passport," with its sense of passing from one port to another, its imperious *laissez-passer* demand—and then, with due delay and officious formality, let us pass.

I remember countless details from those trips, but only now does it strike me how odd it is that in my memory of all the driving we did as a family, even in England, I place my father sitting behind the wheel on the left, not the right. My memory has made him a European. Or an American, like his daughter.

★

I had a pile of columns to write and tight deadlines to get them done in. But drafting a reply to the kids was far more important. And a lot more fun.

"Dear Alberto, Bianca, Chad, Chris, Colt, Danny, Diana, Hans, Heather, Jasmin, Jessica, Joey, Jorge, Kristen, Martin, Mireya, Niles, and Ricky," I began—important to include them all from the start—and I was off, telling them what great letter writers they were, what wonderful drawings they'd done, thanking them for writing. I left big spaces between the paragraphs, imagining that Nancy would want to deal with them one by one. I'd only intended to write a brief letter, but the pages began to mount up. I was enjoying being a pedagogical tool.

I told them why I was driving to Detroit. I explained the idea of doing research for a book, told them the route I'd taken so far, asked if they could find the places I'd mentioned on a map. I wrote about what it was like to live on a houseboat, and promised to enclose a snapshot. I told them what car I was driving and why ("If I need to, I can sleep in the back"). "Now that I know you a little, I'll send you postcards from the road," I wrote. "And I'll answer any questions you want to ask." And then I added a few lines to each one separately, replying individually to their letters. I asked Bianca to tell me about Mexico. Asked Danny to tell me what a Criss Cross Crash was; I had an idea it had to be some game where you sent cars crashing into each other, but couldn't quite get my mind to accept that. Asked Niles to send me a real scary story. Told Martin, "Don't ever stop asking questions!"

And at the end I add a P.S.: "You have a *great* teacher!" Imagining Nancy explaining what a P.S. was.

When I finished, two hours had gone by.

I called Nancy to tell her the letter was in the mail. She and Harry were just back from another rocket-firing trip to the Black Rock desert, and were there the day Breedlove had arrived with the Spirit of America and a by now considerable entourage. "We waited a whole extra day for him to make a run," she said, "but one end of the operation didn't seem to know what the other was doing." Their rockets had been the only fast movement on the playa all weekend.

She told me how excited the kids were. "I've put a big map of the States up on the classroom wall so that they can follow your route, and it's working just like I hoped. They all want to write!" The idea of a class full of eight-year-olds dying to write—especially a below-the-national-average class, the kind that's given to a first-year teacher like Nancy—was wonderful. When I'd agreed to this correspondence back in Black Rock, I'd thought that I was taking on extra weight in the form of a duty. Now it felt more like a privilege.

I must have driven within a few hundred yards of their school either before or after driving the Rubicon, but I was glad I didn't know it at the time. Better this way, with them following this unknown creature in a big red truck around the country. After the journey was over, I'd go see them. After we got to know each other from letters.

I'd been picking up picture postcards here and there on the road ever since Black Rock: a dragster on the salt flats, an old-time prospector posed flat on his face in the desert with a vulture perched on his back, a girl leading a horse along the beach at Malibu, a mountain man trying to persuade a stubborn mule to budge. Now I bought a Seattle postcard too—an aerial view, with Lake Union clearly visible. I marked the location of my houseboat with a big X, and sent that off first. I'd stagger the others, a week apart, until I was caught up with myself.

Over the next few days, I did all the things I'd come home to do: wrote columns, saw friends, spent a day in the library, sailed on the lake, went to the chiropractor, caught up on phone calls. The carry-on case still lay open on the floor, forcing me to step over it every time I came in and out. I tossed items in as they occurred to me—Wintersilk underwear, a Polartec vest, my prized Harley-Davidson leather gloves with cut-off fingers. As I passed by my bookshelves, Ilya Ehrenburg's novel *The Life of the Automobile* caught my eye. I flipped through it and started reading about halfway through:

"Cars don't have a homeland. Like oil stocks or like classic love, they can easily cross borders. Italian Fiats clamber up the cliffs of Norway. Ever-worried specialists in Renault taxis jolt around the bumpy streets of Moscow. Ford is ubiquitous, he's in Australia, he's also in Japan. American Chevrolet trucks carry Sumatran tobacco and Palestinian oranges. A Spanish banker owns a German Mercedes. Citroens in display windows in Piccadilly or Berlin cause dreamy passers-by to halt. The automobile has come to show even the slowest minds that the earth is truly round, that the heart is just a poetic relic, that a human being contains two standard gauges: one indicates miles, the other minutes."

Ehrenburg was writing in 1929, just as the world of money was about to come crashing down. I hesitated, then tossed him into the carry-on too. The case was full by now, its presence like a partner waiting impatiently at the door, saying, "Aren't you ready yet?"

I took the hint and booked myself on a flight back to Los Angeles, planning to pick up the truck and drive east to Phoenix, where I had a date on the racetrack. That evening, with the case locked and standing by the door for an early morning getaway, I flipped on the television news and saw Craig Breedlove crash. At six hundred miles an hour.

His publicity machine must have finally cranked into action, for the network cameras were there to record it as it happened. As newscasts do whenever disaster strikes or is barely averted, they showed the tape again and again. The long metallic tube streaked across the Black Rock playa, a flash of silver even in the slow motion of the televised replay. Then came a slight wobble, an almost imperceptible lift of the rear wheels, and next the car tilted over on its side and veered into a long, wide curve, gradually bleeding off speed in a giant U-turn until it finally came to a standstill.

Breedlove had escaped with minor injuries. The Spirit of America had not. Gradually, the details sifted through the mesh of made-for-TV drama. Breedlove had made two practice runs the day before, and a third one that same morning; he and his crew were rushed and exhausted. They'd decided to go ahead with the record attempt as quickly as possible when they realized a rain-bearing front was moving in. The kind of front preceded by gusty winds.

It was a gust of crosswind that had blown the vehicle off course, they said. I remembered standing on the salt flats with a long strip of newspaper held high as a makeshift wind sock, amazed that there were no real windsocks around.

And then there'd been a little problem with the parachute: it hadn't deployed properly, so Breedlove hadn't been able to brake. A faulty parachute canister, it seemed. That sounded familiar. As did the fact that Breedlove's car had nearly hit a van parked by the side of the course, with a group of sightseers on the roof. As those people excitedly told the camera how fast it had all happened, I remembered the absurd dash of vehicles chasing down the salt flats, and how we had parked right by the course.

Now as I stared at the television screen, watching Breedlove do his aw-shucks gave-it-my-best I'll-be-back-next-year thing, still with that dopey other-worldly smile despite having just been in a six-hundred-mile-an-hour crash with absolutely no means of control, I kept thinking just one thing: How long can a man's luck last?

Chapter Ten

I stood out on my balcony at the Phoenician Hotel in Scottsdale, Arizona, looking over the huge floodlit lawn dotted with pools and well-behaved streams to the glitter of Phoenix, crossed at regular intervals by the flashing lights of planes on final approach to Sky Harbor airport, and ungraciously missed the dust.

Culture shock had set up dust devils in my brain. It had seemed a good idea to accept an invitation from Cadillac to come drive a new sedan at the Phoenix International Raceway. Just the prospect of a Cadillac on a racetrack was wonderfully absurd. And the spa world of the Phoenician promised a couple of nights of sybaritic luxury in among my usual chain of cheap motel rooms. But when I drove up to the front entrance in the dust-crusted Expedition, with every other car in sight scrubbed and polished to Q-Tip perfection, I began to think twice.

The doormen and valet parking attendants were delighted, as if I'd just driven up in a Ferrari. More so, in fact; they saw Ferraris every day. I was definitely something different, a bundle of sweat and dust standing in the Persian-carpeted air-conditioned lobby, head full of ancient palms and Joshua trees and abandoned jet fighters.

It had taken three days to make the three-hundred-and-seventy-mile drive from LAX, not the least because I'd turned it into a seven-hundred-mile drive. I'd spent one day roaming the original palm springs, the canyons south of the city that had taken their name and then turned its back on them. Hidden from the artifice of golf courses and health spas, the springs had been guarded by the Agua Caliente band of Indians, who had refrained from the temptation to "develop" these Edenic canyons. I lounged beneath two-hundred-year-old palms so lush and numerous that they formed a towering umbrella against the desert sun. Lay in the pools and let the water rush over me. Hiked up the canyons, following the water until the rock closed in so tight that I could go no farther. Dozed off on a huge slab of rock right by a stream, and had the good fortune to remember the sign warning of mountain lions only when I woke up.

The next day found me meandering through the high scrub desert of Joshua Tree National Monument, an essential side trip since I knew my father, Jessel—a nickname for his given name, Joshua—would get a kick out of my having been there. I picked up picture postcards at the ranger station, one for the kids, one for Jessel. "You have to come here," I wrote him. "Vast orchards of trees all named for you, in the middle of high desert—the kind of glorious rocky emptiness you see in westerns and think doesn't exist any more. Such a pleasure to know it does."

And on the third day, I'd taken a wrong turn coming into Phoenix and found myself driving in the desert past AMARC—the American Military Aircraft Recycling Center, which is military-speak for a huge airplane graveyard, six miles square. Every mile was densely packed with row on row of aircraft: F-111 and F-15 and A-4 fighters, noses pointing sharp and bright into the sun; HueyCobras and Chinooks and Apache helicopters, stripped of their guns; B-52s and C-5s and thousands of others I didn't recognize, each parked with military precision so that the dirt tracks between them formed a neat criss-cross pattern against the scrub grass growing beneath the planes' bellies and wings. Some were painted in faded camouflage, others in silver or gunship gray. A few had covers thrown over them to shield them from dust and sun. None were rusted, and all, at least from the road, looked as though they were in viable shape: not dead relics but live planes, consigned by politics to early retirement in the desert, where they'd be cannibalized for parts. It was a sight to gladden a pacifist, enrage a tax-payer, and sadden anyone who loved machines.

Especially a pilot. I'd started flying the year I moved to Seattle, seduced by the way messing around in the air can make you forget earthbound cares. Over the next three years, I'd happily flown away all my savings, and didn't regret a moment or a cent of it. And if my experience was limited mainly to ancient single-engine propeller craft, and my license had been gathering dust in a drawer for the past two years, none of that mattered in the face of AMARC's extravagant display of aerodynamic power.

Such a waste to keep superb flying machines permanently grounded, I thought. So tempting to liberate at least one. Just slip over the fence, hot-wire an F-15, taxi it on out onto the desert flats, and take it up into its natural habitat, soaring high into the air in a splendid curving chandelle . . .

After such lofty fantasies, the Phoenician Hotel brought me back to earth. Its luxury was intended to coddle and protect its denizens from the rawness of the desert, but that rawness was inside me, and I resisted the coddling. Where I should have been charmed by the fake Louis-something furniture, the crystal chandeliers, the heavy brocaded drapes, something in me railed at the expense of it all.

The huge marbled bathroom with its chromed faucets and generous bottles of scented designer lotions invited me to spoil myself. Instead I took a quick shower and glowered at the label attached to the downy-soft terrycloth robe hanging in the closet that said if I'd like to take the robe home, I should feel free to do so, and a ninety-dollar charge would be added to my bill. The Lone Ranger had come in from the sun, but she'd grown attached to her mask, and wasn't about to let a dose of luxury charm it off her.

It was a relief to get to the dust-swirled reality of the racetrack early the next morning. There's something peculiarly desolate about an empty racetrack, as though it's haunted by all the races that have taken place there. It's like seeing an actress without her stage makeup on, or a bar in the harsh light of morning. Beneath the whisper of wind and the echo of open space against the grandstand, you can almost hear the memories of the place—cars screaming down the straights, the crackle of the PA systems breaking up, the roar of throats and throttles.

Six new Caddies were lined up incongruously in pit row. Not that these really were Caddies. That is, they both were and weren't. In an effort to shuck its old land-yacht image, the automaker had introduced the Catera, an American version of Europe's Opel Omega. With rear wheel drive and a tight suspension, the Catera promised to be fun to drive on the track, with an added kick from the idea of squealing tires in a Cadillac.

But first, as a kind of refresher course on the dynamics of driving, we spent an hour or so on the skidpad: a small circle of concrete kept nice and slippery by occasional sprays of water. Most drivers hate the skidpad; perversely, I love it. Love the idea of learning to control a skid by first producing an uncontrolled one. The idea, that is, of controlled lack of control. Gradually feed in more speed, lift suddenly off the gas, and you produce a delirious spin. Correct for it at the very first hint of the rear end's veering out to the side, remember to counter-steer so that you avoid the vicious hook slide that otherwise follows the initial recovery, and you create order out of seeming chaos.

Take the whole sequence onto a tight mini-course laid out between orange cones, and you learn how to trail-brake, using a controlled skid to drift around corners, accelerating out early and fast. Take it onto the real track, and you have the seductive illusion that you too have the makings of a race driver.

The track we'd be driving was a one-and-a-half-mile circuit incorporating half of the raceway's oval, together with a road course winding through the infield. I drove it slowly the first few times, exploring the racing line. Each track has its own ideal line, and it's never the shortest one. It's the line that allows you to use the dynamics of the car to maximum effect, sweeping from one side of the track to the other to create momentum and speed in the turns. You trace the line by figuring out the apex of each corner—the ultimate point of the turn, which dictates when you brake and when you accelerate. You want to brush the apex with the outside of your wheels. To kiss the edge of the track even as you speed on by. And if you do this well, the car itself seems to learn the line, to take in the pattern of curve and straight, find the rhythm of it, and when all is perfect, enter the dance of speed.

The smoother the dance, the faster you go. Doing laps—driving the circuit again and again—you take the course just a shade smoother each time around, shaving off time: whole seconds at first, and then tenths of seconds, and then, if you're very good and have been doing this for years, even hundredths of seconds.

★

Time is of the essence on a racetrack, but to such a fine degree that few non-racers can grasp it.

Lap times are measured with surgical precision. They have to be. The first dozen cars in qualifying time trials may finish within a second of each other over a two-mile track. The pole winner—the fastest car in qualifying, which then gets the most favorable position on the starting grid—has been as little as three one-thousandths of a second faster than the runner-up.

A modern Indy car is designed for such finesse. On the one hand, it is old-fashioned, massive power; it consumes half a gallon of methanol fuel per mile, produces nearly nine hundred horsepower, and can rev as high as 15,000 rpm. But it is also a space-age creature. In fact, as veteran motor sports writer Carl Ludwigsen once said, "The only other small wheeled vehicles that compare with racing cars in cost, complexity, and design-for-purpose are now parked, abandoned, on the moon." And, since then, on Mars.

Radio telemetry allows for up to sixty channels of information to be transmitted from the car's on-board computer to engineers in the pits—everything from brake and throttle pressures to gearbox temperatures, suspension travel, wheel-bearing pressures, tire pressures, wheel speeds, boost, ride height, and of course, numerous engine parameters. Yet the actual driver controls are surprisingly sparse. Or not so, considering the split-second amounts of time the driver has to look at them. The steering wheel has only four control buttons, one in each of the primary colors. Yellow and blue move the boost up and down; green limits the speed in the pits as required by rules; red allows the driver to talk to the pits by radio. And that's it.

There are no gauges as in regular cars. Liquid crystal displays in front of the driver display essential information: rpm, boost, speed, fuel remaining, and what gear the car is in, since except for in the pits, nearly all shifting in an Indy car is done by matching revs, without using the clutch pedal. Those electronic transmissions with rocker switches on the steering wheel are only on Formula One cars.

Warning displays flash if engine temperature or oil pressure rises too high, and the driver can scroll through a series of optional displays too, though he's unlikely to do so unless the race is under the yellow caution flag—usually as emergency crew clear debris from a crash, with the surviving cars merely maintaining position at relatively slow speed instead of racing.

Indy cars are highly customized creations. Each one uses a standard chassis, often from Lola or Reynard in England, but nearly every part is lightened, strengthened, or otherwise modified. Aluminum, titanium, or magnesium may be used instead of steel. Carbon fiber, lighter than aluminum and stronger than steel, is used to mold the body. The cockpit width is matched to the precise width of the driver's shoulders, and the seat molded to his frame—or, in the case of Lyn St. James, her frame. The result is starkly functional, the car stripped of all but the raw essentials of the creation of speed, its maintenance, and its control.

It's hard to assess the price of an Indy car, but by the time a team has fine-tuned one to their satisfaction, a million dollars may be a good ballpark figure. And this million dollars provides a machine that is utterly terrifying to a rank amateur like me.

Imagine that you are the driver. You're sitting two inches off the ground, and the whole machine is shaking and vibrating so badly that the world seems to be in a continuous state of earthquake. The car is on the outer edge of the limits of control, and you're going to keep it that way for two hundred laps.

You can't falter even for a split second; the slightest lapse of concentration is potentially fatal. Your mind must stay tuned to a perfect pitch of focus, even as the physical pressures mount. The cockpit is so cramped you can't move a muscle that isn't needed to operate the machine. The heat is stifling; every part of the car radiates heat, and it's made all the worse by the triple layer of flame-resistant clothing you're wearing. The sheer monotony of taking the same lap again and again begins to wear on you. As does the immense physical stress of speed.

Acceleration is a massive sensory experience. It literally sends the senses into overload. Like all human bodies, yours is made to move at a certain speed, and at a certain angle to the world. Exceed that speed, or that angle, and the G-force takes over.

Essentially, this force is dislocation. It works with such pressure that it seems as though your skeleton is moved first and your insides unwillingly follow after. You are, literally, thrown at an angle to the world. Where you usually think of gravity as a vertical force, pulling you down, the main G-force you feel in a race car is horizontal. Take a sharp turn and you can feel it pulling inexorably at you, pushing the car and all the fluids in it, and in you, to one side or the other. Take a high banked turn, and you may find yourself subject to three or even four times the normal force of gravity. Your head turns to a block of lead, lolling heavily to the side as you strain everything in your neck and back in the attempt to keep your eyes more or less level with the track.

From a standing start, an Indy car reaches a hundred miles an hour in just under three seconds. In the first second alone, the force of acceleration pushes your head back so violently that your face distends into a ghostly Halloween grimace. By the end of two seconds, you've changed gears twice and been smashed back into the seat each time. After the third second, accelerating toward two hundred miles an hour, your peripheral vision is completely blurred. You can only see straight ahead. You no longer feel like you're moving over the road; instead, the road seems to be moving under you. If you had the time to think about it, you'd realize that what you're seeing is almost precisely what anyone who plays an electronic video racing game sees. In one of those postmodern ironies, reality reflects virtual reality.

Meanwhile all your vital signs are in high gear. The force of acceleration makes blood pool in your legs so that less is delivered to your heart. Your pulse rate rises to compensate. It may reach two hundred beats a minute, and stay at eighty-five percent of that maximum for almost the entire length of the two-hour race.

Your breathing quickens as your muscles call for more oxygen—speed literally takes your breath away—and your whole body goes into high-adrenaline emergency stance: mouth dry, eyes dilated, hands and feet responding in the kind of reaction times only top-flight athletes can muster. Everything in you is primed for instantaneity.

The good news is that you're barely aware of all this. You have too much else to think about. It's not enough that you drive fast and skill-fully; you need to be a master strategist too. At this level, the pressure of competition is relentless. And ruthless. Short-term strategy demands the ability to pounce on the slightest opening given by an opposing racer, because that one split-second moment is all you will get. You need to calculate the overtaking point to within a fraction of an inch, to know where that other driver will go as well as where you will. And long-term strategy demands that a plan for the whole race be put into effect. You may lead for a hundred and ninety-nine laps, but it means nothing if you're not leading at the end of the two hundredth one. You're calculat-ing gas and distance, how much longer the tires will last, whether you should delay the next pit stop or take an early one. And you're doing the same for your opponents, second-guessing them, trying to assess their strategies so that you can out-maneuver them.

What you are doing, under the most intense physical pressure, is essentially this: you are playing a highly sophisticated game of chess at well over two hundred miles an hour. With yourself as the king.

And by the end of a long, hard race, you'll have lost as much as four percent of your body weight. If you weigh one seventy-five, that's seven pounds. Mentally and physically, you've sweated it away.

But at least you'll have the good fortune to be so focused on the race that you have no awareness of what goes on in the stands and behind the fences. Because what happens there, among the spectators, is not pretty.

Motor racing is the biggest spectator sport in the United States, far outpacing football in terms of attendance. As the perfect expression of the national obsession with mechanistic power, this seems to make sense. As a sport that allows spectators to follow strategy, let alone what is happening at any particular moment, it makes none at all.

There is only so long you can sit in a grandstand seat watching car after car scream by so fast that your neck aches with the impossible effort of keeping up with their movement. If you want to know what's happening, you need a radio, and even then you'll be hard put to hear it above the noise of the cars. So people with access to the best seats in the grandstand can usually be found sitting in the hospitality tents of various sponsors, where they can watch the race on television. I've done it myself: sat in an enclosed tent, cool drink in hand, and watched the race on the small screen as though it were happening in another country instead of a mere thirty yards away. The victory once again of the virtual over the real.

For those without access to the tents, the attraction seems to be a mix of beer and blood. Most of the spectators, in short, are waiting for a crash. The standing joke in racing circles is that when there's a crash at an Indy-car race, a collective gasp goes up from the crowd; when there's one at a stock-car race, the gasp is followed by cheers. It's not the race that's exciting, but the risk. Skill is confused with drama, disaster with entertainment.

I once worked my way down to the fence by the chicane during a race at Connecticut's Lime Rock Park. "Who's leading?" I asked the beer-toting man beside me, his fair skin sweating and burning in the sun.

He shrugged, like I'd asked a really dumb question. "Beats me."

A large cooler stood on the ground beside him. "Looks like you're settled in for the day."

"Sure am," he said, puffing up in territorial pride. "This is the most dangerous corner. If anything happens, it's gonna happen right here." He rested his belly against the fence. "And I've got the best seat in the house."

★

They say that if you have to crash, a racetrack is the best place to do it. There is no traffic coming toward you, the corners are equipped with banks of tires to cushion hard landings, and most tight bends have run-off areas in which you can spin out if you have to. A good track, in short, is made to accommodate a crash.

I'm talking road tracks here—ones like Sears Point and Watkins Glen and Laguna Seca, where the courses loop up and down hill and round crazily tight hairpin bends, as opposed to the pure symmetry of the ovals, which terrify me. If a road track forgives mistakes, an oval does not; the oval looks deceptively easy, but the outside of the curve is a solid concrete wall, and that wall is far too absolute a test of nerves and control for me. A good race driver uses every available inch of track, which means driving within an inch of the wall; err by that one inch, and there is no forgiveness.

At least on a road track, I can pretend I know what I'm doing. Even when I clearly don't.

I made a bad mistake some years ago on one of the most famed road tracks: Road America, the four-mile, fourteen-turn circuit at Elkhart Lake, Wisconsin, some ten miles inland from Lake Michigan. It was the first day I'd ever driven the course, and that fact alone might seem to have called for some caution. But after a morning spent doing laps, I was full of the exhilarating illusion that I had gotten the hang of it.

The laps, and the cars, were courtesy of General Motors, which every year holds a big press preview of all its products at Road America. Brand-new cars line the pits. Pick a helmet from the wall, choose any car you want, hop in, and take off for as many laps as you like. Since most automotive journalists have either some amateur racing experience or, like me, have taken intensive competition courses, this is less a recipe for chaos than it might sound at first, especially since there is no car-to-car racing. But it's still a racetrack, and wristwatches still include split-second timers; unofficial lap times become the focus of competition, if not with others, then at least with yourself. Each lap, you vow, you'll take it smoother and cleaner and just a tenth of a second faster. Or maybe two-tenths. Or three . . .

The last car I drove before the lunch break was the newest and most powerful of the Corvettes. It handled the course superbly, taking me at speed even through Turn Three, which I'd found especially tricky since while it seemed at first to be a plain ninety degrees to the right, it kept turning, so that it was really well over a hundred degrees. The Vette made me breathless and high. I had such a ball in it I kept right on doing laps, and so came late to lunch, which meant that by the time I got back to the track, everyone else was there before me and the cars I most wanted to drive were already gone. The only car left that stood fair to improve my lap time was a Camaro Z28. In red, of course. With an automatic shift.

Ordinarily, I'd know better than to take an automatic anything onto a racetrack; I don't know how to handle an automatic with the same precision as I do a manual shift. But I was full of a very good meal, still a bit high from those laps in the Vette, and hot to trot. As they say in aviation, I was fat, dumb, and happy. So I made for Turn Three at eighty miles an hour just as I had in the Vette, turned far too late into the corner—and realized I wasn't going to make it.

I could struggle to hold the car on the pavement, but I knew I'd risk rolling it. So in the split second available, I made what seemed to me a calm and wise decision: let the car spin out onto the large run-off area of earth and gravel designed for just that purpose. Spin it to a stall, start up the engine again, and get back onto the track. I'd done it in open-wheel race cars, so why not in the Camaro?

I found out why not. The spin began as predicted, and all might have been fine—or so I tell myself—if the run-off area had not been heavily corrugated from bulldozer tracks. The right rear wheel caught one of those tracks at precisely the wrong angle, and burst. All predictable properties of a spin went flying. As did the car.

Still barreling along at some speed, the Camaro began to tip. As more and more weight came over onto the left wheels, it tipped farther, then farther still, until it reached the point where I knew it was going to roll. And as it went past the point of no return, I sat there quite calmly thinking one thing over and over again: "What a stupid way to go, Lesley. What a *stupid* way to go." As though somewhere, somehow, there had to be an intelligent way.

It seemed I sat with extraordinary calmness, hands and feet still on the controls. The roll itself was not what disturbed me. I'd made several forays into aerobatics in the previous year, and while being upside down was what was called in aviation an "unusual attitude," it was not an impossible one so long as there was air enough beneath you. What did disturb me was the fact that I was in a car, not a plane, which meant that there was no air at all beneath me. Just extremely solid ground.

The car rolled a hundred and eighty degrees, and slid several yards farther on its roof. When it came to a stop, it took me a moment to realize I wasn't moving any more. Then another one to register the fact that I was still alive. And a third to start thinking.

Thought came in the form of a single word of fear and warning: "Fire." There was none yet, but there could be at any moment. I reached for the ignition and switched off the engine. Pulled out the key for good measure. Set about getting out of there as quick as I could, reaching for the seat-belt latch with one hand and stretching out the other to brace myself so that I wouldn't fall head first to the ground.

But the ground was not where I thought it would be. It was right up against my nose.

This puzzled me, as did the fact that for some reason I couldn't turn head first to the open window beside me. I squirmed around to wriggle out feet first instead, which worked fine until I reached my head. It wouldn't go through the window. I undid my helmet and pulled my head out of both helmet and window together, vaguely wondering why the opening was suddenly so narrow.

I stood up and did a quick check: neck, shoulders, hips, legs, everything was still connected. Just a couple of cuts—one on my wrist, the other on my knee. Across the track, I could see the corner worker shouting into a field phone. I looked down at the car; it seemed peculiarly small and crumpled. Then I saw the two roof panels on the ground some thirty yards away: the body must have twisted as I'd rolled, and the panels had torqued out. That's why the ground had been right beneath my nose when I came to a stop. That, and the fact that the front pillars, the ones either side of the windshield, had crushed.

I stared at the wreck, amazed that I'd squirmed out of it in one piece. The only deep cut was to my pride. Especially my female pride. "You're one of only a handful of women in this field, and you had to go crash," I kept thinking. It was as if I'd betrayed not just my own sense of ability and skill—now indubitably and most publicly disproved—but the whole female race.

The ambulance came and the attendant fussed, delighted to have something to do. I rattled off my name, Bill Clinton's name, my social security number, and the date. "No concussion," he concluded. He couldn't quite hide a certain disappointment. I let him apply a couple of Band-aids, and drove with him back to the pits, where I stepped out falling over myself in embarrassed apologies: to the General Motors people for wrecking their brand-new Camaro, but mostly to my colleagues for closing the track for twenty minutes while the emergency crew cleared the car away and checked for debris. "So stupid," I kept saying. "So stupid of me."

I'd expected sneers, but to my amazement, I got sympathy. One by one, the most experienced and respected of my colleagues took me aside to confide the time when he too had done something really dumb on a racetrack—a rollover, a spin, a collision. It was their way of telling me that things like this happen even to the best.

"It's the hardest way to learn, but it can be the most effective," said one.

"I hope you're right," I muttered.

It occurred to me only later that if I had not been wearing a helmet— if I'd been on a public highway instead of on a track—I would have incurred massive head injuries. I half allowed myself to imagine it: my scalp ripped away, my skull opening, my brains spilling out, leaving a trail of red and white and pale gray as the car slid on over the corrugated ground . . .

But that was just hypothetical. The cuts healed quickly. The ego took far longer.

★

It is generally agreed that one of the most intelligent of race drivers is the only three-time winner of the World Series Indy Car Championship, Bobby Rahal, a man I've had a weakness for ever since I first saw a photo of him driving—a photo, that is, of round, steel-rimmed spectacles peering out from under the helmet. The glasses gave him something of a gnomic face, and defied the stock image of the dashingly handsome daredevil race driver.

The last time I was back east, I'd driven down from Detroit to see Rahal at his race team's headquarters in an industrial park just outside Columbus, Ohio. I'd been spurred by a description of him by *AutoWeek*'s

Leon Mandel as "a cerebral, complex man, ferocious and at the same time attentive and gentle." Mandel is a good writer; his use of the words "ferocious" and "cerebral" in the same sentence had me thoroughly intrigued.

With his well-balded head, neat mustache, and slight overbite, Rahal looked like he could well be a doctor—a cardiologist perhaps, maybe even a neurosurgeon. He smiled when I said so: "I played with the idea of being a doctor when I was in college, but the chemistry eluded me. I ended up majoring in history. My specialty was Victorian England and the dawn of the industrial age."

"Dark Satanic mills," I said. He nodded. This was a race driver who'd read his Blake. Perhaps that explained the airy, light-filled design of the Team Rahal building. Full of interesting angles, it was a standout in the usual industrial-park environment of copy-cat boxes. Bobby Rahal was producing the filthiest of all cars—cars that burn half a gallon of fuel for every mile they travel—in a structure that was an esthetic pleasure to be in.

His office, an aerie built into a mezzanine floor, had the clean elegance of that of a CEO of a small company. But of course that's exactly what he was: the majority owner and manager of the team, a third of whose operating budget went into research and development. With sixty-five employees, including eleven engineers, Team Rahal wasn't just racing cars: it was designing and testing them, and its workshops were a showcase for the highest-tech new processes and materials.

I asked about his name. "Isn't that Arabic?" I said. "Rahal"—pronouncing it the Arabic way, *rah-hal* instead of *ray-hall*—"meaning 'traveler'?"

He looked at me in surprise. "How did you know that?"

"I lived in Jerusalem for thirteen years, and learned some Arabic."

He smiled. His grandparents were Greek Orthodox immigrants from Lebanon, from a village near the Golan Heights. In the Middle East, we'd be on opposite sides of the conflict, but here in Columbus, Ohio, we'd come together to talk racing. Which made the world of cars either very large or very small, though I wasn't sure which.

Now forty-three, Rahal was at perhaps the roughest stage of a successful racer's life: wondering whether to retire as a driver. The winning is the dramatic part—the victor's wreaths, the trophies, the endorsements, the fame. But it's when the winning stops that things get really interesting. Rahal was old for racing, and he knew it.

He'd had the foresight to set himself up for retirement. He was managing his own race team, with a good younger driver in Bryan Herta and an attention-getting business partner in David Letterman, who was clearly determined to go *mano a mano* with Jay Leno in the automotive world as well as in the late-night television one. There was also a string of successful Rahal car dealerships in Pennsylvania. But literally half this man's life had been spent as a race driver, and though he hadn't been winning races in the past couple of years, he had been placing in the top five rankings, and was still a contender for an unprecedented fourth world championship. How does anyone let go of all that?

"Motor racing is very fleeting, very fickle," he said. "You'd better take advantage of the momentum while it's there, because it won't be there forever. It can't be." He arched his fingers together under his chin, like a professor considering his words. "This may be my last year as a driver. I have a responsibility to others now, a responsibility not to let the team suffer because my ego won't let go. In your forties, it gets harder and harder to create the level of intensity you had in your twenties, and at some point, I have to acknowledge that."

"That could also be called maturity," I pointed out.

He grinned, owlish eyes becoming almost predatory. "It's true that right now I can still use the wisdom and guile and treachery of age to overcome pure youth. But at some point youth will overcome all the wisdom and guile in the world, and I'd like to retire before that happens."

"Do you feel intimations of mortality on the track that you never felt before?" Aware that I was speaking to one of the few men in racing who'd catch the reference to Wordsworth.

He nodded in acknowledgment, and considered the question. "No," he said finally. "I don't think so. I've always been a careful driver. No race-car driver I've ever known is interested in dying. But if you're realistic and honest, you have to constantly check: Do you still have the intensity and commitment and focus? These things are sacred, and I think you can see when they're missing."

Intensity and commitment and focus . . . "Is that what Mandel meant when he talked about you being 'ferocious and cerebral'?"

"The cerebral part is true in that I think I understand the pace of a race and the needs of the car, know when to push and when not. That's part of the experience—the treachery and guile. You need intelligence to win. It doesn't just happen; it's created."

"And what about the ferocious part?"

"Maybe he saw what my wife calls my 'race face.' She says she can see the focus on the race building in me. On the Monday, maybe five percent of your brain is thinking of the race and ninety-five percent of everything else. By Wednesday, it's fifty-fifty. By Friday, the morning of practice, it's ninety-five percent the race and only five percent everything else.

"Then comes the race itself, and when you're in that car, there's only you, and it. Everything else is just color. You focus so tremendously you lose all concept of time and place. A two-hour race goes by"—he snapped his fingers—"just like that. And that level of concentration, the intensity of it, consumes you. So when the race is over, even if you win, you're completely drained and beat. You feel a tremendous letdown. I know the Hollywood image of the race winner is champagne and babes and party all night, but all I want to do is be with those who are close to me and get away from the track and go to bed."

Somehow it was easy to ask Rahal the questions I'd always wanted to ask other drivers, but never dared, too aware that I'd be stepping on taboos or superstitions. "And fear? Does that play a role? The increasing awareness with age of what can happen? That loss of the youthful conviction that you're bulletproof?"

He considered a moment, took his time. "To me," he said finally, "the definition of faith is going into Turn One at Indy at 241 mph and knowing that when you turn that steering wheel, the car's actually going to turn. The concept of faith and belief is immense: in yourself, in the people around you, and in the machinery. Motor racing centers on that.

If a driver is afraid, it's because he no longer has faith. He questions everything he does, everything the mechanics do, even the car itself. And you can't get into a race car questioning."

Now I saw why he'd used the word "sacred" earlier. Not a careless use of the word; there is nothing careless about Bobby Rahal. A carefully chosen word, used with the very intensity he requires of himself.

Faith was not what I'd expected to talk about with him, but perhaps I should have expected it. Perhaps that is what is necessary to do such a crazy thing as drive a race car. "Have faith," my instructor had screamed at me the first time I took a competition course and balked at taking my single-seat Formula Ford open-wheel race car through the S bend at Lime Rock the way he wanted me to—that is, go into it full tilt, and what felt like a good three seconds too late, brake hard, then turn the wheel a mere two inches to the left when several hefty wrenches of the wheel seemed called for. Something prevented me from doing this. I assumed it was called the survival instinct. "You have to override instinct," my instructor explained. "Remember Hebrews eleven, verse one: have faith!"

Being a rather literal creature, I couldn't bring myself to follow his instructions until I'd looked up the verse that night in my motel-room Bible, courtesy of the Gideons. "Faith," it said, "is the substance of things hoped for, the evidence of things not seen."

That seemed to just about cover it.

I went back to the track the next morning, took a deep breath, and thought—God help me—"Hebrews eleven, verse one." I was vaguely aware of the tires screeching dramatically as the G-force pulled at me, the car rounded the S fast and high on the rim of each turn as though it were a self-guided missile, and I came roaring out full tilt onto the following straight with a smile on my face as broad as the track. For a brief, glorious moment, I'd discovered the rhythm of the racing line.

"You can't drive a race car without faith," Rahal was saying. "People talk about it being a risky profession, but I don't see the risk, because I believe. I have faith that I can get myself out of trouble, out of any incident. I don't think it's a matter of overconfidence or cockiness, because there's an element of humility in faith. As much as you need belief, you need respect too. You have to respect what this car is capable of doing. The moment you think you can make it do something it can't or won't, that's when you're in trouble."

"So it's a matter of eliminating chance, as far as possible?"

"As far as possible. But when you come out of a turn to see a crash happening right in front of you, and cars are spinning back and forth across the track and there's debris flying, and yet you come through okay, what's happening there? Fate? God? Pure damn luck?"

"It's generally attributed to skill."

"Maybe, but some drivers go through a situation like that with their eyes closed, on a hope and a prayer. I don't know. Some things are better left undiscovered or unsaid, I guess. We try to explain everything, but some things we can't have an answer for."

★

Speed is the only truly modern sensation. The early modernists knew that. "A car driver, always speeding across space like a tempest or a cyclone, is something of a superman," raved Octave Mirbeau, part of the literary *anarchisme* movement in France in 1908. His Italian counterpart F. T. Marinetti aimed higher still. The car was a mechanical centaur, "a vehement God of a race of steel," and to go fast was god-like: "The intoxication of great speeds in cars is nothing but the joy of feeling oneself fused with the only divinity."

The thought of these artists and writers whooping their way into religious revelation behind the wheel might seem almost comical ninety years later, but they had that clarity that comes with doing something for the very first time. There is something about speed that grasps the imagination and will not let go. It seduces the mind: hooks you in, encompasses you, obviates every other part of you. It makes you high, and an essential part of that exhilaration is the awareness of being at the very limits of control, hovering just this side of that thin, fragile line between life and death where gods play and humans stumble. If speed were not dangerous, it would lose that intoxicating vehemence. If it were safe, the sharp aura of the divine would pale, dull, and dilute into the mundane.

I nosed the Catera gently around the first couple of laps at Phoenix, getting used to the line and getting a feel for what the car could do on it. On the third lap, I began to go down hard on the throttle, and as I did so my eyes opened wide, tears gathering at the corners as I struggled to assimilate the blur of the track racing toward me. Every synapse in my brain told me I wasn't going to make this turn or the next one, and every muscle in my body strained to prove my brain wrong. The G-force pulled at me in the corners, and I heard the tires squealing as I rounded a hairpin bend and came tearing out onto the oval, running high up against the wall . . .

And suddenly the wall was my friend and it felt good up here, high on the edge, zooming past the pits with the tach needle reaching for the red line and the odometer nosing over a hundred, one ten, one twenty, and plenty more power to go, and all I wanted to do at that moment was drive lap after lap all day, taking the course just a little smoother each time until I could muster the courage to keep my foot down all the way and drive one perfect lap.

I could feel the desire for that perfection in my muscles and my bones, a physical ache for it as I took each lap better, laying down the line like the melody of a jazz riff and then fine-tuning it, faster and smoother each time until I could sense perfection within my reach, could even taste it, acrid yet sweet on the roof of my mouth: the taste of adrenaline.

I was high on the rim of the track, up on the edge of the world with the engine roaring and the wheels thrumming and the music of the track vibrating through every cell of my body, and life was terrifying and life was perfect and even as all I wanted to do was slow down, I yearned for nothing more than to go faster. I was getting there, reaching for the perfection I knew was waiting for me on the next lap, or maybe the one after that, and then on one magnificent pass along the straight side of the oval, the needle hit one thirty and the electronic speed limiter kicked in, cutting back fuel to the injectors.

I heard the revs drop, felt the engine slow, and was suddenly and cruelly bereft, brought back to the real world by the sophisticated safety technology of a luxury sedan. The perfect lap would not be mine. Not today.

I came back into the pits the next time round, eyes gleaming and body limp with a mix of relief and exhilaration, and surrendered the car to another driver. I took off my helmet, found a can of something—anything—to drink, and went to sit on the pit wall, trying to assimilate the fact that I was no longer in motion even though my heart rate told me I was.

"Better than sex, huh?" someone said.

I'd heard it said many times before. Fortunately he didn't seem to expect an answer.

"You drive really well," he said. I smiled, a sucker for a compliment even as I knew just how badly I was capable of driving.

"You must really love cars."

"No," I said, my guard down in the afterglow of the drive, "I don't love them. I'm fascinated by them. Intrigued by them. But love? They move too fast for love."

The poor man stared at me dumbfounded. So far as he was concerned, this conversation had just left the safe prescribed limits he'd had in mind and gone veering off into uncharted territory. He mumbled a lame excuse and made his escape, leaving me to catch up with what I'd just said.

"Speed," Milan Kundera wrote slyly in his novel *Slowness,* "is the form of ecstasy the technical revolution has bestowed on man." And on woman too. But like Kundera, I am aware of other forms of ecstasy, moments that depend not on speed but on slowness. Sex to be sure, but so many other kinds too.

There was the pleasure of flying lazy eights in an old biplane, for instance, letting the plane bleed off speed as it noses upward until, just as it's about to lose all momentum, you let the nose arc over and zoom down, tracing an imaginary ribbon in the sky. Down you swoop to the bottom of the loop, and then at just the right moment, you apply power, climb up the other side, arc over, and do it all over again. Or there was the brisk exhilaration of driving at dawn along a back country road at twenty miles an hour with the windows wide open and your nostrils full of the crispness of frost or the softness of dew. Or the lost pleasure of Thoreau's idea of sauntering, ambling the road to the *sainte terre,* the holy land, with no thought of healthy exercise, no measurements of heart rates, no "making time," but the simple pleasure of movement itself.

Slowness connects, speed disconnects. The one makes you see the world, the other makes you the center of the world. At speed, there is no road, no sense of place, not even any time. Speed is annihilation: it eats everything up into the sensation of the moment. Only when you go slow can you think and absorb. Only when you go slow do you have time to see.

That evening, I leaned over the balcony rail and watched the sunset paint the distant mountains red and then purple. In the middle distance, the airliners sailed in and out of Sky Harbor. On final approach, they were going twice the speed that I'd driven that day on the track. Yet they seemed to be moving extraordinarily slowly, as though at any moment they'd stall and fall out of the sky.

Chapter Eleven

I have always been leery of Mexican Day of the Dead dolls, those bright plaster skeletons clad in multicolored finery, kicking up their heels in an afterlife. Teeth bared and joints clicking, they indulge all the pleasures of the flesh despite—or perhaps because of—the complete absence of flesh on their bones.

They make me nervous, these dolls, as though just to have one in the house is to tempt fate. Whenever I see one in someone else's living room, I look away quickly, and position myself so that I have my back to it.

Yet now, a few days after leaving Phoenix, I found myself buying one.

I'd checked in to a motel in Albuquerque, New Mexico, with a day to spare before the start of a crash conference—the Fortieth Annual Stapp Car Crash Conference, to be precise. I wasn't too sure about the idea of going to this. In fact I was downright edgy. As with a crash on the road, my impulse was to look away and speed up, not slow down and gaze. The very act of attending a crash conference seemed somehow to be tempting fate. But that, perhaps, was what had attracted me to it.

I used the spare day to drive up to Santa Fe and visit Denise Mac-Cluggage, a former racer who was now a journalist. Black clouds loomed menacingly behind me as I drove north, the wind began to gust hard, and lightning slammed jaggedly into the mountainsides. The clouds lowered and rolled in, sending down rain so hard that the noise of it drowned out an Indian rally for gaming rights being broadcast live on the radio, which was just as well: the chants and drumbeats were beginning to hypnotize me. By the time the worst of the storm had passed, I'd switched to a performance of Brahms's Double Concerto for Violin and Cello instead, played by the Detroit Symphony Orchestra—an appropriate way to roll up in the driveway of Denise's house.

The place was full of automotive memorabilia—framed photos, model cars, certificates, trophies—hung and displayed side by side with an extensive array of Indian wall hangings and baskets and masks. I couldn't imagine any other home where the two collections could exist side by side. We settled in by the juniper fire in her living room, had a bite to eat, and swapped stories of experiences on the Hopi mesas in northern Arizona, where I'd spent the past few days. And when the rain tailed off, we went downtown to visit an old racing friend of hers in his arts and crafts store. The Day of the Dead doll was there.

It was a skeleton driving a car. A black convertible Porsche, it looked like. The windows were painted white, the headlamps red, and the lines were picked out in yellow, with a touch of gold on the wheels. A turquoise bubble waved absurdly on top of what I supposed was the radio antenna. The whole thing was everything Day of the Dead dolls always are: garish, kitschy, and frightening.

I stared at it, shuddered, and turned away. Then turned back again, fascinated despite myself.

While Denise and her friend talked about race meets, I roamed the store and drank coffee and came back again and again to the doll. This was sick, I thought. This was asking for trouble. The toy seemed to celebrate death and tempt it, defy it and deny it, all at the same time. And yet I couldn't leave the store without taking it with me. If Denise thought my purchase odd, she made no comment. Perhaps she thought that anything anyone would buy before attending a crash conference would have to be somewhat skewed.

At the time, I had the vague idea that the skeleton and his Porsche—I instantly thought of it as him, not her—would sit on the dashboard of the truck as a kind of road-runner's icon, fending off the worst by anticipating it. But later, I'd wonder if my purchase of it wasn't a small, strange act of recognition. In the past few days, eight thousand miles away, my father had come close to death and once again, defied it.

★

I'd been on the Hopi reservation in northern Arizona at the time. The drive up from Phoenix, on the two-lane blacktop of Route 87 the whole way, had been superb—the kind of drive an ideal high-school geography teacher would take students on. Within a couple of hundred miles, the landscape changed so abruptly that at times you could practically stand with your left foot in one climate zone and your right in another. One side of a low pass was the cholla and saguaro cactus of the Sonoran desert; the other, deciduous forest, which then changed with elevation into alpine forest. Next came open rangeland, which gave way to high scrub desert, which in turn led into the six-thousand-foot-high painted desert, where the mesas glimmered in the distance of late afternoon and pillars of red rock stood sentinel either side of the road.

The lower the sun dropped, the larger it seemed the sky became. "Unearthly," I kept thinking, even as I smiled at the very idea of such a word for the sky. But unearthly it was.

The light became a palpable presence, the single dominating factor of that vast rockscape. Huge swathes of it reached from the horizon to the very center of the sky. Bands of dark and light glowered to the northeast, while off to the west, the sun lowered into technicolor splendor and cast an Old Master varnish of gold over the mesas.

I pulled in to ask directions at a small supermarket at the base of the mesas. Fluorescent light bounced harshly off the walls and the shelves, both of which were practically bare. I walked around: the bread section consisted almost entirely of Wonderbread; the dented cans had faded labels and rusted rims; the "fresh" vegetables were pale and droopy with age. The aroma of pesticide hung in the aisles. It reminded me of markets in inner-city ghetto neighborhoods, where you have the feeling that the goods on display are those rejected from markets in more upscale areas. There was no mistaking the aura of the place: it was the aura of poverty.

Since I was the only customer, I picked out a few basics just to be polite.

"Staying a while?" asked the checkout clerk, and sneezed.

"Bless you," I said. "I'm just here for a couple of days."

She blushed and smiled at my "bless you." "Then you're coming to the dance."

"The dance?"

"The basket dance, tomorrow, up in Sipaulovi. You didn't know about it? You must come. You're invited. I invite you. It goes on all day, from sunrise to sunset."

"What's a basket dance?"

"It's what we call a social dance. A women's dance. The women dance, and everybody is invited, from all the villages on the mesas." She smiled, woman to woman. "You'll like it," she said, as though she knew who I was and what sort of thing I liked.

She gave me directions to the motel attached to the Hopi Cultural Center. The sun had long set by now, and I made my way up the steep hillside road in a darkness so absolute I could see the Big Dipper ahead of me even with my headlights on. The motel was a concrete huddle on the rim of the mesa. There was only one other car in the parking lot, and it belonged to the desk clerk. "I guess you're going to the basket dance," he said. I guessed I was.

The rooms were a series of concrete cubes facing inward onto three small, empty courtyards, each one lit with a single buzzing yellow light. A freezing wind had come up out of the southwest, and it soughed around the corners, raising wisps of sand and dust. The complex was evidently intended to be a modern interpretation of pueblo style, and maybe it had looked great on the drafting table. In reality it was bleak and lonesome, all the more so when you were the only guest. Aside from the dogs.

They were the gentlest, most sweet-natured, most flea-ridden pack of mutts I have ever come across. Curled up in the corners of the court-yards, scratching themselves and huddling for shelter against the wind, they leaped to their feet at the sight of me and crowded around, all six of them. Tails wagged, noses snuffled, dark doe-like eyes peered be-seechingly up at me as I opened the door to my room. They were so pathetically eager that it was all I could do not to squat down, give them the pats and hugs they so clearly wanted, and accept their fleas.

The concrete beneath the worn carpeting gave the room a permanent chill, not helped by the dull lighting from two forty-watt bulbs. There was none of the Hopi-themed furnishing I'd expected, but by now I was grateful for that. The dogs whined outside the door, begging for access, and I opened it to shoo them away. Two of them were mating half-heartedly. The others crowded the door, retreated a couple of steps when I shooed at them, then came back and, as I closed the door again, lay down in a heap across the threshold. I put on an extra layer of clothing and drifted off to sleep to the scuffling pants and moans of canine mating, oddly secure in knowing that my door was guarded.

In the clear, cold light of a below-freezing morning, the motel and cultural center were even sorrier than at night. The center's dark, poky museum held the barest basics of Hopi life; all the good stuff was gone to museum collections in cities around the States, even around the world—anywhere but here. The cafe was closed, so I breakfasted on the Wonderbread and processed cheese and saccharin-flavored orange juice I'd bought at the supermarket the night before, and set off to explore the mesas, feeling horribly conspicuous in my big new Expedition when every other car I saw was at least ten years old, and many were twice that age.

At a small repair shop by the gas pump at the bottom of the mesa, a mechanic was working on an old Datsun. It was a faded turquoise color, livened here and there with a splash of rust, except for the front passenger door, which was metallic purple, with a pink-tinted window.

I bought some gas. "That's quite some color scheme," I said.

He nodded. "Found just the right door off another one, same model."

"It'll look great once you paint it all the same color."

He looked at me in surprise. "Why paint it? The door fits, the engine works. What more could you want?"

I got back self-consciously into my heap of brand-new metal. No rust, no dents, no cannibalized parts, it was like a purebred dog compared to flea-bitten mutts. On the radio, the Indian station was full of news about the gaming initiatives on the election ballots, which would allow all Arizona's reservations to open casinos. I'm no fan of what gambling does to both the people who run it and the people who indulge in it, but it's easy to take the high moral ground when you're not living in the squalor that gaming revenues could alleviate.

High up on First Mesa, built so closely into the rock that it was hard to tell where the rock ended and the stones of the houses began, was the oldest and most sacred of all the clifftop pueblos, Walpi. With steep cliffs on three sides and only a narrow stone causeway linking it to the main part of the mesa, it had the desolate splendor of an abandoned fortress. And abandoned it was, except by a few elders who, I'd been told, stuck to "the old ways." The wind blew hard and sharp, and I tried to imagine how those elders survived without electricity or running water. Faith didn't seem to be enough.

The remains of a stone pillar had an eagle's feather and a small cairn of stones tucked into a rough niche. I caught a glimpse of a face staring out at me through a small dirty window. The door opened a crack, and an old man's head appeared, wisps of rank-smelling damp smoke escaping above him into the wind.

"You want to buy kachina dolls?" The words barely decipherable for lack of teeth to pronounce them. "You see me in *Arizona Highways* magazine? September 1980. Everyone knows me from there. D'you read it?"

But when I admitted that I hadn't, he gave a "hrrmph" of disgust and slammed the door shut.

Feeling forlorn and lonesome, I headed to the dance in Sipaulovi.

I left the truck halfway up the mesa, alongside several dozen worn old pickups, and climbed steps cut into the rock the rest of the way, emerging into a small pueblo whose square, sheltered by the four rows of houses enclosing it, was full of people. Even the roofs were full. Men and women sat with legs dangling over the edges, children ran giddily from one roof to the next, friends and relatives yelled and joked from roofs to ground and back again.

The mood was festive. People nodded and said hello as though there was nothing strange in my being one of exactly four Anglo faces in the crowd. The others, two men and a woman in their twenties, wore that tolerant, knowing smile that somehow combines both respect and condescension. Anthropologists' smiles.

Just as I was going to ask if I'd missed the dance, a line of about thirty women emerged from the kiwa below the pueblo—an underground room carved into the rock, where participants prepare themselves for ritual events. Each woman held a woven yucca platter. They carried the smell of juniper smoke with them as they threaded into the square, weighed down by heavy red and white ceremonial shawls with black trim. White leather leg bindings poked out beneath, and white moccasins. Many could have been grandmothers, some even great grandmothers, and they moved with a heavy, slow solemnity, impervious to the jollity around them. The crowd made way for them as they formed a large inward-facing circle, but otherwise paid no attention as they began the dance.

The only motion of the dance was of the straw platters. As they began to chant in a low monotone, the same phrase over and over again, each woman raised her platter a few inches in slow, rhythmic accompaniment to the chant, then lowered it. That's all. Up, and down. Up, and down. Their faces betrayed nothing: no emotion, no animation. If anything, they looked mournful. They certainly sounded mournful.

This went on for a good half-hour or so, and then the chant changed slightly. It was still a monotone, but had risen perhaps a half-tone higher. Three women wearing feathered green head-dresses entered the circle, dragging huge bundles wrapped in white bedsheets, and the crowd in the square began to push up close. A man wearing a fox skin suddenly appeared—a kachina, or spirit dancer. He was naked to the waist; the fox's tail hung down behind him, and its head covered his. Everything went almost quiet except for the chanting; the women didn't miss a beat as the fox man made a few passes at the white-sheeted bundles with his arms, shouted something at them—a blessing, I assumed—slipped out through the circle, and disappeared.

"Who was he?" I asked the young man beside me in the crowd.

He shrugged. "Shaman. Kachina. What does it matter? Now the fun starts."

"What happens?"

"Now they throw us gifts," said his friend.

"You mean they give everyone gifts?"

He laughed. "If you can catch them. Get ready to jump."

"Why do they do this? I mean, what's the ceremonial reason? Is it a harvest festival?"

They both laughed now. "You're asking the wrong people," said the first one. "We just came for the fun of it. We're not *proper* Indians. Not like the old people want us to be."

I tried a row of teenage girls standing on a low stone bench, but they were as puzzled as I was. One nodded toward the women in the circle. "They're the ones who know," she said. "We just came to watch, same as you."

The three women in the center of the circle now dipped into the sheeted bundles and began to toss the contents, one by one, out over the heads of the chanters. They tossed well, like expert Frisbee players. They started with a barrage of plastic bowls. Then came plastic trays and trash cans and bundles of clothes hangers. Plates, colanders, cooking utensils, and windshield scrapers followed. Bars of soap and boxes of teabags spun into the crowd, then packets of Ramen noodles and dried soups and thousand-island salad dressing. Rolls of toilet paper unraveled as they flew. Bags of candies burst open and showered everyone with hard sweetness.

The young men in the crowd jostled and shouted, vying with each other to leap high for each item that came their way. People oohed and aahed as a round metal tray soared over the roofs of the pueblo; they burst into applause when someone up there leaped to his feet to make a spectacular catch, then bowed with a flourish in acknowledgment.

On and on it went, a vast aerial flow of plastic, processed, K-Mart riches soaring on out over the circle of women, who kept up their mournful chant as though completely unaware of the joyful chaos behind them.

Something came flying my way. My hand went up into the air and caught it, and the young men beside me cheered. I looked at it in astonishment: I'd caught a packet of car deodorizers, those little cardboard pine trees you hang from the rearview mirror. My gift from the Hopis.

I was thoroughly chilled by the time I got back to my room. The dogs sprang out of their huddles to greet me, then retreated in whining disappointment when I closed the door. I took a hot shower, boiled some water for instant soup, checked the messages on my answering machine in Seattle, and made my weekly phone call to England.

"How goes it?" I said.

I could hear the dogs scratching and scuffling at the door as my mother told me that my father had been hospitalized for severe angina. "It was touch and go for a while, but he's all right now. Just came home today," she said.

"Why didn't you call me? Leave a message on my phone at home?"

"We didn't want to worry you. I wanted to, but Jessel said no, not to worry you."

"I can catch a plane from Phoenix and be there tomorrow . . ."

My father's voice came on the extension, warm and laughing. "No, no, really, no need to do that. A bit dicey there for a moment, but everything back to normal now. Your mother exaggerates, you know."

"Darling, you know it was much closer than that," she insisted, as usual the two of them talking to each other on the phone as much as to me. "Honestly, Lesley, I thought I was going to lose him this time . . ."

"Nonsense," he said. "I'm fine. You stay on the road, Lesley. Where are you calling from, anyway?"

I painted a quick idyll of the Hopi mesas. The basket dance achieved the grandeur it possibly once had, while the cultural center became the very picture the architect had in mind before it was built.

"Mm, it all sounds very romantic," he said suspiciously. That's the trouble with parents: even from eight thousand miles away, they can sense a lie. And that works both ways: I could sense theirs too. By the time I put down the phone, I felt as cold and miserable as the dogs huddled outside my door.

★

Three days later, I turned up bright and early at the crash conference headquarters in the Marriott Hotel in Albuquerque, armed with a double espresso, only to gulp the whole cup the moment I sat down to read the program. The session titles alone were enough to send a lay soul running for the hills. On foot.

Parametric Finite Element Studies of the Human Pelvis: the Influence of Load Magnitude and Duration on Pelvic Tolerance During Side Impact.

A Three-Dimensional Finite Model of the Human Ankle: Development and Preliminary Application to Axial Impulsive Loading.

Proposed Provisional Reference Values for the Humerus for Evaluation of Injury Potential."

Human Subject Kinematics and Electromyographic Activity during Low Speed Rear Impacts.

The Effects of Subfracture Impact Loading on the Patellofemoral Joint.

In Vivo Thresholds for Mechanical Injury to the Blood-Brain Barrier.

The Dynamic Responses of the Cervical Spine: Buckling, End Conditions, and Tolerance in Compressive Impacts.

Welcome to the field of biodynamics. J. G. Ballard would have felt right at home here, creating fiction from the point where hard science meets soft flesh. He'd have soaked up the medical-textbook photographs projected onto the meeting-room screens, the detailed diagrams, the computer simulations, the precise and dispassionate language. He'd certainly have loved Colonel Dr. John Paul Stapp, who organized the first of these conferences at Holloman Air Force Base near Alamogordo back in the fifties, not far south of Trinity Site, where the first atomic bomb was exploded on July 16, 1945.

As a young man, Stapp had been the original guinea pig for high-speed crashes, long before the invention of modern crash dummies equipped with sophisticated electronic monitors. He'd walked away from more high-impact crashes than anyone else in the world. Twenty-six of them, to be precise. Crashes so strong that in the moment of collision his eyes literally squished into ovals.

Now eighty-seven, the colonel was something of a leonine presence, even if the lion had put on weight and become somewhat long-toothed and thin-maned. We settled down for a drink—"He really shouldn't," said his wife, to which he replied, "Nonsense"—and despite the extraordinary things he'd done to his brain and body in the name of science, he was excellent company.

He told me happily about researchers who make their life's work collecting and measuring "high-velocity events" such as accidental falls from high buildings, suicide leaps from bridges, even the clashing of helmets in college football games.

"Isn't that kind of sick?" I asked.

He laughed. "Not if you want to know how humans can survive a car crash," he said.

He'd been a flight surgeon in the Army Air Corps in 1946—or as he put it, "nineteen and forty-six"—when he transferred to the corps' aeromedical lab to work on the new technology of seat ejection. As the project officer for the test trials, he volunteered to be the ejectee. In official terms, he was "investigating human tolerance to deceleration and windblast environments occurring in escape from high-speed aircraft." In simple fact, he was the first person to be shot out into the air 1,800 feet above Edwards Air Force Base at 360 miles an hour.

A year later he began "riding the sled," a rocket-propelled device designed to test the effects of sudden, sharp, and immense acceleration and deceleration on the human body. Jet fighters could take the human body far beyond the known envelope of tolerance. His job was to expand that envelope.

He was strapped in to the sled, then shot down a short indoor rail and stopped practically on a dime—from 154 to 34 miles an hour in twenty-six feet and one-quarter of a second—creating the same force as a car hitting a solid concrete wall at sixty miles an hour.

"In that two or three milliseconds," he said, in typical fighter-pilot understatement, "you really get hammered."

It seemed impossible at the time that anyone could survive such impacts, yet thanks to the straps, he did. "The point is, you can walk away if you've got suitable restraints."

Most of this crash work was for air force and later NASA research—

Stapp was one of a select group that would come to be known as "the pre-astronauts"—but when the air force realized in 1953 that it was losing far more pilots in car crashes than in plane crashes, Stapp decided to expand the work into cars, and set up an annual conference where research scientists and automotive engineers could exchange information.

"Of course the proceedings used to be closed to the public," he said, making me uneasily aware that I seemed to be the only member of "the public" around. "Then Ralph Nader betrayed our confidence—that was nineteen and sixty-six—and published findings from the conference in that book of his, and that forced us to open things up."

Since Nader's *Unsafe at Any Speed* got automotive safety standards established and led to the formation the following year of the Department of Transportation, I would have thought that Stapp would be all for it. He shook his head sorrowfully. "It wasn't the professional way to go about things," he said. "We would have dealt with everything ourselves."

I could see exactly why Nader took the step he did.

Still, if Stapp felt somewhat proprietary about car crash research, it was understandable. In effect, he'd created the field, and now he could look round the lobby and meeting halls of the Albuquerque Marriott and take pride in over three hundred auto-company, university, and government researchers who were capable of deconstructing a crash to the point where they could predict exactly what would happen to what size bone or joint under what circumstances. Stapp's brain, his eyeballs, and his bones had survived despite all odds. He was a happy man.

Before his wife came back to claim him for a midday rest, he pressed a copy of his "little red book" on me. The self-published edition was called *For Your Moments of Inertia: from levity to gravity,* and was a collection of truly awful puns, epigrams, limericks, and other verse that included such gems as "The inept parachute rigger who was known as Rigger Mortis," "The United States is no bed of roses, just a car-nation," and the old medical-school rhyme, "It isn't the cough that carries them off, It's the coffin they carry them off in."

To balance Stapp's little red book, I browsed through the publications on display in a side room, and found a volume called *Crash Injuries* by

Alvin Hyde. It had breezy subheadings like "How to wreak musculo-skeletal havoc" and "Wrecking joints." This was language I could understand. And since I was at a crash conference, it made perfect bedtime reading that night.

"In simple terms, the car slows as its front end is crushed and then stops when its kinetic energy is used up by the crush," Hyde wrote. "The unrestrained occupant does not slow and stop, however. . . . It may be said that the car stops before the occupant does—that the occupant effectively 'runs into' the slowing or stopped vehicle interior."

Hyde was coolly and horrifyingly precise about the details of this event, known in crash-research circles as "the second collision." In a 30-mph test, a crash dummy continues its forward motion at that speed, which is about forty-four feet per second. The car stops after two or three feet of travel; the dummy does not. Which means the human driver also does not.

Now, take a body from 30 to 0 mph in two feet, and you create a deceleration force of 15 G, or fifteen times the force of gravity. That's three times the 5 G that astronauts experience on lift-off, and two-thirds more than the 9 G fighter pilots pull in the most extreme maneuvers. But since you're still traveling at forty-four feet per second, and colliding with metal, which has little give, the actual G-force is multiplied. It won't be a mere 15 G, but much greater.

Specifically, for instance, if you're not wearing a three-point seat belt, your head will hit the metal bar above the windshield at up to 700 G. If you weigh, say, 175 pounds, that's equivalent to suddenly weighing 175 pounds times seven hundred, which is over sixty-one tons.

That kind of impact would obviously be fatal if it weren't for a couple of additional factors. The first is known as *delta v*, a measure of instantaneous change in velocity: not speed itself, but a very sudden change in speed. The approximate rule of thumb is 1.5 mph of *delta v* for every one inch of frontal crush in the car, a formula that some months later would allow me to eyeball the television image of the Mercedes in which Princess Diana had died and make a coolly accurate estimate of the speed at which it was going when it crashed: some five feet of frontal crush, meaning about ninety miles an hour.

The second additional factor is time. A typical frontal crash, Hyde wrote, begins and is over in 100 to 120 milliseconds, or about one-tenth of a second. And it's this astonishing rapidity that makes it potentially survivable. "Survivability" becomes a delicate dance of *delta v*, G-force, and time. Even 30 G does not do much lasting harm if it's over in thousandths of a second; there simply isn't time for human tissues to be permanently displaced. But if that 30-G force were to last a few seconds, something in you would break; in fact, just about everything in you would break.

Cushioning the force of impact begins to sound like a very good idea.

Seat belts simply can't do enough, Hyde argued. If an average man wearing a three-point seat belt drives into a wall at 30 mph, and his car has no air bag, the issue is not whether he'll hit the steering wheel, but how hard. He'll strike it with between 700 and 1,000 pounds of force, which means his head will have a virtual weight of up to half a ton. The entirely predictable and quite inevitable result: a diagonal two-inch long by half-inch deep cut on the forehead, and a broken cheekbone.

"Anyone for air bags?" Hyde concluded breezily.

I turned the page to a chapter on "how we break and tear the stuff we are made of," and decided that I was not made of strong enough stuff for any more that night. As I turned out the light, I wondered for a moment if I was going to have nightmares, but I was lucky: the pure weight of detail had numbed my brain, and allowed me to sleep the night through without any dreams at all.

★

On my way out of town, I stopped in at Kirtland Air Force Base to go to the Atomic Museum. My pass read "Warning: Consent to Search. By accepting this pass you give your consent to search of this vehicle while it is entering, on, or leaving this installation (AFI 31-209)." I accepted the pass, signed in, and was allowed past the guardhouse, driving with the self-conscious care of someone who thinks someone else might be watching.

A few blocks past the guardhouse, I pulled right and drew up under the huge wing of a B-29 bomber parked outside the museum—the same type of plane as the *Enola Gay*, which dropped the Hiroshima bomb. Inside the museum, a movie was about to start. I sat down on a rickety folding chair, one of only five people in the dark, as the title came up on the screen: *Ten Seconds That Shook the World.* Presumably a none-too-sly poke at John Reed's famed account of the Communist revolution, *Ten Days That Shook the World.*

The movie was in black and white, and so was its message: the atomic bomb had saved democracy and won the war. In the deep, overly dramatic tones of old newsreels, breathless and measured at the same time, the voice-over narrator limned a heroic battle against time to develop the atomic bomb, and sang the praises of brave politicians in Washington and steadfast scientists in Los Alamos.

There was no mention of radiation. No mention of how many people were killed in Hiroshima and Nagasaki. No pictures of the damage done by the bombs, aside from a single brief aerial shot of Hiroshima. We were shown exactly what people were doing at the time the bomb was dropped: people in New York, people in Los Angeles, people in Saint Louis, people in Paris, people in London. But not people in Hiroshima.

When the credits rolled a half-hour later, I saw that the movie had been made in 1963.

I emerged somewhat shaken, not by what I had seen, but by what I hadn't. The other viewers, two retired couples, were clearly quite satisfied.

"Them Nips got what they were asking for," one of the men declared.

"Asking for the same thing again the way they're taking over our roads with those cars of theirs," said the other.

The wives smiled sweetly at me and asked if I knew where the bathroom was. I pointed them back to the reception desk and they went off, chattering about grandchildren while their husbands replayed the Second World War and plotted the Third.

I wandered around the museum, and belatedly realized why it was here: Kirtland had provided the air support for the atomic bombs. Or as they put it, "the delivery systems." The whole display was based on the engineering of the bombs and their delivery, with esthetic relief provided by a long series of photographs of mushroom clouds blooming over Trinity Site and of the craters left behind.

Walking past bomb after bomb, then missile after missile as the exhibit developed into a metallic history of the Cold War, I listened as the two retired couples examined the exhibits behind me. The women were talking real-estate prices in Arizona. The men swapped service stories; they were evidently Korean War vets, with the kind of knowledge about weapons systems that enabled them to stand in front of a missile head and say, "Now there's a beauty."

I'd just spent two days with researchers who analyzed nightmare events in order to prevent their happening again—engineers who far from being soulless, based their work on the most precisely detailed imagination of cause and effect. But here, at the Atomic Museum, there seemed to be an echoing absence of imagination, and this, combined with a total lack of any sense of irony, let alone compassion, was utterly depressing.

On the way out, I stopped in at the museum store and checked the bookshelves. A single slim paperback copy of John Hersey's *Hiroshima* was all but hidden among the glossy photo albums of weaponry, but at least it was there. With that small consolation, I turned to leave, and caught sight of a pile of presentation boxes of chocolate. Two pieces of chocolate, to be precise. One in the shape of Little Boy, the other in the shape of Fat Man—the Hiroshima and Nagasaki bombs.

What could I do? I bought a box, tossed it on the passenger seat of the truck, left Kirtland Air Force Base without being searched, and headed east on I-40. I'd been on the road an hour or so when I realized that the chocolate was going to melt, so I ate it. Little Boy first, then Fat Man.

I could taste them in my mouth all the way to the Texas border.

Chapter Twelve

At the edge of a cornfield three miles west of Amarillo, Texas, where Interstate 40 runs right alongside the blacktop of the old Route 66, ten half-buried Cadillacs look as though they've been flying in formation and taken a simultaneous nosedive into the ground without breaking line. I'd seen so many photos of them that the real things seemed smaller and farther away than I'd expected. If I hadn't been on the lookout, I could easily have driven right past.

This was Cadillac Ranch, commissioned in 1974 by one of that archetypal Texan breed, an eccentric multimillionaire, and designed and constructed by the now-disbanded San Francisco art collective called the Ant Farm as "a roadside monument standing as a symbol of our nation's passion for the automobile and our dream to escape in it." Not that anyone could dream of escaping anywhere in one of these.

The collective—multimedia artists Chip Lord, Hudson Marquez, and Doug Michels—cataloged the installation as follows:

"Dimensions: 120 feet long, 6 feet wide.

"Material: Ten Cadillacs, 1949, 1952, 1954, 1956, 1957, 1958, 1959, 1960, 1962, 1964, buried, with the tail fins pointing east, at a sixty-degree angle.

But put ten old Cadillacs together, and they become more than the sum of their parts, or their years. They achieve a kind of iconic splendor. The enforced immobility, the Stonehenge permanence, the surreal nos-

talgia of seeing that line of tail fins jutting up into the sky have made this lonely row of cars a familiar part of popular American culture.

In 1980, Bruce Springsteen paid homage to the ranch in his song of the same name: "I'm gonna pack my pa and gonna pack my aunt, I'm gonna take them down to the Cadillac Ranch." In a big black Cadillac, of course, "a little bit of heaven here on earth," which sounded just fine until you paused for a moment to think about the other titles on the same side of the album: "Stolen Car," "The Price You Pay," "Drive All Night," and "Wreck on the Highway."

With the sole and sobering exception of the Vietnam Memorial in Washington, D.C., art installations don't usually register in the mind of America. And while the Vietnam Memorial is surely America's most revered piece of modern sculpture, Cadillac Ranch is probably its best loved. Maybe because it's all things to all people. You can see it as an acerbic comment on Detroit or as a kind of *memento mori;* as the best-known stop on the American list of "major roadside attractions," or, if you're a local teenager, as a place to go and make out on a summer evening.

I pulled off the highway and parked by a gap in the fence. There was no sign, just a path trodden by visiting feet across a hundred yards or so of plowed earth leading between the road and the Cadillacs. A chill wind was blowing—winter in the air, even in Texas—and as I neared the cars, I could hear it rustling through the field of dying corn behind them, and whistling around the tail fins.

I'd heard that the place was usually littered with beer cans and condoms, which seemed a good enough tribute to the spirit of what the cars once were, but today the ground was clean. Which is not to say that the beer drinkers and condom-users hadn't left their mark. They had, and all over the cars themselves. The bodies were entirely covered in graffitti, indecipherable words and obscure images spray-painted one on top of the other in a palimpsest of drunk desire.

"You know why people like Cadillac Ranch so much?" the multimillionaire proprietor had scrawled in a fax to me. "Because it's impossible to take a bad photo of it." And he was right. I walked slowly up and down the line, and every step gave me a different viewpoint, each one perfectly set up for the camera. Whether I crouched down or stood erect or clambered up onto one of the cars for a higher vantage point, positioned myself at the end of the line or halfway up it, at a ten-degree angle or an eighty-degree angle, the viewfinder of my cheap automatic camera showed me a perfect shot. Too perfect to make clicking the shutter interesting. I shot a few frames, but there didn't seem much point in it, so I headed back for the truck and drove into town in search of the man who'd commissioned Cadillac Ranch.

★

Why Texas should specialize in eccentric millionaires surely has to do with the place itself—the vastness, the huge distances, the sense that to make yourself heard and assert your existence in this landscape, you need to shout very loud.

Stanley Marsh 3—"*never* III or the Third"—had spent most of his sixty-odd years shouting as loud as he could. This was the man who sent letters to Pat Nixon asking her to donate her best dresses to what he said was his Museum of Decadent Art. Who showed up at John Connally's bribery trial in Washington, D.C. carrying a bucket of cow manure. Who bought up a whole zoo and then gave the animals the run of Toad Hall, his ranch home outside town. Who took delight in ordering suits made in the same fabric as his chairs or sofas, so that he'd disappear into them, just his round mustachioed face and goggle eyes behind thick glasses floating in space like the Cheshire Cat. Sometimes dubbed the "Puck of the Panhandle," he was one of the state's merriest pranksters.

He also happened to be the scion of one of the most prominent oil and gas families in West Texas—a member of what in these parts they call "the lucky-sperm club"—as well as a major landowner in the area around Amarillo, and the proprietor of the city's main television station. Stanley, in other words, could afford to shout.

Yet at the same time he'd acted as an extraordinarily open-minded patron of the arts. The world's top conceptual and environmental artists beat a path to the door of Toad Hall, entranced by the idea of someone who could afford not only to install their huge artworks on his land, but also maintain them. And if some of Amarillo's most established citizens didn't share his enthusiasm for giant art installations—especially when, like Cadillac Ranch, they were right at the entrance to the city—so far as Stanley was concerned, that was just an extra bonus.

I'd been carrying on a kind of electronic flirtation with him, exchanging a flurry of faxes in the past couple of weeks. I'd faxed him from the road, and he'd sent his faxes to my machine in Seattle, where Gene had read them into my answering machine, adding his own bemused comment: "Who *is* this man?"

I wanted a chance to find out for myself, but uncharacteristically, and for probably the first time in his life, Stanley was refusing to talk face to face. Not because of any prior appointment, but because "I can't keep my mouth shut."

"Sounds fine by me," I'd faxed back.

"My lawyer doesn't think so," he'd replied.

Stanley's mouth, it seemed, had gotten him into trouble. Again. Only this time, there was a serious chance it might land him in jail.

The cause of his trouble was art. At least, Stanley called it art. It was his latest project, which involved placing road signs all around town. Not quite your typical road signs. Though they were the right size and the right diamond shape, in standard black on yellow, they bore slogans such as "Unnatural Practices," "Unspeakable Acts," "Blood," "Afoot," "Ostrich X-ing," and the long-disappeared "Steal This Sign."

In the past two years, the road-sign project had run wildfire, despite a battle with the city council over placement of the signs. The final compromise had been to place them on private property at least nine feet from any official road sign, so Stanley began to hand them out free to anyone who asked for one. Two thousand signs now stood in people's yards all over Amarillo, usually as close to the road as possible. By now, five percent of Amarillans had one in their yard.

"We're aiming for forty-nine percent," Stanley had faxed me.

"Why not fifty?" I'd shot back.

"Art must always remain in the minority."

But the road-sign project had sparked a new outbreak of that other great Texan tradition: the long-standing family feud. The feud in question was between Stanley Marsh 3 and George A. Whittenburg II, a

lawyer whose father had been one of the city's most powerful businessmen, and who, like Stanley, was a member of the lucky-sperm club.
Once apparently resolved by a court ruling that neither could ever sue
the other again—and understood by all in town never to be resolved no
matter what any court might say—the feud had flared up anew with
Whittenburg's college-age son, Ben, as the main litigant.

The *casus belli* was the Rabid Rabbit sign. This was surely perfect. I
imagined the words glowing, black on yellow, warning of this latest haz-
ard to transportation, and was disappointed to learn that my ear had
betrayed me and that it was in fact the Rapid Rabbit sign—a picture of
a rabbit, with the word *rapid* beneath it—stolen one night by Ben Whittenburg.

Since teenage Amarillo had made stealing the signs into a late-night
hobby, this was not the slightest bit odd. Stanley's reaction was. According to Ben Whittenburg, Stanley took a couple of his employees, found
Ben, threatened to hit him with a hammer, and locked him in a chicken
coop, yelling all the time: "The goddamn Whittenburgs. Everyone hates
your dad. He's just an arrogant fucker. Your granddad was a scum. Y'all
used to have money, but you don't any more. You're just poor white
trash."

This seemed a slight overreaction, even by Texas standards. But then
so did the fact that an Amarillo grand jury had indicted Stanley Marsh
on felony charges of aggravated assault and kidnapping. Which is what
had sobered him into silence.

"I'm coming in any case," I'd faxed him.

"You're welcome, but you won't see me," he'd responded.

"What about the art?"

"I'll arrange everything for you."

Still, as I made for his headquarters at the top of the one high-rise in
town, I nurtured the hope that he would be around somewhere, if only
to see who on earth it was who'd sent him a copy of Harry Crews's
gothic satire *Car,* in which a man eats a Ford Maverick, bit by bit. I
resolved to keep a close eye on the upholstery; Stanley might be hiding
there in camouflage.

The elevator doors opened onto a large reception area lined with fake

Rothkos, about twice the size of Rothko's real work, and with none of
the subtlety. There was no receptionist, so I wandered on in. To the left
were elegantly appointed offices; to the right, what looked like a giant
playroom running the whole length of the building. I went right.

It was a Hollywood moviemaker's dream of an artist's studio, crammed
with the stock paraphernalia of arty trash: a crushed-car sculpture, canvases painted in a kind of primitive-modern style stacked haphazardly
against any vertical surface, bits and pieces of old silk and velvet drapes
spilling out of a big wicker basket, the inevitable vintage barber's chair,
croquet mallets lying like pickup sticks in one corner, a plastic blow-up
pink flamingo, ornate gilt picture frames, a couple of cigar-store Indians, road signs evidently still in progress. I nearly stumbled over a
stuffed pig with wings tattooed on its sides. There was so much junk in
the room that it took a moment to realize that there were two people in
here too. Both young, both male, both studiously ignoring me.

"Who are you?" I said, feeling oddly like Alice in Wonderland.

"Doug," said the one with red and yellow and orange hair.

"Jamie," said the other, who was wearing a pith helmet.

"Am I in the right place?"

Doug cracked what might have been the glimmer of a smile. "Sure
you are. This is the croquet room."

"Ah." A pause. "Croquet?"

They exchanged a glance that said, "Is this one dumb or what?" I
spotted a pack of Marlboros on Jamie's table. "Can I bum one of those?"

If you want to break the ice with an eighteen-year-old with an attitude, do something his elders keep telling him not to do. The three of
us lit up together, and the two boys, both barely out of high school,
showed me the croquet hoops still embedded in the floor. "Been some
time since anyone last played croquet here though," said Doug. "We
can't find the balls."

They were, they told me, Stanley's "artists-in-residence." Neither had
any art training; what they did have was a salary and a free hand. And
Stanley's charge of showing me around for the day. So after I'd said hello
to his personal assistant and searched the zebra-striped office chairs for
any sign of Stanley's corpulent form—none that I could see, though I

had a clear feeling that he was observing me from somewhere—Jamie and Doug and I piled into a battered old Jeep, stocked up at a fast-food stand on burritos and pink lemonade, and set off on the road out of town past the Big Texan Steak Ranch, where if you can eat a seventy-two-ounce steak in one hour, you get it free (and if you can't, you pay fifty dollars for the attempt).

"Has anyone ever done it?" I asked.

"Oh sure," said Doug.

"How many?"

"About eleven hundred," said Jamie.

"One guy did it in seven minutes," said Doug.

"An eleven-year-old-boy did it," said Jamie.

"A sumo wrestler ate two of them," said Doug.

Jamie let it rest.

On top of everything else, George Whittenburg had told reporters that Stanley had been sexually molesting the young men who worked for him. "Would that have been you guys?" I asked.

"Yeah, in George Whittenburg's dreams," sneered Jamie.

"Stanley likes skinny-dipping on a hot day," said Doug. "Who doesn't?"

"Whittenburg just wishes he could do it too," Jamie added. "That's why it bugs him so much."

"Were you guys along with Stanley when he went and shut Ben Whittenburg in the chicken coop?"

They didn't quite answer that question.

"It's not like it was any kind of big deal."

"So Stanley tossed a couple of plastic chairs in the pond."

"And took the license plates off Ben's truck."

"So what? It wasn't even a proper door on that chicken coop."

"Even a chicken could figure out how to open it."

"That's what really upset old man Whittenburg, that all his chickens got loose."

We were way out in the country some seven miles west of Amarillo by now, driving along a narrow, curving farm road improbably dignified with the designation Highway 1071.

"Are we still on Stanley's land?" I asked.

"Stanley's all the way," said Jamie.

We went up a rise, rounded a bend, and there, off in the distance, was the Floating Mesa, smack in the middle of what most people would call absolutely nowhere.

Andrew Leicester's installation was astonishingly simple, and even more astonishingly effective: a 300-foot-long steel wall painted grayish blue—the color of the early November afternoon sky—placed just below the rim of a mesa, so that the top seemed cut off from its body and looked as though it were floating in space.

"There it is," said Doug, and began to turn the Jeep around.

"Closer," I said. He gave the kind of shrug that said, "Okay, humor the lady," straightened out the Jeep, and drove another few miles to the base of the mesa. Even from close up, where you could see the fence clearly, the illusion held. Stanley may have been a pain in the backside to the upright citizens of Amarillo, but as a patron of the arts he was brilliant.

"It's quite haunting," I said.

Jamie laughed. "The old girl'd love to hear you say that."

"What old girl?"

"The one that's buried up there. You know, the one that wrote that book *Fried Green Tomatoes*."

"Fell in love with the place," said Doug. "She was a good friend of Stanley's wife, and asked to be buried up there when she died. So there she is up there right now."

"What does Andrew Leicester think of that?"

Doug grinned. "Doesn't matter, does it?"

I would have gone on up to check out what Fannie Flagg could see from her grave, but the boys clearly considered it beneath their dignity to walk, let alone climb. "What else do you want to see?" said Jamie.

"What about the Amarillo Ramp?"

"Sure, we'll show you where it was."

Another half-hour of bumping over back roads, the burrito making its presence felt by remaining stubbornly indigestible in my stomach, and we were overlooking the site of what had once been a mammoth ramp of earth spiraling into a man-made lake. Like the Floating Mesa, this site was all but hidden unless you knew exactly where to look for it. Designed by Robert Smithson and built in 1973 by three other sculptors including Richard Serra, the Amarillo Ramp promised a magnificently surreal grandeur in the photographs I'd seen, but death haunted this artwork too. Smithson had been surveying the nearly completed work from the air when the pilot lost control and the plane went into the infamous and aptly named graveyard spiral. Smithson, two photographers, and the pilot were all killed. The spiral ramp was never finished. Without upkeep, the lake had dried up and the ramp eroded into earthly oblivion.

Still, that seemed to be entirely in keeping with Stanley's notion of art as ephemeral. His own creations appeared and disappeared at whim. They included Claes Oldenburg derivatives like the Phantom Soft Pool Table, whose balls, cues, and rack were made out of giant plastic beanbags, as well as the Great American Farmhand, which consisted of planted maize and was visible as a hand only from the air.

We turned back toward town. Doug and Jamie picked up more burritos—I demurred—and we set off in search of road signs. There'd been a large wall map of the city back in Stanley's offices, studded with pins, one for each sign. But neither Doug nor Jamie seemed quite sure which sign was where, even though they'd installed them all, so our tour had something of a scavenger hunt feel to it:

"There's the Low-Flying Pig."

"Marilyn Monroe's around here somewhere."

"How did Short Stop get here?"

But the one that truly entranced me stood all alone at the edge of an empty field just outside town:

ROAD

DOES NOT

END

To someone who'd driven some five thousand miles and still had at least as many to go until she reached her goal, it shimmered with evasive meaning like some kind of Zen koan.

★

The next day I drove south from Amarillo on Route 207, with the morning's economic news streaming out of the radio:

"Pork bellies are down fifty-three, cash hogs fifty to a dollar lower, Omaha market at fifty-three fifty. December Kansas City wheat down three, three ninety-six and a half, March down four and a half, and July down six at three forty-nine and a half. In Chicago, December corn off three and a half at two fifty-eight and a quarter, March down three and three quarters at two sixty-four . . ."

I felt like a landlubber who'd accidentally tuned in to a marine forecast. I was sure it all made perfect sense to a Stanley Marsh, but to my urbanized ear it had the ring of an exotic code:

"November beans up two and a half at six sixty-eight and a half, December meal up a dollar thirty at two nineteen eighty, December oats down two at one fifty-six, and December cotton down twelve at seventy-two forty. December crude oil up seventeen cents at twenty-two ninety-six. The dollar is stronger. December gold up fifty cents at three eighty ten, December silver down a half cent at four eighty. On Wall Street, the Dow Jones industrial average . . ."

Ah, back on familiar ground. But here in the heart of Texas—or at least of the Texas panhandle—I didn't even want to think about Wall Street. I went hunting on the dial and found some bluegrass music, which felt more in tune with the country I was driving through.

There was something utterly familiar about this country, though I'd never been here before. It wasn't spectacularly beautiful like the painted rockscapes of Arizona and New Mexico, but it had a quiet, homey kind of peacefulness, and it made me feel that if I were to get out and go walking off into the shallow canyons, I'd find my way with no problem. I drove slower and slower, half expecting to see John Wayne on horseback, fording a red clay wash.

"Howdy ma'am," he'd say as I wheeled on past, lifting the rim of his stetson just an inch or two in greeting.

"Hey there, cowboy," I'd reply. I've always wanted to say that.

Deer bounced into the road ahead of me, and hawks circled overhead, hovering, waiting to pounce. Occasionally one dived, and I'd stop to watch as it disappeared from view for a moment, then rose up into the sky with some small furry delicacy squirming in its claws. Every few miles, I'd go past another dead raccoon lying by the side of the road. Roadkill, and probably old roadkill at that: oncoming traffic on this blacktop worn to the color of sand amounted to maybe one pickup truck an hour.

I found myself wishing for a trusty old Bowie knife so that I could hop out, cut off the striped tails, and arrive in Dallas festooned Davy Crockett style. Since all I had was a Swiss Army knife, I could happily indulge this fantasy without having to deal with any of its more gruesome details.

"You'll get so bored driving through Texas," friends had warned me, and now I saw why. They'd never driven these back-country roads. Instead, they'd driven through on the interstate, subjecting themselves to that peculiarly asphalt form of alienation that makes so many people think of driving cross country in terms of Ilya Ehrenburg's "two standard gauges: one indicating miles, the other minutes."

As I watched an eagle riding the air way ahead of me, I remembered a sharp revelation of asphalt alienation on the way north from Phoenix to the Hopi mesas, when the road I was on had crossed Interstate 40. Dazzled and distracted by the golden varnish spreading across the landscape as the sun lowered in the west, I'd missed the turning and found myself driving east in multi-lane traffic. And suddenly, peculiarly, everything changed.

I drove only five miles to the next exit, where I turned, headed back, and found the road I wanted. But those five miles existed in a world entirely different from the one I'd just been driving through. It was the same place—the high desert—and the same time—late afternoon—and yet both place and time had been utterly altered. The moment I joined that interstate, with its huge semis and high speeds, I seemed to have left Arizona behind and entered another world that existed only in long, straight two-hundred-foot-wide swathes. I was driving at an enforced remove from the landscape, as though someone had placed a clear, plastic tunnel over the road. The world of the interstate forced out the real world. All I could hear was traffic. All I could smell was burned gasoline. And with ears and nose assaulted, even my eyes felt dimmed.

The interstate, I realized, is an exercise in sensory deprivation. Either side of the asphalt, the landscape is kept literally at a physical remove. Trees, bushes, any sign of encroachment of natural vegetation is banished behind fences. The highway makes no concession to the land, as regular roads often have to; in places, it literally cuts through the land, and you find yourself driving between the innards of rock laid obscenely bare to the human eye. The land itself becomes irrelevant. You lose the sense of connection to it, and that loss means that you also lose dimension. Your sense of motion goes all awry. Seventy miles an hour feels like thirty on a regular road. Put your foot down, and the only way you know how fast you're going is by the gauges. Driving is reduced to a mechanical act, the landscape to a blurred ribbon, the world to the monotonous thrum of wheels on asphalt.

The result is the unblinking stare. Eyes glued to the road, seeing everything and nothing, you zone out. You're "making time," a strange phrase since what it really means is that you're losing it. Interstate time is felt as time wasted. The drive has only one purpose, and that is its end. And so, bored, you drive faster, checking road sign against gauge against clock. Life has been reduced to a matter of computation—how much farther, how much longer—and though all the world is there for you to see, you barely register its existence.

It had happened to me again just a few days before, when the prospect of bearding Stanley in his lair had lured me onto the three-hundred-mile stretch of I-40 between Albuquerque and Amarillo. The few towns I saw consisted almost entirely of mobile homes, and it occurred to me that at any moment the owners might up and join the stream of traffic rushing past them, as though it made no difference if they were there or not.

Not that the back-road towns I was going through now, south of Amarillo, were in much better shape. Every twenty miles or so, a sign proclaimed a township and its population: 441, or 309, or 216. I wondered how often they had to repaint those signs, revising the population numbers downward. Half the houses seemed to be boarded up or collapsing in on themselves.

In Turkey, "pop. 507," I saw a sign for a "historic hotel." That seemed a good idea until I walked in to the cluttered foyer, inhaled the smell of stale frying oil, and saw the faded chairs and sofas, their once-fancy brocade and yellowed antimacassars slip-covered in clear plastic. The rubber plant just inside the door drooped, its leaves curling brown at the edges.

A bony woman with tight gray curls appeared out of what I assumed was the kitchen. "What do you want?" she said accusingly, as though I wasn't the Lone Ranger at all but a masked robber come to do her in.

Mine was the only vehicle outside, so I thought it best to check: "Is the hotel open?"

"How else did you walk in here?"

This wasn't quite the famed Texan hospitality I'd expected, but I persevered nonetheless. "How much is a room for the night?"

"Eighty dollars."

"I mean your least expensive room."

She pursed her lips. "Eighty dollars," she said, and watched with apparent satisfaction as I left.

Did she know I'd been consorting with the minions of the infamous Stanley Marsh up in Amarillo? Was she afraid a woman traveling alone would bring "bad company" to her room? Could she tell at a glance that I was an immigrant liberal in the rock-hard heart of Republican country? Probably the last. As I drove out of town I searched the radio for some company—the bluegrass music had long faded—and found Rush Limbaugh. I kept hunting the dial, and found Limbaugh again. The only other station I could pick up was playing hard rock.

I went with one of the Limbaugh stations. At least he made me laugh. But his callers didn't. They were Limbaugh without the humor, mouthing the phrases of the Master back at him to prove what good disciples they were. They ranted against immigrants and welfare and single mothers and abortions. They ranted against government and they ranted against the President, who they didn't even refer to by name. The men called him "that man," the women "you know who," in the same way they might refer to Satan, superstitiously evading the personification of evil by not naming it.

Such animosity toward somebody who seemed to me so amorphous—at best determinedly centrist—was ominous, even frightening. What came over the radio was hate and fear. It had never occurred to me that Bill Clinton was even worthy of such strong emotion.

I checked my map. Some fifty miles farther south was the town of Dickens, Texas. Surely the perfect place for a writer to spend the night. Darkness fell as I drove through Motley County. By the time I saw the sign—"Dickens (pop. 322)"—it was pitch black, and all I could see of the town was a crossroads boasting a convenience store, a gas station, and a crudely painted red arrow containing the words "Motel, 100 yards." I followed the arrow.

It was one of those fifties motels with rooms around three sides of a gravel yard. Even in the dark, I could see the paint flaking off the cinder-block walls. But this was the only bed to be had for miles in any direction, and besides, the price was right: twenty-five dollars.

A man stood silhouetted in the doorway of his room and watched as I backed the truck up to my door. He smoked a cigarette slowly and deliberately. His face was hidden beneath his stetson, but he had the gaunt, menacing stance of a man who found trouble with ease. There was no car in front of his room. I nodded cautiously to him. He raised his cigarette slightly in response, and watched as I opened my door.

Someone else had opened it very thoroughly in the recent past. The wood of the doorjamb was torn and splintered where the chain should have bolted into it; a very hefty shoulder had clearly busted the bolt. Why anyone would have wanted to get into that room so badly was another question. A ratty, threadbare carpet was spread directly over an unevenly laid concrete floor. A single overhead light cast its forty-watt glory over a frayed gray blanket on the bed, and a rickety table with an old rotary-dial phone on it. Faded plastic shelf-liner was still half-attached to the tabletop. I could just make out the pattern: blue ducks swimming inside a border of yellow daisies.

I picked up the phone and dialed the 800 number that would connect me to my long-distance carrier. I got a strange series of beeps and buzzes, and then nothing. I tried again, with the same result, then walked over to the manager's office—a small cubicle walled off from the front room of the Pakistani family who ran the place. His English wasn't up to the intricacies of the phone system, and finally his wife had to come out and explain that I could only make local and collect calls from my room. She clearly thought the idea of a long-distance calling card very strange.

At least I'd called England the night before from Amarillo, checking on my father's health. He seemed to be doing fine: walking two miles a day, he assured me, and no angina.

"I hope you're being careful with those motels," he'd said. Even from eight thousand miles away, worrying that his little girl was safe. "You don't want to be in one like in that film . . ." And shouting to my mother in another room, "Sybil, what was that film?" Pause. "You know, the one with the motel and the shower."

"I know the one you mean," I heard her saying. She must have come into the room with him. "Why?"

"I'm telling Lesley to be careful where she stays."

"Oh really, Jessel, she's far too sensible to stay in a place like that. Wasn't that a Hitchcock film?"

"Psycho," I mouthed silently my end of the line, wishing my father hadn't thought of it.

"Psycho!" my mother said triumphantly in England.

"Yes, but what was the name of the motel?"

"You know you must be getting old," she teased him. "Let's see, it was Anthony Perkins, wasn't it? I always rather liked him. I haven't seen him in anything for a long time."

"Bates Motel," I said out loud.

"That's it!" he said delightedly. "Darling, Bates Motel," he said to her.

"Don't worry, I'm very careful," I assured him. "Only the best motels for me." And heard the dissatisfied harrumph of a man convinced that the very phrase "best motel" is an oxymoron.

I was relieved he couldn't see me now. But the bed didn't sag too badly, there was only one cigarette burn in the blanket, and if I could smell mold in the bathroom, it didn't matter: after the previous night's phone conversation, I had no intention of taking a shower.

I'd gotten into the habit of airing out a motel room before settling in, opening the door and the window and letting out the fusty stale air with its remnants of past inhabitants. No matter how cold the night outside, I did it every time. There are too many ghosts in motel rooms. Even in the best, I would stare at a faint stain on a chair or a bottle ring on the table and wonder who had put it there, where they were coming from, where they were going to. Even whether they themselves knew the answers to such questions. I'd wonder how many people had coupled on the bed, how many prostitutes had spent part of a work night here. How many arguments had taken place, how much violence been committed.

The gaunt man with the stetson was no longer there. Now it was me standing silhouetted in a doorway, thinking how much sadness there was in motel rooms. That's what Hitchcock saw, of course. Perhaps it wasn't such a long way from sadness to madness. The sense of temporariness, the restless nights, the solitary fifths of whiskey, shared quarts of cheap wine, cigarettes burned to the filter slipping from television-numbed fingers, sheets stained from illicit or loveless or solitary sex, the weird disorientation of the road . . . Yes, these could drive a person to violence.

Even in the more upscale motels by the interstates, the Holiday Inns and Ramada Inns and Best Westerns, the roar of the traffic invades your sleep and haunts your dreams. You close the drapes as tight as you can against the sound, but it slips around the edges of the window, along with the yellow of the security lights outside. Even as you lie still, your mind is still in motion, hurtling through space, the ribbon of the road unfolding beneath your closed eyelids.

There is sleep in motel rooms, but not much rest. In Amarillo, I'd come wide awake in the middle of the night to the sound of the couple next door fighting.

"You'll do what I tell you."

"I'll do what I want."

"You little whore."

"I'm a whore? Well then, maybe I *will* . . ."

"You bitch!" And a huge thud as something—someone—was hurled against the wall, followed by a silence, and then deep, retching sobs.

I had my hand on the phone to call the desk, the police, anyone, when I heard the equally horrifying sound of her making up to him.

"Don't go. Don't leave me. I'll be good to you. Don't I know how to be good to you?"

And then, eventually, the rhythmic rattling of their bed against the wall.

At least here in Dickens, there was nobody in the rooms either side of me. I locked the door, looked once again at the useless chain, jammed a chair beneath the doorknob, and fell into the restless sleep of exhaustion.

I was up and out of the place at dawn. A gentle, silvery mist hung over the landscape, reminding me of early mornings back home in Seattle. I headed east along Route 82, angled off onto 222, and found my predilection for deep-country back roads rewarded by the sight of cowboys riding in and out of the mist, herding cattle. One drove a herd of horses in front of him, some fifty or sixty perhaps; I saw them for just a few seconds until the mist closed in again, but I could swear that just before he disappeared from sight he tipped his stetson and mouthed a "Howdy, ma'am" in my direction.

The sun began to break through as I entered O'Brien, which boasted a population of 152. Two farmers standing by a pickup truck directed me to the Cafe and General Store. "Down the road, just past the gin," said one. "Don't look like much from the outside," said the other, "but they'll take care of you there." I was grateful for his choice of words. And the heaped plate of scrambled eggs and hash browns, with solidly meaty bacon and fresh-brewed coffee, eaten at a red-checker-clothed table while a half-dozen women sat quilting and comparing notes about their offspring nearby, was just what I needed to feel that all was right with the world again.

I was sorry now that I'd agreed to a well-meaning talk-show host's plan for me to do some media interviews in Dallas. I'd far rather have kept on these back roads, working my way south and east and south again to Houston, avoiding any place with a population over a few hundred. But within an hour of O'Brien, the land began to change. Water appeared in the form of ponds and shallow streams. The towns became larger, more prosperous, and less interesting. And the low hills were no longer dotted with cattle, but with oil pumps doing their mechanical nod, grazing deep into the ground.

The back roads ran out about a half-hour outside the city. I cruised on in, surrounded by traffic and strip malls and advertising signs, found a three-story motel with an elevator just off I-20, grabbed an early dinner with the talk-show host, and vegged out for the rest of the evening in front of the television set, getting myself in the mood for the next day.

It didn't quite work. The artifice of studio lights and heavy makeup made me long to be back driving through a misty dawn. And though my media friend did me the courtesy of taking the afternoon off to show me round Dallas, the unreality of television lingered. We made a double circuit of Dealey Plaza, grassy knoll and all, but all I could think was that it looked far smaller than the familiar television image from that November day all those years ago. Or perhaps JFK's assassination had granted Dealey Plaza a grandeur it never really had.

I caught myself replaying the tape in my mind—the President crumpling, Jackie reaching for help. Tried to put it together with the city traffic going about its normal business. "Surely these cars should stop moving," I thought. "Go into freeze-frame. Acknowledge what happened here." But life went on as normal, as sooner or later it always does, and I felt a sudden desire to get out of town as quickly as possible.

Besides, I was eager to get to Houston: I'd heard about a great junkyard there, and I had a date to go crush a car.

Chapter Thirteen

Two large black dogs, one of them very pregnant, eyed me suspiciously from behind the chain-link fence dividing the entrance area of the junkyard from the rest of the barn-like main building, but didn't move. A third dog, a small brown mutt, made up for their inertia. He kept flinging himself against the wire in his eagerness to get at me.

"Don't worry, he's already been fed," said Dave McKee, one of the two brothers who run the yard. The moment he let me through the gate in the fencing, the dog was all over me. Ears flapping, tail wagging, he licked my hands and nuzzled my crotch. I've always been a sucker for dogs who nuzzle crotches.

"Great guard dog," I said.

Dave grinned. "That's what you call a real junkyard dog," he said. "Salvaged."

Junkyard dogs are a stubborn breed. They know about survival, and they survive against all odds. Dave and his brother Rick found this one floating down the bayou that runs by the yard, half-dead. They fished him out, pumped his belly by hand, and took him back to the office. "That dog just lay there for five days before he decided to live."

The ABC Junkyard's entrance area was full of things that seemed suspended somewhere between life and death. A quick inventory of the wooden walls and rafters had revealed an assortment of grease-stained stetsons and thoroughly scuffed cowboy boots, a rusted machete, a set of wooden Ninja nunchuks, old framed photos of cowboys, more old framed photos of Indians, a single large photo of John Wayne, a small

Confederate flag, a stuffed rabbit head with horns, a once-stuffed deer head with the stuffing hanging out behind, old wooden tennis racquets with only a couple of broken strings, two pairs of blunted ice skates, and three dust-crusted Oriental masks. "Time was we had quite a collection of knives and swords," said Dave as he cleared space for coffee among the clutter on his desk, "but someone broke in one night and stole them."

Every one of these items had been left behind in a car that ended up in the junkyard. Along with the occasional dog. The pregnant black dog, for example, had been in the back seat of her owner's car when he pulled up by the side of the road, had a heart attack, and died. By the time Dave and Rick got there, she was starving, but still fiercely resisted any attempt to get her out. They towed the car with her in it, and she'd lived in the yard ever since.

ABC is one of the oldest junkyards in the country. It was started by a character with the irresistible name of Frog Todd, who bought the land for a proverbial song back in 1943. It was low-lying land, and nobody imagined that it would eventually be right on the edge of downtown Houston, just off the portion of I-10 still known as the Katy Freeway, which is now the main road to San Antonio. Nobody, that is, except canny Frog. Back then was when contractors were busily reducing the past to rubble, and Frog graciously consented to accept payment for each truckload of old Houston he could take away and dump on his lot. By the time he'd done, he had a level five acres standing thirty feet above the banks of the bayou, which would soon become just a tame trickle of muddy water at the bottom of a concrete channel. When the McKees drilled down for a new well a few years ago, they found remains of Corinthian columns, old decorative tiles, and gargoyle heads. Frog's idea of salvage, it seems, hadn't quite extended to architecture.

Or maybe it had. What I'd thought was a barn was in fact another of Frog's paid-for favors to a contractor; he'd disassembled a wooden aircraft hangar from the city's old Town and Country airfield and resurrected it on his lot. What had served for Stearmans would serve just as well for junked Chevys.

The McKees' father bought the place from Frog in 1967. "It didn't even have a fence back then," said Dave. "There'd be a trailer full of people across the road waiting for us to go home in the afternoon so's they could come over and steal the parts."

McKee Senior soon put a stop to that. He was what you might call a forceful character. "One of the old-school fathers," said Dave. "We were terrified of him." An alcoholic who spent a good part of his time ensconced in the corner office of the hangar playing cards and drinking with various friendly members of the local police force, he'd terrorize not only those who'd steal his junk but also those who'd steal his daughter. When she brought boyfriends home, he'd sit there tossing knives into the ceiling above their heads and saying "You treat my daughter, right, you hear?" They didn't come back to be told a second time.

If the sons had other ideas for their lives—at one stage, Rick wanted to study medicine—the father wouldn't hear of it. He made them work in the junkyard during school vacations, so that when a bout with cancer eventually forced him to retire and give up drinking, "more or less," he made Rick the president, Dave the manager, and took off for the golf course. "Now he just turns up once a week to check out how much money he's got coming."

The sons pulled the place together into a computer-efficient operation, each part listed and tracked. And a legal one. The phone kept ringing as Dave and I talked, with people looking for parts or wanting to sell cars. One call ended abruptly after Dave asked about the title. He raised his eyes heavenward in exasperation. "Said a friend gave it to him. You know what that means."

ABC insists on titles, and pays by check. Many salvage yards come and go; some quickly outlive their purpose as means of laundering drug money, others rake in the cash by dealing in stolen cars until the owners cut and run. "The only way to last a long time as a junkyard is to be straight," said Dave, and followed this up with a disarming grin: "Besides, I'm the kind of guy who'd get caught." It was the sort of grin that made me wonder why on earth his wife had recently divorced him, and yet explained it perfectly at the same time.

No matter what the computer said, however, Dave often priced parts by his own criteria: how much he liked someone, or knew they could afford. "Like for our father, I'll price them real low."

"Your father?"

"That's what we call him. Our padre: Father Jim. He's a priest, and in many ways you could say he's been more of a father to us than our real one. All the trouble we've had with our dad, he's been there for us. He's a great guy, you'd like him. He cracks some of the dirtiest jokes you've ever heard in your life, he's just as poor as can be—doesn't have a pot to piss in—and he's always in trouble with his supervisors."

I had to admire Dave's assessment of the kind of person I'd like. "What does he get in trouble over?"

"Well," said Dave, drawing out the vowel as he sized me up further. "He's for birth control, for instance, and he's something of a political activist. I suppose they think he's a radical. In any case, he's in here once or twice a week."

"A parish call?"

He laughed. "Hell, no. Didn't I tell you? He's a mechanic, always looking for parts. That guy can get anything working again. Rick always jokes that if the church kicks him out, he should come work with us. What he does is fix up people's cars for free so's they have what to get to work in. Word's gotten around, so now people donate old clapped-out cars to the rectory, and he gets them running again and then gives them away. He has a small parish down south of the city, out in the country. I'll give you his number. Jim Gaunt, his name is. You two should meet."

The phone rang again. He sighed. "Rick should've been back by now. I know he needs to get a few cars crushed this afternoon, make some space for new ones. He's real tickled that you want to crush one your-self."

"Why don't I look around for a while until he gets here?" I said.

"Sure thing. We get a lot of people like to do that, just wander around the yard. They say it makes them feel kind of peaceful."

He walked me out past rows of engine blocks to the open yard behind. A weathered sandwich board stood right in front of us, hand-printed in faded red and black block letters, with certain words heavily underlined. On one side was the following:

YOU DO NOT
TAKE ANY PART
OFF ANY MOTOR
DO NOT TAKE ANY
PARTS OFF ANYTHING
UNLESS YOU GET
PERMISSION FIRST

On the other:

TO ANYONE
CAUGHT THROWING
PARTS OVER
FENCE OR STEALING
ANYTHING
THIS COMPANY WILL DO
EVERYTHING IN ITS POWER
TO MAKE YOU VERY SORRY
IT MAKES US MAD AS HELL
WE WILL PROSECUTE!

The disdain for any punctuation other than that sole, final exclamation mark was extraordinarily effective. I didn't need to ask who'd made the sign; it had all the hallmarks of McKee Senior.

"Don't throw things over the fence?" I asked.

"Sure," said Dave. "One guy inside, one outside, heave the stuff over the fence and then walk out."

"It's really so valuable?"

He flashed that grin again. "How do you think we make a living?"

A good salvage yard will completely reverse all your preconceptions about junk. To the uninterested eye, that was all that was here. But if you happened to need a steering column for a '76 Chevy, or a drive shaft for an '84 Accord, or a fender for a '69 Mustang, you'd think of this place not as an automotive graveyard, but as heaven on earth.

In a real-life illustration of the anatomy of a car, the yard's fifteen employees had thoroughly stripped incoming cars of their components, separating metallic wheat from chaff. Then they'd sorted the parts by type and make, marked them by model and year, and put them out for display on rows of shelving, hanging off industrial racks, in piles under sheds.

Doors, engines, transmissions, alternators, starters, cylinder heads, cranks, axles, hubs, wheels, fenders, grilles, front lights, rear lights, whole front ends, windshields, steering wheels, driveshafts, steering columns, shocks, rotors, brake calipers, radiators, radios, batteries, bumpers, manifolds, fans, gas tanks . . . It's easy to forget how many parts go into a car until you see them like this, separated out, and become suddenly aware of just how many pieces of metal, plastic, rubber, and glass have to be inserted, threaded, welded, snapped, locked, and bolted into place.

The reality of running a junkyard slowly dawned on me: this was the ultimate recycling center. There was really no such thing as junk. Everything, one way or another, could be salvaged. Oil drained and reprocessed, radiators rebuilt, valves cleaned, rubber shredded, and even what was left, the metal hulk itself, eventually crushed and sold by the ton. But first those hulks got a respite of a few weeks so that people could come and pick over whatever was left. In the classic image of the automotive graveyard, some six or seven hundred at a time were stacked two and three high in row after row of dented metal frames, waiting for the crusher.

Moviemakers love this easy symbol of urban decay, not the least because it's so perfectly photogenic. What Stanley Marsh said of Cadillac Ranch was just as true here: it's impossible to take a bad shot. Even the dumbest amateur can't miss, while a professional can create instant poetry. Every year, *Hemmings Motor News,* the bible of the vintage automobile world, publishes a wall calendar with twelve artistically framed shots of abandoned classics rusting out in gullies and backyards, weeds and even trees growing up through the floorboards. You'd think it enough to break a collector's heart; instead, the collectors collect the calendars too.

Since ABC was right by a major city center, photographers had sought it out more than most. There was an obvious irony in that it was a fashion photographer who'd first told me about the place. The cover for the ZZ Top album *Recycler* was shot here. The cars for both *Robocop* movies came from here. And the Houston police chose this place for their first demonstration of the Jaws of Life, with local TV news cameras drinking up all the atmosphere.

I wandered slowly up and down the rows. Wires hung loose, windows were splintered, engines and hoods were missing. Here and there, weeds grew up around the bottom row of cars—thorns mostly, though under the trees at the back of the lot, there were patches of what might almost be called grass. Some of the cars were rusted, some not, but all were crumpled. Metal that had once gleamed and shone was now tossed aside like a Lurex dress taken off after a hard night on the town and left discarded on the floor, having done its job, perhaps too well.

Which cars were crumpled from a crash, and which from simply being forklifted into place? It was hard to tell. A good guess would be that anything from the nineties had crashed, while anything from the seventies had succumbed to age. But since most of these cars seemed to be from the eighties, such a guess left me none the wiser.

I caught an occasional glimpse of dark shadows skulking through the metal skeletons: a rump disappearing from view beneath a contorted fender, or hind legs and a tail wriggling deeper under a floorpan. The two black dogs were staking their territory, silent enforcers of McKee Senior's dire warnings. So long as I behaved myself, it seemed, they'd let me be, so I settled down on a patch of grass in the sunlight, and as I leaned back against a rusted fender in Houston, Texas, remembered another day, years before and halfway across the world, in another kind of junkyard.

There'd been dogs there too—heavily gravid curs, dugs hanging low and swollen by disease, slinking into the shadows of the ruined Egyptian temple where the colossal head of Rameses II still lay on its side on the ground, one stone eye staring fixedly at the relentless blue of the sky. The place had inspired Shelley to his famous ode mocking grandiose pretensions, and I chanted what I could remember of *Ozymandias* as I roamed through the ruins. "Look on my works, ye Mighty, and despair," yes. Poor Rameses, destined to suffer the indignity of my climbing up onto his face, lying alongside his nose, and resting my head on the cushion of his eyeball.

I'd come to this Houston junkyard in a fit of automotive romanticism, ready like Shelley to reflect on inevitable decay. Rust to rust, and all that. Instead, to my surprise, I felt relaxed and comfortable. I'd have been quite happy to sit here all day, blinking slowly in the sun and watching the weeds grow.

These bare metal hulks had suffered neglect and misfortune, been subject to every human fault that accounts for why people wreck and abandon their cars—poverty or drink, carelessness or drugs, bravado or just sheer exhaustion—and now it was as though they'd taken on the humility that their owners had lacked. Released from the flashy sameness of new metal, each one had crumpled in its own distinctive way, blotched and scraped and rusted in its own individual pattern.

Yet I had no sense of decay. Instead, there was something here of the quiet peacefulness of an English country graveyard. There'd been so much motion in the life of these cars; now they were at rest. And this way, pared down to their essence, they seemed to me far more moving than they had ever been in their glory days.

Humility is hard come by in a culture that celebrates newness and grandeur. There is good reason why the Vietnam Memorial moves people to tears as they see their own images reflected across the engraved names of the dead. That long, low, horizontal gash in the earth is human-sized. It bypasses grandeur, forgoes the traditional sense of awe, and goes straight to the heart.

I've seen people hush and whisper in great cathedrals, but rarely seen them cry. Architectural grandeur intimidates. It makes us shrink and cower into a sense of our own insignificance, and we emerge chastened, like children punished for some wrong we didn't even understand. Most of us, I think, are far more truly moved by a small adobe chapel somewhere in the Southwest, where the desert dust stings your nostrils, and the silence, broken only by the low keening of the wind outside, makes you all the more aware of how alive you are, and how fragile life can be.

★

"There you are!" said Rick. I opened my eyes, startled. I had no idea how much time had gone by. "Thought we'd lost you to the dogs," he joked, and offered a hand to help me up.

He was the older brother, sandy-haired instead of dark, and more serious than Dave, as the first-born often are. I imagined he'd had that worried half-frown on his forehead since he was a young boy. He asked careful questions about who I was and what I was doing, checking to see if he could trust me at the controls of the giant hydraulic Mac press that stood up against the side fence.

The press was basically one huge slab of solid metal suspended over another. It cost $85,000 back in 1977, Rick said. A new one would cost $650,000 today, "and it still wouldn't be as good as this one." Operating on a 200-hp electric motor, it exerted forty tons of pressure per square inch.

"Tons?" I checked.

"Tons," he calmly confirmed. That was the kind of pressure needed to flatten the cars into pancakes, which were then sold to be shredded and resold, melted down and resurrected, often as part of a brand-new car.

Rick and I watched as Pedro, the forklift operator, jockeyed around the first crushee, a gold-colored Oldsmobile circa 1975, making sure there was no rubber left in the car before it went into the press. He nicked open the trunk with the sharp blades of the lift so that his partner could get out the spare tire. Both of them worked with finesse, as though it were important that they not harm the metalwork of this car about to be flattened beyond recognition. Finally, Pedro inserted the blades carefully through the window frames and hoisted the whole car up into the air and over into the press. He placed it perfectly the first time, dead center on the lower slab.

The Olds sat between the two giant metal rectangles as though framed for an art exhibition, the kind that uses industrial artifacts to make some sort of postmodern statement of impending doom. It looked very vulnerable in there, its gold reduced to a mere dirty ocher in the ominous shade. I almost felt sorry for it.

"All yours," said Rick.

I moved over to the controls by the side of the press, pressed the green button to start the motor, then slowly pulled on one of the two tall levers beside it. The lever was stiffer than I'd thought it would be, and I had to put some body English into it. But as I hauled, the top slab began to descend. The farther I pulled the lever, the faster the slab came down; when I pushed on the lever instead, the slab slowed.

I opted to keep it coming slowly: I wanted to draw this out, to savor the moment. Like a child given a match to light a bonfire, I was entranced by the idea that with so little effort, I could effect such a radical change in seemingly solid matter. I felt possessed by that heretical impulse to play God, seduced by the idea of so vast an extension of my own strength. I peered into the press. The slab was almost touching the roof of the car. I licked my lips.

"Nice and easy now," Rick was saying. "Work both levers together, keep it on a level plane."

The second lever shifted the angle of the slab forward and backward, so that I could ensure an even crush over the whole surface of the car. "Keep it level," I muttered to myself. "Nice and easy now." And lowered the top slab just a few inches more.

As though in a slow-motion replay, the sides of the car bulged, and the windshield pillars buckled. The hood broke free of its latch and sprung up at a jaunty angle. I stopped to admire my handiwork, half aware of a manic glitter in my eyes. Then I pulled again on the vertical lever and resumed the pressure. The pillars gave way completely, and the car was suddenly roofless.

"Wow!" I said.

It occurred to me that I should have been used to this extension of power granted by a machine. That's what cars were all about—what struck me so strongly that first time I lifted my foot off the clutch and pressed down on the gas and made a car move. But this was different. There was an alchemy at work here. I was transforming matter.

Inexorably, unrelentingly, the enormous weight of the slab bore down on the car, like the pendulum of death in Edgar Allen Poe's *The Pit and the Pendulum.*

"Down—steadily down it crept . . . Down—certainly, relentlessly down! . . . Down—still unceasingly—still inevitably down!"

What had been four feet high was now three feet. Metal began to fold on metal, like pleats in a skirt. I kept the pressure on, jockeying the two levers to keep it even. The pleats became sharper and more pronounced. The folds began to crack. And suddenly the Olds was lost. It went past a certain, specific point and lost all recognizable aspects of a car. Two feet high, a foot and a half, one foot . . . and I'd reduced a whole car to a compact pancake of indecipherable matter in less than a minute.

"Lift it back up now," said Rick, and I felt a surge of disappointment. If I could just keep the pressure on, it seemed I could reduce that metal pancake to nothing at all—keep pressing it down into the bottom slab until metal blended with metal in cold fusion.

I pushed the lever away from me, watched the upper slab move back up to the top of the press, then moved round into the sunlight to get a good look at my work. Pedro was smoking a cigarette, and I bummed another one off him, lit up, and inhaled. We stood there staring at the flattened car. It had crushed so easily that I'd barely heard the buckling metal over the sound of the motor. I wondered how easily a human body would crush under all that weight.

I shivered in the sunlight, and the manic sense of achievement evaporated. You can identify with a car; people do it all the time. You can even project yourself into a wreck. But this flat slab of tightly creased metal defied identification. I had taken something and rendered it into nothing.

I turned away, caught sight of the pregnant black dog slinking into the darkness of the engine shed, and wondered idly if she'd give birth in there, snuggled into a corner behind the row of Chevy V-8s, the puppies' first smell of life a mix of blood and the stale remnants of motor oil.

★

I called Jim Gaunt the next morning. The idea of priest-mechanic intrigued me. So did how he sounded on the phone.

"You have a car?" he asked, and assured that I did, said: "Why don't you come on out right now?"

"Let's make it in an hour or so," I replied. "I've got to grab some breakfast first."

"I can make you breakfast here if you like."

Since I tend to fall in love with men who cook for me, this offer from a Roman Catholic priest took me off guard. But when you're on the road, you yearn for such things as a home-cooked breakfast. I jotted down the directions to the Sacred Heart Rectory and Church in Manvel, about a half-hour south of Houston.

"I'll be out back working on an MG Midget," he said. Could this man be for real?

The moment I saw him, I knew he was. Jim Gaunt, in perfect contrast to his name, looked more like a trucker than a priest. Tall and burly, he was wearing old pants, a well-worn shirt, and workshoes. He gave a big "Hulloo" as I drove up, followed by a warm, firm handshake. The MG was there, alongside a stunning little white Mini Mark—a convertible roadster based on a VW Beetle, with black and white upholstery and purple shag liner on the roof. "I'm fixing it up to raffle off for the high-school scholarship fund," he said.

He was in his early sixties, but looked a good ten years younger—the youthful look that comes on a man who's living out his vocation the way he knows is best. He saw me studying his clothes. "I do wear a priest's collar sometimes," he assured me, creating the clear impression that he avoided it whenever he could.

Inside the modern bungalow that served as the rectory, he put together a grand breakfast of coffee, poached eggs, bacon, toast, even marmalade in deference to my English origins. I was hungrier than I'd thought, and kept going back to the toaster for more. He understood: "Must be hard out there on the road with nowhere to make food for yourself."

Jim Gaunt, it turned out, was a Detroit boy born and bred. I'm not sure why this should have surprised me, but it did; I hadn't expected to encounter Detroit so directly in Houston, let alone in the form of a priest. His father had been a research engineer at General Motors, one brother worked for Detroit Diesel, and of his three brothers-in-law, one worked at Chrysler and another at Cadillac, while the third was a vice-president in charge of parts and supplies at Ford. That's how it goes with Detroit families: a mishmash of conflicting name-brand loyalties.

Jim sidestepped the family destiny by joining the Congregation of Saint Basil, also known as the Basilian Fathers, after college. He took graduate degrees in both theology and geology, and was a teaching father for many years. The geology made sense; it has always seemed to me that geologists are extraordinarily well-centered, balanced people. Grounded, I suppose you might say.

Vows of obedience kept him in teaching and training, eventually as the superior and novice master in several of the order's houses. "And then they finally said, 'Okay, so what do you really want to do?' And there was this little parish, a poor one, open in south Texas. Five hundred families, fifty-fifty Anglo and Hispanic, and half the houses with wheels on them. 'There,' I said, 'that's what I really want to do.'"

All through his long journey to this parish, he'd fixed cars. Hundreds of them over the years. And bought and sold and maintained them too: "If you're from Detroit, knowing mechanics comes with the territory. At one point I picked up two old T-bird convertibles, made one new one out of them, and sold it. But I guess I really got into wheeling and dealing with cars when I was the principal at the order's high school, Saint Thomas, up in Houston. I did it because the kids were intensely interested in working on cars. Word got out that I'd accept old cars and that people could donate them as a tax write-off. We'd fix them and sell them cheap to poor people, and the whole thing took off from there. And when I came to this parish, it just continued."

"Dave McKee says you give cars away."

He shrugged. "Yes, I do that sometimes. Maybe I'll give away five a year, and sell six or seven. Sometimes, if a poor family needs a car, you can't give it away to them, because there's the issue of dignity, so I'll charge them for it. I may come up short on what I charge, but they don't know that, and they'll have reliable transportation for two or three hundred dollars."

He got up to make a fresh pot of coffee. "You know, poor people get hosed on again and and again at these used-car lots. The dealers tell me they *want* the cars to break down because then the payments will stop and they can come and repossess the cars. That way they can sell the same car five times over, since they never hand over the papers until the final payment is made."

Any profit he makes on the cars goes to good use. Some goes to scholarship funds for the order's high schools and college, and some to maintain a religious retreat he runs farther out in the country, donated to him by a Jewish businessman. And some also goes to anyone in dire need in the form of small loans, "five hundred dollars, say, that I never expect to get back and that's fine."

I smiled. "I know that five hundred dollars," I said. And told him the story of how a good friend back in Jerusalem had once given me precisely that amount when I was dirt broke, calling it a long-term loan. When I'd tried to pay it back, he'd waved it off. "Someone else will need it," he said. And sure enough, years later, five hundred dollars stood to make all the difference in the life of a student of mine in Pennsylvania. I gave it to him, together with the story of how I came by it, in the unspoken hope that in another few years, he in turn would be able to pass it on.

We took our fresh coffee out into the yard, where there were two worn Adirondack chairs on a small patch of grass shaded by a pecan tree. Jim's dog, a drooling mutt with a coat the color of clay and the unlikely name of Maybelline, waddled out behind us. What she lacked in looks, she made up in friendliness. Like the McKee brothers' dogs, she'd been salvaged—found by a parishioner starving and wounded by the side of the road, named by the parishioner's daughter, then delivered to Jim, who'd nursed her back to health.

The McKees, he said, were "hard-shell Baptists," which surprised me; I'd assumed from the way they talked of Jim as "our padre" that they were Catholic. But Jim seemed to think this nothing unusual.

"I've been adopted as a father by quite a few sons and daughters," he said. "I see a lot of homes where there's no father living there, and many others where the father lives at home but doesn't function as a father. There are so many brave, great mothers making a life for their children by themselves, but how many great fathers do you know? This is what worries me—not as an anti-feminist issue, but more as a criticism of men. We're losing the idea of being a father, the concept of fatherhood."

And as we talked on, I realized that this man was blending the different concepts of fatherhood—the Catholic father, the biological father, God the father—into his own very human kind of Trinity.

A faint breeze rustled the pecan tree, and large black nuts plopped to the ground. I found myself telling Jim about my own father, and to my surprise, heard the pain in my voice as I spoke. "I know it's just a matter of time until he dies," I said. "That is, it's a matter of time until we all die, but with him, it was real close for a while back in the spring. And again, apparently, quite recently, though he says he's fine now. I tell myself I'm ready for it, but of course I'm not. And if we really have gained him an extra year, then that's an extraordinary gift. It gives me the grace of time. So once I finish this journey I'm on now, I'll go spend some time with my parents in England, or bring them over to visit in Seattle, and enjoy being my father's daughter a little while longer."

I'd never actually said this to anyone before. Not even to myself. I'd clung to the stubborn insistence that my father would always pull through, somehow, as though I would never have to face not having him. And when I'd finished, Jim didn't utter any of the usual pious platitudes like, "I'll pray for him," as I'd trusted him not to. He just nodded, and said nothing, because we both knew there was nothing to be said. There was understanding in that silence, and a companionable solace.

Maybelline nuzzled Jim's hand as I sat there wondering at the roundabout ways in which people meet and talk. Here in this pocket handkerchief of a garden, we were a Catholic father and a wandering Jew—a priest who knew the importance of humanism and a writer who knew she wasn't really an agnostic but stubbornly resisted calling herself anything else.

Cars had brought us together, in an interest as seemingly unlikely on his part as on mine. Yet the more we talked on through the morning—about the encroaching corruption of spiritual life, and his concern with bridging the sometimes yawning abyss between religious life and "real life"—the less unlikely cars began to seem, at least on his part.

His work as a mechanic grounded him. It kept him from getting too holy, too removed from the lives of real people. With his hands covered in grease, he had found a physical as well as a spiritual way of working for others. Or maybe, in essence, they were the same thing.

It had never occurred to me to think of mechanics as a spiritual calling. Yet absurd as it may sound, it seemed that Jim Gaunt had found a way to make it so. Which is why he had that youthful look of a man doing his best work. His life as a priest spanned the limitations we usually impose by dividing the world every which way: into physical work and intellectual work, or "real life" and spiritual life, or family father and Christian father, or Roman Catholic and hard-shell Baptist.

Before I left, he offered me a test drive of the Mini Mark. "Just on the church grounds," he said. "It's not licensed for the road yet." He tossed me the keys and I squeezed into the little white hot rod, revved it up, took it around the parking lot a few times, and then went roaring up and down the access road.

"What do you think?" he asked when I brought it back.

"Sign me up for a couple of those raffle tickets," I said. Knowing that if I won, I'd auction it off and donate the proceeds back to him. Much as I loved the car, I couldn't imagine doing anything else.

Chapter Fourteen

On Thanksgiving weekend, Houston would host the Autorama—my chance to crack the esoteric world of hot rods and custom cars. Just the name of the show conjured up glitzy visions of the newly technicolored fifties and their adulation of all things bright and shiny. But that was still a week away. I thought of driving on down to Miami, then checked the map. Even if I stayed on the interstates, it would mean a two-thousand-mile round trip in holiday traffic. The same applied to flying home for the holiday: air travel anywhere around that most American of dates was just too much to face.

Then it turned out that good friends in Houston were going up north for the week, and they offered me the use of their home, a little cottage close by the De Menil art museum. News of an early-winter ice storm spreading from North Texas up through Oklahoma and Missouri clinched the matter: it was time to hunker down in the sun for a bit, and prepare for what was to come.

I called Gene in Seattle, asked him to FedEx my bills, faxes, and any interesting-looking mail to my friends' address—"Keep an eye out for a large envelope from Sierra House Elementary School," I said—and settled in. I savored the prospect of staying still for a few days, especially with a lemon tree outside my window and an outstanding private art collection as my neighbor.

The FedEx man arrived in due course, and sure enough there was a big packet from the kids in with all the regular mail. I tossed everything else aside, sat out under the lemon tree, and opened it. Drawings and letters spilled out onto the flagstones, the letters full of questions. These eight-year-olds had taken my advice to heart.

Did I go trick-or-treating on Halloween? What did I dress up as? Did I get a lot of candy? What was my favorite candy? What was my favorite animal? What was my favorite color? Could I tell them more about living on a houseboat? Had I been to New York yet? Had I been to Florida yet? Would I go see the White House? When would I get to Detroit?

> Dear Lesley. Hi Lesley it's me Alberto. And I want to tell you about how come I like to write about cars so much. Because I like it when they go realy realy fast. My mom has a mustang gt and her mustang is yellow. I wish I could be just like you so that I can go that far like you. I have a question for you. Do you have a husbend? Lesley I have another question for you. Are you married?

He'd included a drawing of a tiny figure smiling and waving from the driver's seat of a big yellow car; an arrow pointed to the figure, and above it were the words "It's me Alberto."

Danny updated me on his car situation:

> I have a Lexus SC400 and a B.M.W. 850I but there are only toys. Thoes I dont run on my Chris cross crash. Oh ya Chris moved and he was my frend. He moved to Reno and I dont know if he likes it ther. A Chris cross crash is a car launcher and it crashis cars it is fun.

He'd signed it "sinsely" and drawn another dragster, this one purple and green with orange flame coming out the back. The sun in the upper left-hand corner seemed to be wearing a black eyepatch.

Two letters were from newcomers to the class. Nancy had warned me that families who work in the casino industry move around a lot depending on the season and the general economy. Chris had already left, while one of the newcomers was busy adapting to geographical and other changes in her life:

Hi my name is Kameron I live in south lake tauha. I like it here it snows and I eat it. I forgot were I went but I did go some were to see my dad sun day. his name is L.L. and I spint the night at his sisters house. and when it was my birthday and then when he said happy birthday and I said happy birthday to him we lafhed."

Bianca thanked me for the "posters" I'd sent from the road, but her heart clearly wasn't in writing this time round. It was, literally, in the drawing she'd attached. A jaggedly divided heart seemed to be caught in the center of a giant spider's web. Growing out of the top was what looked like a crown of thorns. The whole was crayoned in deliriously bright purples and pinks and oranges and yellows. I was stunned; both sinister and hauntingly beautiful, this drawing would have done credit to Frida Kahlo.

Diana wrote about her new puppy, Macarena. Jorge told me how he liked to ride his bike and play baseball—"my favorite shoo Reebok." Chad listed his collection of Hot Wheels. And Martin took what I'd said about asking questions one inquiring step further:

Dear Lesley. I'm going to ask question like you. But what people do you ask question? Just people that you know or people that work on cars. Let me ask you a question do you have a husben. I'm asking this becaus he would ride with you. When I grow up I want to drive a mustang and be a docter and make people well. Your friend Martin.

I smiled, remembering when I'd also wanted to be a doctor. A car had been involved with that for me too, though it wasn't a Mustang. It was a model nobody could ever have imagined achieving anything so grandiose as classic status, yet I'd seen it recently in a new coffee-table book of classic cars, photographed and written up with the same loving detail and appreciation as the Ferraris and Jaguars, Mustangs and Corvettes: a lumpy little Morris Minor. I'd photocopied the pages and sent them to my father. "Remember this?" I'd scrawled across the top.

★

My father went through a whole series of cars, reasoning that he needed a new one every three years or so since his profession demanded that his transport be utterly reliable. As a general practitioner in Britain's National Health Service from its inception in the forties, he'd spend mornings "in surgery," receiving patients, and afternoons "on rounds," visiting patients too sick to get out of the house. "Too sick," when I was young, meant anyone running even the mildest fever, so he might do a dozen house calls or more on any afternoon.

And then there were the nights. There were three doctors in his practice, which meant he was on night call at least twice a week.

The ringing phone would wake me, and I'd hear him, calm and authoritative: "Yes . . . Yes . . . I see . . . Aha . . . Running a temperature, is she? . . ." A longer pause, and then: "I'll be there as soon as I can."

There'd be my mother's soft protest as he left the bed, and after a while, the creak of the floorboards as he passed my bedroom door and went down the stairs. I lay there listening: the front door closing, the car starting, the sound of it backing down the driveway and then off up the street.

I'd sleep through the car's return an hour or so later, but he tried so hard not to wake us as he came back up the stairs that of course he ended up doing exactly what he was trying to avoid. Half-awake and half-asleep, I'd hear his brief report to my mother.

Sometimes it was good news: "Easy delivery," he'd say. "A girl."

Sometimes it wasn't: "The Grigsby baby. Had to send the poor thing to Battle." And I'd imagine this unknown baby lying in bed at Battle Hospital, the unfortunately named complex of red-brick buildings that seemed to be on emergency duty far more than the posher Royal Berkshire, the other hospital in town.

This might happen two or even three times a night. Always, he went to visit his patient again the next day, whether still at home or in Battle. Which might explain why, when he eventually retired, patients sent so many cards of thanks and appreciation that they covered every surface in the living room, including the floor.

Occasionally, when I was eight or nine and on vacation from school, he'd take me with him on his rounds. I felt very grown-up then. My brother was deemed too young for this, so it was just me and my father, and it seemed like I'd been conferred a particular honor. These were the only times I spent alone with him—an English family doctor's equivalent, perhaps, of taking his daughter to a ball game.

He knew the streets of our town, Reading, as well as any London cabbie knows every alley in Whitechapel or Wimbledon. He never needed a map; the whole town was there in his head, from the meanest little red-brick rowhouse to country mansions with long gravel driveways. I'd sit in the passenger seat of the Morris Minor with his call list in my lap, reading out the next destination each time he got back into the car. And once we reached it, he'd give me an old stethoscope to play with, get his big black doctor's case out of the trunk, and tell me he'd be back soon.

He'd knock on the front door—"Doctor, thank you so much for coming"—and then he'd be ushered in and the door would close behind him, leaving me alone in the car with the stethoscope.

I'd listen to my own heart for a while, but it just kept on doing the same thing over and over, and besides, I'd discovered a far more interesting way to play doctor. So sooner or later, I'd slide on over to the driver's seat, grasp the wheel, pull myself up to the edge of the seat so that I could see the road, and imagine myself in my father's place.

I was rushing out in the middle of a snowstorm to deliver a baby. No, not one: Twins! A boy and a girl. Sometimes even triplets. I was off to prescribe bitter potions and big black and red pills that would stop pain and bring down fevers, for it was clear that the more unpleasant the medicine, the more effective it had to be. I was speeding to the rescue with a rare antidote in my case, driving as fast as I could so that I'd get to my dying patient just in the nick of time, when I'd plunge in the hypodermic, fearless of needles so long as I was the injecter and not the injectee, and watch color come back to his cheeks and his eyes flutter open. I was driving into the night with the power of life and death in that black case in the trunk, ready to work miracles of modern medicine, and I felt very large and very important.

And then I'd hear my father coming out of the house, his voice the cheery professional one that always seemed to reassure:

"If she's not feeling better by tomorrow, phone me at the surgery."

Or: "I'll stop by tomorrow and see how he's doing."

Or: "Nothing to worry about: just a bit of a virus that's going around."

I'd slide back over to the passenger seat before he could see me, and sit there demurely as he replaced his case in the trunk, got into the driver's seat, and started the engine, all unaware of the powerhouse sitting beside him.

"Right," he'd say, "where are we going next?"

★

I settled down to write back to the kids. Since the husband question seemed to be weighing on their minds, I tried to explain my unmarried state of semi-domesticity. "He travels a lot on business," I said, "so he understands when I go away for a long time to do research, like I'm doing now."

I told them a little about where I'd been and who I'd met since I'd last written, dutifully listed my favorite color (green), animal (jaguar), and candy (mints), and told them more about life on a houseboat. "Sometimes it rocks," I said. "I'm used to it, and hardly notice. But when friends come to visit, they tell me it's really weird. They sit inside what seems to be a normal house, and then they suddenly realize that it's moving up and down."

Martin's question about asking questions deserved a serious answer, and this letter got to be even longer than my previous one:

"I ask all kinds of people," I wrote. "When I write about cars, I talk to engineers and designers, test drivers and race-car drivers, people who make cars and people who fix them and people who sell them. But I also talk to the people who drive the cars—people like your Mom and Dad, and your teacher, and anyone who owns a car. Because though they may not know everything about how a car works, they do know if it works well for them.

"By now I have a long list of people I can call and talk to, and it gets longer all the time. I keep their names in a Rolodex on my desk." And I took off into a minor riff on the advantages of the Rolodex system:

"You can keep expanding it just by slipping in extra cards. So when I get home, I can add the priest who fixes cars and the guys who own the junkyard where I crushed the car. Then when I want to write a letter, send a fax, e-mail someone, or call them on the phone, it will be easy to find their addresses and numbers.

"You are all in my Rolodex. Your card is filed under 'S' for Sierra House Elementary School, and I've written all your names on the back.

"How do I know so many people? Other people tell me about them. 'Oh, you should talk to so-and-so,' they'll say. Or 'So-and-so is the person who can answer that question.' And then even though I haven't met that person before, I can call, say that I'm doing research, and they'll talk to me.

"The thing is, people *like* to answer questions. Once they know you're really interested, and really want to know the answer, they'll take the time to help you."

I read through what I'd written. It seemed a bit dry. The words needed something extra. So I took my cue from their letters to me and got out a couple of felt pens. I can't draw well, but then aside from Bianca, neither could they.

I drew a Rolodex, open to the card with Sierra House Elementary on it. I drew my houseboat rocking away on high waves. I drew me dressed up for Halloween in a big black wig, looking like Morticia Addams.

"I've just realized, I haven't given my truck a name," I added at the end. "Do you think I should? And if you do, what name do you suggest?"

As I'd done the first time I'd written, I called Nancy to tell her the letter was on the way, and discovered that my postcards had been subjected to intense analysis in the classroom: a kind of eight-year-old deconstructionism.

There'd been a long discussion about whether the old mountain man in the Sierras ever got his mule to move. This had led to a debate on the relative merits of different ways of inducing it to move, with some of the class touting the virtues of sugar lumps, and the majority, two-by-fours. "They're not sentimentalists," said Nancy succinctly.

The postcard showing a vulture perched on the back of a dehydrated prospector in the desert had led to an even longer discussion as the kids tussled with the idea that the photograph had been posed, and that what you see might not necessarily be reality.

It hadn't even occurred to me that they might think the scene was real. "Would it be better if I sent regular scenic postcards instead?" I asked.

Nancy laughed. "No, I can handle it. The discussions open up all sorts of issues that are on their minds, like what's real and what's not, and what death is."

"Good questions," I said, mired in my own confusion of realities as the rest of the country took to the road to go home, while I stayed still.

★

The FedEx packet had also included the press kit for the 37th Annual Hi/Lo Auto Supply Autorama at Astrodomain. The first thing I saw when I opened the folder was a photo of *Baywatch* star Gena Lee Nolin, crouched provocatively on California sand. Call me naive, but my first thought was, "They've sent me the wrong kit."

The moment I stepped through the entrance of the Astrodome on the morning after Thanksgiving, all such misconceptions were instantly erased. The first vehicle I saw or, rather, encountered, was an acid trip on wheels: a 1989 full-size GMC pickup entirely covered in comic-book graphics. Psychedelic robots and wild beasts cavorted over the sheet metal and rampaged on the underside of the hood. The background color was a pearlized apricot, and the interior was appointed in lavender and pale apricot.

Everything that could be gold-plated on the vehicle, had been. Not just such minor items as door handles, but every metallic part. This included the whole of the underbody, visible since the vehicle was displayed at a thirty-degree tilt over a large mirror. Hubs, engine block, pipes, struts, oil pan, tie rods, drive train, radiator—all were coated in 24-carat gold. And then engraved. In ornate curlicues and flourishes.

The owner sat beside his creation. In his late twenties, he had long blond hair, one hoop earring, and the kind of goofy grin you get somewhere in the middle of your second reefer. He introduced himself as Mike, told me the truck was called Wild Thing, and said he'd spent three hundred thousand dollars to make it over. He didn't look like the kind of man who could get his hands on that kind of money.

"I thought only drug money could pay for something like that," I said.

His grin widened. "It's cheaper than a drug habit, and easier to sell," he replied.

He laid out the specs for me: a 355 Chevy engine and a 6-71 blower, meaning it was a supercharged six-cylinder 71 cubic-inch dual-carb . . .

The words flowed over me, the usual litany of male automotive appreciation, recited entirely in numbers. My eyes glazed. Visibly, it seemed. Mike slowed down, stopped, then shrugged. "It's kind of a good idea gone berserk," he finally admitted. "Some of the things I did started out as a joke."

But the joke had worked. Wild Thing was the current *Lowrider* magazine's Truck of the Year. "Three and a half years to make," Mike said, "and at least one person working on it eight hours a day, six days a week. There's only four parts left on it the way GMC made them." Everything else had been, in custom/hot-rod lingo, smoothed, chopped, slammed, frenched, plated, "or just thrown away and replaced." The aim was to modify the whole vehicle in some way, shape, or fashion, and in this Mike had been superbly successful.

"Which parts did you leave untouched?"

"The windshield, the left door glass, the right door glass, and the gas pedal."

"Why the gas pedal?"

That loopy grin again: "I just plain forgot."

I wished him luck and wandered farther into the hall. Wild Thing began to seem almost tame. Everywhere I looked, cars and trucks had been turned into phantasmagoric canvases. The graphics were called "murals," and seemed to favor heavily bearded Merlins and full-bosomed Gena Lee Nolins in flowing robes and Court of King Arthur head-dresses, all larger than life, set against landscapes of the American sublime: lakes and mountains and Disneyland castles. I couldn't decide if some of the female figures were intended to be lascivious bimbos, Queen Guinevere, or the Virgin Mary; I wondered if the men who painted them might have the three confused.

Occasionally there was something a tad more up-to-date, like the Chevy minivan with machine guns as its main decorative motif—real ones, set inside neon-lit panels in the quilted velvet doors. The railings around the van were made of handcuffs, and its sides were painted with intensely detailed and just as intensely violent scenes of inner-city gang warfare. The van was called Thug Life.

The latest thing in customizing, it seemed, was to cover the whole of the interior in deeply quilted crush velour, with piping and tassels. Literally the whole of it. Not just the seats and the roof, but also the floor, the insides of the doors, the dashboard, the steering wheel, even the cupholders. The favored colors were deep purple, midnight blue, carmine, and a particularly bilious bright turquoise. The piping and tassels were invariably gold.

These interiors were clearly supposed to be the ultimate in richly plush luxury. To me, they looked more like hearses. I thought of this as "the funereal look," and enjoyed it as an absurd joke until another proud owner told me that the companies that do the quilting work, known as "diamond pleating," in fact do most of their work for funeral parlors.

The deeper I wandered into the hall, the more I realized how completely lost I was in this world. The hot-rod and custom-car culture was indeed a separate and distinct culture. It had successfully instituted a fully alternative esthetic, elevating kitsch to a standard of cultural pride and identity that defied, challenged, and thumbed its nose at accepted standards of good taste. And did it all with absolute sincerity.

Perhaps my mind had been affected by the sheer volume of acid-like visions on vehicle after vehicle, but the more I saw, the more I began to simply enjoy what was there to see. After all, who said that this was not good taste? "Society's definition," true, but then who is society? The arbiters of taste in the big-city art museums and magazines, or the majority of people living in the real America?

This whole show began to appear as a message from the majority culture to the minority one that has claimed culture as its own. It was a forceful assertion of majority standards. And if it had taken kitsch to the nth degree, wasn't that a perfect comment on cars in general? Was there anything intrinsically less kitschy about the heated leather seats and onboard compass of my forty-thousand-dollar Ford Expedition? Or for that matter, about a Ferrari or a Lamborghini, with their flash and flamboyance and primary reds and yellows?

And what, I began to wonder, made the metallic visions of the Autorama any less admirable than, say, the BMW collection of "art cars." Each year, the German automaker asks a well-known artist to paint a 3-series car. By now they have quite a collection—Rauschenberg, Warhol, Hockney, Lichtenstein, Stella—but though the cars look impressive in photographs, in real life they seem cheaply done, inept and amateurish compared to the superb craft and finish of these vehicles at the Autorama. Was a badly done Rauschenberg better than a superbly done Thug Life?

It comes down, of course, to the issue of class. Place the Autorama alongside Pebble Beach, and that becomes clear. On the one hand, the eighteenth hole of one of the world's most famous golf courses, the exclusive Lodge, champagne, sorbets, Cuban cigars, white-jacketed waiters, Ascot hats, Dior cravats, and bodies toned and shaped by personal trainers and discreet surgeons. On the other, the ur-plebeian interior of the Astrodome and the Astrohall with their bare floors, loud rock music, T-shirts, baseball caps, fuzzy dice, hot dogs, root beers, ice creams, screaming kids, and beer paunches. At Pebble Beach, you overheard tense discussions of auction prices; at the Autorama, impassioned debates as to the relative virtues of triple and quad carbs.

Yet in terms of pure creativity, what was here at the Autorama far outdid Pebble Beach's antiques. Every car here was unique, a one-off. Like the Pebble Beach cars, the Autorama cars were the fruit of years of work; but where the vintage exotics had been meticulously restored by hired professionals, the custom cars had been molded and sawed and plated and engraved by backyard enthusiasts in the spirit and esthetic of the streets, not the golf course.

I suddenly remembered a scene from Pebble Beach: Tom Gale, Chrysler's chief of design, and Bob Lutz, the company's chairman and CEO, huddled together over snapshots of Gale's latest hobby car. It wasn't a "better-than-new" restoration of an antique, as I'd expected, but a custom car based on a fifties Chrysler sedan. Gale had chopped the roof—lowered it by shortening the pillars—and added to the side panels, making them taller and achieving the distinctive "highboy" look. The two executives were as excited about the snapshots as teenage boys about their first set of wheels, faces flushed with pleasure as they ignored the riches around them and focused in on what Gale was doing in his own backyard. And something clicked in my mind as they handed me the snapshots and watched my reaction. These two were the team responsible for the Plymouth Prowler, Chrysler's modern version of a hot rod, a limited-production car intended to give the company a high-profile, radical image. And they knew where to look for their cues. Not on the manicured lawns of Pebble Beach, but where the action really was: on the boulevards of Los Angeles and Miami, in backyard garages around the country, and at events like the Autorama.

Of course to a real hot-rodder, the very idea of a production hot rod is an oxymoron. "Kustom kar" culture, as many of its members insist on spelling it, is individualist to the point of pathology. Reyner Banham, writing about Los Angeles in the seventies, saw "the art of customizing, of turning common family sedans into wild extravaganzas of richly colored and exotically shaped metal," as "delinquent in its origins"—an irresistible turn-on to a professor at University College, London. That very delinquency, he argued, leads to "the uninhibited inventiveness of master customizers like Ed ('Big Daddy') Roth."

"Delinquent?" spluttered Ed Roth when I told him this. "The man don't know his ass from his elbow."

Roth, of course, was here at the Astrodome. An Autorama is just not a proper Autorama without Big Daddy. Bearded and top-hatted, in paint-smeared T-shirt and baggy pants, he was holding court at his booth. He was the king of the road, the king of kitsch, the king of the whole shebang. He was the king, in fact, of whatever you liked, so long as you paid due respect and were willing to fork over cash for his auto-graph on anything that could take pen and ink.

Big Daddy Roth made his reputation by creating a tiny bubbletop custom dragster called the Beatnik Bandit, back in the days when he was whooping it up with Ken Kesey and his Merry Prankster crowd. The Bandit was still the best known of all his cars, gems such as the Outlaw and Tweedy Pie notwithstanding, and a fourth-generation in-carnation of the car was on display behind tasseled ropes beside his booth. Roth also invented pinstriping, which in custom-car lingo is the antithesis of a straight pinstriped suit; thin byzantine curlicues dance over hoods and trunks, and sometimes over everything else too. But most lucrative of all, Roth was the creator and copyright holder of Rat Fink.

This cartoon creature might be called a nightmare version of Mickey Mouse. There's something Robert Crumb–like about him. His egre-giously ugly features include huge sharklike teeth, grotesquely bulging eyes that somehow look more like a porn cartoon of a woman's breasts, a giant drooling tongue, and stick-thin arms and legs that always seem about to do something unutterably obscene. On T-shirts, he says things like, "Life begins at 200 mph," "Once a fink, always a fink," "Hip hop burn out" (very big in Japan, apparently) and, infamously, "Get out of my garage and back into the kitchen."

In the thirty years since Roth first sketched him on a paper napkin, Rat Fink has achieved worldwide fame. Or rather, infamy. He's ap-peared in one pose or another not only on T-shirts, but also on caps, patches, decals, plaques, jewelry, and belt buckles, in calendars and posters, comic books and kids' coloring books, and as "lawn art" and "garage art" statuettes. All of these and more were selling like hot wheels at the Autorama, along with models and model kits of Roth's hot rods.

Fans crowded around the booth, tended by two of Roth's sons as the man himself sat placidly in the middle, drawing more Rat Finks on tin sheets while at the same time exchanging one-liners with prospective buyers. I must have had the right name by way of introduction, for he instantly gestured me into the booth, sat me down on a low stool beside him, and with no prompting at all, began to expound his philosophy of life.

The trouble was, Big Daddy waxing philosophical was either above my head or beneath my feet. The ambient noise was so loud that sometimes I couldn't make out what he was saying. What I did get seemed to fade in and out of making sense like a shortwave broadcast on a radio with worn batteries. The free-association rap blended new-age spirituality with old-time religion, a Zen-like insouciance about earthly belongings with a highly honed sense of capitalism, and hard-gut conservative moral principles with an ageing hippy lingo.

It occurred to me that Big Daddy may have taken far too many drugs back in the sixties.

But one thing emerged quite clearly: Big Daddy was sad. Big Daddy was unhappy. Big Daddy, he confided in me as I sat staring up into his kindly, lined, profane face, needed a wife.

I moved quickly to forestall where I feared this was leading: "Oh we can find you a wife. I know lots of women who'd be delighted to meet you."

"No," he said, shaking his beard lugubriously, "you don't understand."

"Come now, it can't be that hard."

"It is," he said mournfully. "She has to be Mormon."

At first I took it as a joke, then realized he was serious. "But why a Mormon?"

He looked at me as though I was a perfect idiot. "Because I'm Mormon," he said. "Always have been. Both my previous wives were Mormon, and the next one has to be too."

Big Daddy Roth? Big Daddy the hard-drinkin', fast-livin', multi-druggin', whoopin', hollerin', free spirit? Big Daddy who named his cars Outlaw, Beatnik Bandit, Peace Rat, Asphalt Angel, Pink Bazooka, Yellow Fang, Candy Wagon, Rubber Ducky, and Tweedy Pie? Big Daddy who made an icon of an obscene rat? *This* Big Daddy, a man of faith? A practicing Mormon?

Could it be that beneath that hard-living, tough-talking persona beat the heart of an old-fashioned sentimentalist? But of course it could.

That was the essence of this whole Autorama world. The essence, in fact, of kitsch. The Autorama was a retro, comic-book world where cars were fifties fantasies, men tucked Marlboro packs into the rolled-up sleeves of their T-shirts, and fuzzy dice dangled in abundance from rearview mirrors. It was a world where men could be knights and women sexy Madonnas. A world in which burly Big Daddy could be, at heart, a teddy bear. Sort of.

"Will you give my girlfriend a ride in the new Bandit?" shouted one guy hovering at the booth. The girlfriend giggled, and thrust out her chest to show off her Rat Fink T-shirt.

"Sure," said Big Daddy. "Four thousand dollars."

The guy grinned and hesitated. For a moment I thought he was going to negotiate the price. But he ended up buying a copy of Roth's book on hot rods instead—"the last fifty copies, right here in this box," Big Daddy declared with absolute conviction—and was rewarded for his hundred-dollar largesse with a large on-the-spot Rat Fink cartoon drawn on the title page and signed with a flourish.

"If he'd offered one thousand, would you have taken his girlfriend for a ride?" I asked after he'd left.

"Are you kidding? Sure I would. The guy was a cheapskate."

Volume was increasing now at the booth, item after item being passed back to Roth for an autograph. A spiffily dressed young man was buying a sateen Rat Fink jacket for his girlfriend back home. "Where's home?" asked Roth. And when the answer was New Jersey, nodded as though he'd known it all along.

"You know the difference between East Coast hot-rodders and the rest of us?" he said as I got up to leave, clutching my own copy of one of those rare one-hundred-dollar books. "On the West Coast and in the Midwest, guys treat their cars like a wife; on the East Coast, they drive a car to find a wife." He shook his head lugubriously. "There's no spiritual connection with the car any more out there."

★

Back at my friends' house, I took a couple of headache pills, and as I waited for the clamor of the Astrodome to subside in my brain, studied the drawing Big Daddy had penned across the first two pages of his book. I must have told him I lived on a houseboat, because Rat Fink was caught in midair, arms and legs akimbo, about to plunge into a considerable body of choppy water and looking none too happy about it. "Lesley, keep on truckin'" was written above the signature. It seemed like a good idea.

I'd intended to spend the whole weekend at the Autorama, but my head couldn't take more than one day. Besides, I was antsy to get back on the road again: get out of town and take a long, lazy drive through the back roads of Louisiana, heading for Natchez, Mississippi. There I'd join the Natchez Trace, the four-hundred-mile long parkway that angled up through Mississippi and into Tennessee, following the route of an old foot and horse trail.

I packed up the truck, ready for an early start in the morning. Just before I went to sleep, I remembered that I hadn't called my answering machine back home for a couple of days. I doubted if there'd be any messages on a holiday weekend, but if there were more motels like the one in Dickens, I should probably check while I could.

And there, the first message, was my mother's voice. Barely recognizable. Tremulous across a continent and an ocean.

"Lesley, Jessel died at seven thirty this morning. Lesley, where are you? Where are you, darling? Can you hear me? Please phone me, darling. Please. As soon as you can. Please . . ."

I sat hunched on the edge of the bed, so shocked I hadn't even started to shake yet. My heart was thumping, my vision blurred. And then I heard her again, a second message left an hour later, panicky that I wouldn't get the news in time to fly to England for the funeral.

Chapter Fifteen

There is something surreal about death. The practical part of the mind accepts it as real, but the rest of the mind is all to sea. Everything that seemed fixed, permanent, becomes as shifting as water. Nothing holds in quite the right place. As with the landsickness you feel when you come ashore after a few days on a sailboat, what you thought was stable begins to reel and heave. Your whole existence is at a different angle to the world.

I flew back to Houston two weeks later. The plane from London landed at about three in the afternoon, and since it would soon be dark, I intended to spend the night in a motel near the airport. Maybe call Father Gaunt and go see him; he'd be a good person to talk to right now. But the moment the shuttle bus reached the Park'N'Fly lot, everything from that night two weeks before came rushing back at me, and I knew I had to get out of this town, as though if I stayed it could all repeat itself, and my father would die again.

Absurd, of course, for an airport parking lot to be so evocative, but when I saw the truck standing there, life went into replay: the phone calls to the airlines, the unexpected kindness of the British Airways people, Ann and Gene back in Seattle finding my passport and going to extraordinary lengths to courier it to me, a journalist colleague who brought round a bottle of brandy and sat there miserably dumb and embarrassed while I babbled incoherently about how sick and self-deluded I had been even to permit myself to laugh at the funereal look of the custom cars while all the time . . .

No, I had to get out of Houston. I opened the driver's door and saw the sprig of rosemary from George and Liz's garden in Ojai still on the dashboard; it was all brown and withered. I remembered the Porsche-driving skeleton, still stowed in a box at the back of the truck. How could I have played so lightly with the idea of death?

Ann sounded shocked when I called to tell her I was back in the States and continuing my journey. She'd assumed I would fly on back to Seattle and take a formal break. "You can't drive away from grief," she said.

I tried to imagine myself back home, mooching around the house, lost and restless. No, better by far to be on the road. Because driving away from grief was not my intention. Driving into grief was more like it. I'd give myself over to the hardscrabble American romance of taking to the road in times of trouble, driving mile upon mile with the thrum of tires on pavement, the relentless hum of the engine, the wind tearing past the windows.

Months ago, in Seattle, I'd seen the long oblique line of the Natchez Trace cutting across the right angles of the map, defying the ninety-degree grid. An ornery kind of road in this nation of verticals and horizontals. One that followed the topography instead of some arbitrary platting measure. Four hundred miles made by usage, not by a bureaucrat's fiat.

The name itself—the Trace—had an almost otherworldly attraction, as though if you didn't pay attention, it might disappear. As indeed the old, original Trace had nearly done. The new Trace was a two-lane blacktop, the longest scenic parkway in the country, with not a single commercial sign the whole way. It ended south of Nashville not far from Spring Hill, Tennessee, where I planned to work the night shift on the assembly line at the Saturn plant. And, I'd heard, it was all but untraveled.

"It will take you forever to drive the Trace," they'd said at Saturn when I called to tell them I'd be there in three days' time. "Why don't you take the interstate?"

But right now, forever was exactly what I wanted.

I drove east out of Houston, intending to take I-10 for a couple of hours just to get some distance between me and the city, but I missed the turnoff and found myself on Route 90 to Beaumont. I could have turned and retraced my way to the entrance to the interstate, but didn't bother. So long as I was going the direction I wanted, any road would do.

Night came quickly. To the south, oil derricks and refineries were lit up like fairy-tale cities, sparkling with light. Strings of colored lights threaded the outlines of the homes I passed, making them into ginger-bread houses. A herd of deer picked out in tiny white lights raced across the front of one house, but I was well past it by the time it occurred to me that they'd been reindeer, and that these were Christmas lights.

I vaguely remembered hearing Christmas music everywhere I'd gone in England—carols tinkling in the pharmacy, in the streets as we walked to the lawyer's office, in the hotel lobby where we gathered for mid-morning tea before the funeral—but the music hadn't really registered. I tried to get my mind around the fact that it was now mid-December. It seemed such a short time ago that I'd been lying in the streams of the Palm Springs canyons, submerged in watery relief from the ninety-degree heat.

I turned on the radio to help dispel the sense of displacement, and only increased it with a Cajun station out of Louisiana. I listened, mes-merized, though I could make out little more than half the heavily southern-accented French. Banjos twanged in seasonal dissonance as country-and-western went Gallic:

> *Oh ho ho ho,*
> *Oh ho ho ho,*
> *Joyeux Noël,*
> *C'est le Christmas en la Louisiane . . .*

followed by the announcer's enthused reading of the commercials: "Ce soir c'est Toys for Tots Night . . ."

I spent Toys for Tots Night in a motel outside Beaumont, near where Route 90 hooked up with I-10, with the continuous growl of traffic drowning out the sounds of neighbors' ablutions through the rickety bathroom walls. I took a sleeping pill to ward off coming wide awake in the middle of the night with jet lag, let alone emotional lag. How brilliant the man who named it Halcion, using the association with halcyon days, sunshine dappling through the big plane tree as I lay on the lawn listening to my father hum to himself as he washed the car.

I crossed into Louisiana early the next morning, and the Cajun station kept me company over the Atchafalaya Swamp Highway. Mile after mile it went, all on stilts, elevated above a waterscape so profuse with vegetation that it was hard to tell where there were islands and where simply clumps of trees and grasses sticking out of the water.

Here and there I saw an abandoned flat-bottomed boat, and at one point, an old shack had slid half into the water as though it had tried to become a houseboat and failed miserably in the attempt.

"I could live down there," I suddenly thought—me, who hated slime and jungle and the rank smell of rotting vegetation. The idea seemed immensely appealing: just leave the truck at the side of the elevated highway and climb down, get into one of those flat-bottomed boats, paddle off into the bayous, and lose myself in that vast confusion of dank and rotted life, to emerge—perhaps—a few weeks later, slime covered, a creature from the swamp . . .

The Cajun station faded into static. I played with the dial, and came up with an added layer of dislocation: the familiar voices of Click and Clack broadcasting "Car Talk" all the way from Cambridge, Massachusetts, and sounding as oddly normal as a regular Saturday morning trip back home in Seattle to buy groceries for the weekend. The program was a replay, but I listened with the rapt attention of a child being read the same bedtime story for the umpteenth time, as though there was security in each word, each joke, each caller's remembered tale of automotive woe.

I crossed the Mississippi at Baton Rouge and turned north on Route 61, angling up to Natchez and the start of the Trace. It was a homely kind of road. The traffic was local, mainly battered old pickups, and when I stopped here and there at a diner or a fruit stand, people were friendly with directions. "You're a long way from home," they'd say, looking at the Michigan plates on the truck. I didn't tell them just how long a way.

Even the antebellum homes dotted here and there off the road seemed friendly, not at all the grand mansions I'd anticipated. Now and again, lured by a small sign by the side of the road, I'd nose down a long, winding, dirt driveway. Sunlight dappled through old elms draped with Spanish moss, eerily beautiful in an abandoned sort of way. Some of the mansions, like Catalpa, were little more than cottages hidden away in the woods, distinguished by a few architectural grace notes. Others tried to be more imposing but didn't quite make it, as though their builders had seen *Gone with the Wind* but misjudged the scale.

I didn't really want to stop at Natchez; I sensed that if I spent too long not moving, something would catch up with me. But I had a certain duty to perform. The kids had gone two weeks without a postcard from me, so I left Route 61 and drove on down the hill on postcard patrol.

Natchez, it seemed, was one of those summer towns that closes in on itself for the winter, even though winter here felt like spring back in Seattle. The few people on the sidewalks looked up suspiciously as I drove past, searching for a diner. Most of the stores were closed.

On a side street, a police cruiser stopped by a harmless-looking group of skateboarding teenagers, and the sheriff got out. I slowed to a stop, lowered the window, and listened.

"I'm giving you all one minute to go on home right now before I'm forced to take you in and call your parents," he declared, one hand on the butt of his pistol, the other on his nightstick. It seemed a tad extreme.

"It's not like it's midnight," I wanted to protest. "It's only lunchtime." I kept quiet and waited for the kids to argue the point, but they just shuffled their feet, and one by one went off in different directions.

The sheriff turned to get back in his car, saw me watching, and threw me a hard glance. I took the hint and moved on. This cop liked his streets empty. Tidier that way.

I finally found an open gift store packed with such southern gems as General Robert E. Lee refrigerator magnets. I was the only customer. When I quizzed the owner as to why Natchez was closed down, he said: "Christmas parade."

"Oh, when?"

"This afternoon," he replied, but with a surly unwillingness, as though afraid I might stay and watch.

He kept a sharp eye on me as I browsed the single rack of postcards. Maybe the sheriff had warned him that there was an unsavory element in town. Most of the cards showed the antebellum homes of Natchez, but after the ones out in the country, hidden away down mossy oak-lined tracks, they seemed pretentiously charmless. I was looking for a card showing the Mississippi, but there was none. There was nothing showing the Trace either. I had to settle for one of the crinoline mansions. I could at least draw myself on the verandah, waving hello to the kids.

"Do you have any books about the Trace?" I asked.

He gestured with his head: "You can look over in that corner." I could swear he almost added, "if you must."

There was one, a small paperback called *The Devil's Backbone,* by Jonathan Daniels. I opened it to the contents page, and was delighted to see that the chapter titles lived up to the book's name: "The Grasping Hand," "Harvests of Hatred," "The Devil's Adversaries," "The Trail to Tears." I hadn't expected quite such a soap opera. I read a few pages. Luridly detailed, they seemed to have been written in a state of near-delirium, caused perhaps by Daniels's fondness for alliteration. In no time at all, I'd been introduced to a vast cast of such stock operatic characters as "doomed strangers," "brawny blacks," "great gamblers," "double dealers," "tow-headed children," "swashbuckling soldiers," and "garrulous gaffers."

Who could resist? I bought the book, and thus fortified for the lonely drive ahead, wandered on down to the levee. The river was broad and empty, not a single vessel on it aside from a tourist paddle steamer docked for the winter. From my vantage point atop the levee, I was suddenly very aware that I was back east.

I'd driven cross-country three times before, each time in one of those mad interstate races against the clock. Yet even then, the Mississippi had demanded that I stop and get out, look at the river and recognize it as a border between East and West. Because the moment I crossed it, in either direction, the world had changed.

It wasn't just a matter of a far more intensive use of land east of the river; nor of the scaling down in size of all things natural; nor of the greater number of buildings and barns and houses. It was more than all these: a matter of climate, partly, but above all a matter of culture—culture dictated by the land and the history of its settlement. Cross the river from West to East, and that pioneer sense of space and vastness which is so much part of the West and Midwest simply disappears. The trees close in. The land achieves a certain lushness. You are in more settled country.

I used to puzzle at why the prairie land west of the Mississippi was called the Midwest, even though geographically speaking it's not midwest at all. If anything, it's mideast. But there is a truth beyond geography. The simple act of crossing this river takes you from one world into another.

There was no Charon carting his unhappy cargo from one bank of the river to the other; the Mississippi was a mild silvery gray in the winter sunlight, and far too wide for the narrow blackness of that other, mythical river, the Styx. Yet it seemed to create almost as distinct a boundary. One side felt open and sparse—a kind of death to some, but life to me. And now, here in Natchez, it felt like the world was closing in again.

I didn't wait for the Christmas parade. I had to move. I turned my back to the river, drove up the hill back to Route 61, and headed a few miles north to the beginning of the Trace.

A turn-in at the beginning of the parkway had one of those Park Service displays of informational posters, each glassed in under a small shingled roof. The largest of them gave me the somewhat clumsy official version of the Trace's history:

"Natchez was once a major port of the Mississippi, in the extreme southwestern corner of the United States, threatened by Spain in 1800 and later by France and Great Britain. President Jefferson in 1801 decided that a road from Nashville was necessary for the safety and welfare of our nation. 'This road being completed, I shall consider our southern extremities secured, the Indians in that quarter at our feet, and adjacent provinces laid open to us,' said James Wilkinson.

"United States soldiers built the road, but the road in fact followed a wilderness road called the Old Natchez Trace, made from old animal and Indian trails, and traders, soldiers, 'Kaintucks,' postriders, circuit-riding preachers, outlaws, settlers, and adventurers trampled a national road. Natchez Trace: a bond that held the southwest to the rest of the nation, a channel for the flow of people and ideas, a memorial to the thousands."

To the thousands of what or whom was not clear. Neither was much else. James Wilkinson was not even identified as the revolutionary general who had become the governor of upper Louisiana. I thought I detected a touch of Jonathan Daniels in that long list of tramplers, but suspected that this language had been decided on in the kind of endless interdepartmental meetings that wear everyone down to the point where they compromise just to get out of the room.

Still, I liked those Kaintucks even before I figured out who they were. Men with the mark of Cain on them, clearly. Mad, bad, and more than a little dangerous to know. President Andrew Jackson would have agreed with me, at least as quoted in *The Devil's Backbone.* "I never met a Kentuckian who did not have a rifle, a pack of cards, and a bottle of whiskey," Daniels had him saying, though I had a feeling that the man known as Old Hickory was equipped in much the same fashion at the time.

The Trace did indeed come into being as a series of Indian hunting paths—Natchez, Chickasaw, and Choctaw Indians. Those not killed were pushed to the west of the Mississippi by the Spaniards and the French as well as by the newly arrived Americans; with the flesh-and-blood Indians safely out of the way, the white settlers felt free to use their tribal name for the new town at the base of the Trace. And Natchez might then have had a fairly sedate history were it not for an odd anomaly in time—the thirty years still to go until the steamboat era.

By 1785, American settlers in the Ohio River valley were using the Mississippi to deliver crops and products to Natchez and New Orleans. Flour, tobacco, pelts, iron, and Monongahela whiskey came downriver on flatboats. But without power, there was no way to get the boats upriver again. They were sold for lumber on arrival, and the traders, after a few nights in the whorehouses of Natchez-under-the-Hill, faced the long walk home up the Trace.

Over the next twenty years, the path they stamped was improved into a wilderness road with primitive inns, known as stands, along the way, plus a couple of missions. But if the Trace was improved, it was definitely not tamed. Cutthroats, shifty stand owners, and inexplicably hostile Indians threatened life, limb, and sanity, as did bears, cougars, copperheads, cottonmouths, rattlers, fire ants, and good old poison ivy. When steamboats came in, they offered relative speed and safety. By the time a nineteen-year-old Abraham Lincoln floated a flatboat a thousand miles downriver in 1828, the way home was a cheap berth on the open deck of a steamboat, and the Trace was history.

It literally sank into oblivion. A small section of the original Trace near the beginning of the parkway turned out to be nothing more than a wide ditch: a long-abandoned path sunken in its traces, its banks all but hidden by a profusion of oaks and pines, locust and gum trees, and held together by tangled masses of roots, vines, and mosses.

A four-hundred-mile-long flat-bottomed ditch was not what I'd expected. Let alone one that was sometimes as much as twenty feet deep. Even one that, per Daniels, was so lush with wild strawberries in the summer that horses' legs were stained red to the knees with the trampled juice. In the heyday of the Trace, it had been a ten-day ride to carry the mail between Nashville and Natchez; for me, on the new parkway, it would be no more than a ten-hour drive in all. And my tires wouldn't be stained red with strawberry juice.

I followed the section of the old Trace a hundred yards or so until the banks closed in on me. The ditch narrowed to a mere three or four feet, just wide enough for a single horse to pass if it hadn't been so overgrown with creepers and brambles. The word *snakes* flashed large in my mind, like a neon "espresso" sign in a coffee-shop window but with the opposite effect. I took refuge back in the truck and began the long meandering drive north by northeast.

★

I am in a motel room in Port Gibson, Mississippi, some forty miles up the Trace. I am lying on the bed, reading psalms from the Gideon Bible in the bedside table, and I am crying—slow, gentle, tears, so that I have to keep wiping my eyes as I read.

Somehow it's good to cry in a strange place. I understand all those people who hit the road when they're troubled. There's an odd comfort in being a total stranger.

I called a friend in New York not long ago. She said how weird it must be for me to be surrounded by strangers, people who never met Jessel and don't know Sybil.

"It seems like it should be," I replied, "but it's not. It's a weird kind of comfort." And even as I spoke, I could hear the oddly distant tone in my own voice, as though I were on some strange drug.

In fact I don't feel surrounded by anyone at all. I feel as though I'm drifting loose in space.

I get up and pour myself a glass of brandy from the bottle my colleague brought over that night in Houston, then sit on the edge of the bed, conscientiously sipping, an occasional drinker trying as hard as she can to drink seriously. I think of the brandy I drank the night after the funeral, sitting out alone on the steps of my parents' house. My mother's house now.

My father's brandy. Good cognac. *Eau de vie*, in French. Water of life.

The ritual was stark and horrifying. An orthodox Jewish funeral, with no disguise, no attempt to smooth things over. The coffin under a coarse black shroud. The crude wooden cart, its black paint chipped with use. The long walk to the gravesite, my mother, my brother, and I pushing the coffin on the cart. The shroud removed at the grave. The plain pine coffin with rope handles. The brief, almost curt, graveside prayers. The lowering of the coffin. The shovelfuls of dirt thrown into the grave. The awful, final thud as each shower of dirt and stones landed on the pine box.

And later, shivering in the cold midnight air, with my father's brandy beside me, reciting the *kaddish* prayer for the dead that I, as a woman, had not been allowed to say at the Orthodox funeral.

"*Yisgadal ve-yiskadesh shmai robo . . .*"

I chanted the words slowly, alone, in the dark. Again and again. As though I'd been saying them all my life. Words of ancient Hebrew and Aramaic. Words familiar from too many funerals. Words that send shivers down my spine each time I hear them, as though each time were the first time. Awful words. Words full of awe.

My flesh rises in goosebumps as I remember, and I start the chant again, here, in this anodyne motel room. The words bounce off the bare white walls. They tremble and echo. Echo and tremble.

And suddenly I am in a ball on the floor, curled up on my knees, and great racking sobs are filling the room as though someone were tearing them by force out of my chest.

I hide my head in my arms against the emptiness around me.

★

I took another sleeping pill that night, closed the curtains tight, and blanked out into a deep, dreamless sleep. An early morning frost reminded me that I was heading north, but the sun still seemed springlike, with just enough warmth in it to make me glad to be on the road, ambling slowly along with the windows open.

I spent the next two days on the Trace parkway, grateful for its curving contours and 50-mph speed limit. Not a road to be rushed, the speed limit seemed to say. A road to be savored. A speed that allowed time for thoughts and memories, for the guilts and regrets, good times and bad times, that went rolling through my mind as I rolled along.

I could lose myself here among the ghosts that lined the road: the old Indian burial mounds, the empty sites of mission stations, the Civil War battlefields, the Confederate gravesites, the stand where Meriwether Lewis, his trailblazing to the Pacific Northwest long behind him, died, either by his own hand or at the hands of others, the answer long lost in the brambles of the Trace.

I stopped to climb down waterfalls. Explore caves. Stare at blank headstones. Gaze into swamps. Examine the remains of stands once advertised as "houses of entertainment in the wilderness." And every now and then, I'd walk a short section of the old, sunken trace where it criss-crossed the new parkway, as though to reassure myself that I was still on the right path. That there was truly an ongoing link between new and old. That the Trace hadn't sunk into oblivion.

Chapter Sixteen

Back in 1990, a few months before the Saturn plant opened in Spring Hill, Tennessee, I'd gone to a dinner in New York given by the new General Motors subsidiary. There were a dozen of us around the table: five executives, five journalists, and, to my astonishment, two union representatives. And before we'd even finished the soup, I had a strange feeling that, like Alice in Wonderland, I'd stumbled into the wrong place, or the wrong time, or the wrong something.

They talked of a new mission, one that would revolutionize American business. They'd make cars differently at Saturn; management would work in cooperation with union, and workers would take full part in decision-making. They spoke of a new philosophy of work, as though words like *philosophy* were everyday parlance at General Motors. And the more they spoke, the stronger grew the feeling that I was not at an auto-industry dinner at all, but at a revivalist meeting.

The light of the true believer shone in their eyes—the same light I'd seen in the eyes of student radicals and religious converts. Their voices lifted and lilted with excitement. They spread their arms wide in expansive gestures, as though about to embrace the whole world. By the time dessert arrived, I had an uneasy feeling someone was about to burst into a spiritual or a chorus of Hallelujahs.

What was most disconcerting was that these were hard-bitten executives. They hadn't climbed to the higher ranks of GM or the UAW by being soft-hearted or mushy-minded, yet they certainly sounded that way. In fact, they sounded like the bright-eyed young psychology student I'd been back in the sixties, when I was convinced that with workers' participation in the means of production, industrial work could be revolutionized.

At that point in my life, of course, I had never set foot inside any kind of industrial plant. But where I could at least plead naiveté, these men could not.

It was tempting to conclude that they were quite nuts. Or else that I was. A social innovation from General Motors? From the company that in the past few years had laid off thousands of workers? From what I thought of as the Pentagon of the automotive world, where paranoia ruled the roost? From the largest, most authoritarian, and most wasteful of auto companies? The company that had colluded in the past against tramlines and railroads? Sat on innovations such as antilock brakes for thirty years? Whose CEO, Roger Smith, had just been cruelly but justifiably lampooned in Michael Moore's documentary, *Roger and Me?* This same Roger Smith had given the okay to an outbreak of bright-eyed idealism in his ranks?

I've never been much for evangelism, which may partly explain my unease at this display of quasi-religious fervor. But there was more to it. There was a somewhat antiquated feel to the fervor—something a touch too close, perhaps, to Henry Ford's chilling dictum that "the man who builds a factory, builds a temple; the man who works there, worships there." No matter how sincere the beliefs being voiced around that New York dinner table, it seemed highly unlikely that they could bear any relation to the sheer drudgery involved in actually building cars.

Yet in the intervening years, Saturn had been a remarkable success. It had become the only automaker to make a profit building small cars. It had been quoted the world over as a model of how to run a company. It had changed the way cars are sold, cutting out the haggling process in favor of fixed prices. It advertised itself as "the auto company with a difference," and that difference was clear even in how I had arrived at the plant in Spring Hill: not at the invitation of management, but at the invitation of the union.

"Just call me when you want to come visit," union coordinator Bryan Czape had said. I had, and he'd arranged everything, appealing to my

sense of romanticism when he suggested working the night shift. I tried
to imagine a journalist setting up a visit to any other automobile plant
this way, and utterly failed. I'd never even get in the door.

★

"You're in Tennessee?" my mother said when I called her after driving
east from the top of the Natchez Trace. "I've always wanted to go to
Tennessee. It sounds so romantic."

This seemed a strange romance for someone who'd lived the last fifty
years in the Thames Valley. What was she thinking of, I wondered. Tennessee Williams? The TVA? Davy Crockett? Mockingbirds? Grace-
land?

I didn't tell her I was here to work a shift in an auto plant. I felt
vaguely guilty about it, as though going back to work was being somehow disloyal to my father's memory. Instead, I picked out a postcard
down in the motel lobby. Horses, a pond, an old barn, rolling pasture.
"Sybil, it really is like this," I scribbled on the back. Very like the English woodlands and farmlands where I'd spent my childhood, in fact.

My pen moved to the right-hand side of the card, and I realized with
a jolt how odd it was to address it just to her, not to the two of them.

I took the last Halcion I had and made an early night of it. Like a
long-distance runner loading up on carbohydrates, I needed to load up
on sleep. Bryan had me scheduled to tour the plant from eight the next
morning to five in the afternoon and then to work on the line until three
the following morning. With Christmas so close, our original plans for
me to spend a week at Saturn had been compressed to two days. We had
a lot to fit in, and I wondered if I'd make it. I was still in a shaky state
of mind.

But I slept hard and deep, and woke to a frosty dawn. I grabbed some
breakfast and drove up Route 31, checking my directions every few minutes; I could see no sign of a heavy industrial plant among these rolling
green hills just an hour's drive south of Nashville. It wasn't until I turned
onto a landscaped access road that I finally caught sight of the plant, and
then I did a double take. I'd expected blackened smokestacks and grimy
brick walls. Instead, I saw a low spread of white roofs and towers nes-

tled in a dip between the hills and shimmering downright prettily in the early morning sun.

I'd left England when I was twenty, but what came to mind at this moment was William Blake: "And did those feet in ancient time, Walk upon England's mountains green? . . . And was Jerusalem builded here, Among these dark Satanic mills?" One of the best-loved tunes in the English hymnal.

Saturn was certainly not a dark Satanic mill, but what was it, then? A light Satanic mill? Or indeed a new Jerusalem—the social revolution it claimed to be?

The evening before, I'd read through the Memorandum of Agreement between "Saturn Corporation (Saturn), a wholly-owned subsidiary of General Motors Corporation (GM) and the International Union, United Automobile, Aerospace and Agricultural Implement Workers of America (Union)." This thirty-two-page booklet was hammered out in the late eighties and was the basis for the formation of Saturn. It's still given to every new employee, on the floor, in the offices, and in the salesrooms. And to every visitor too.

It was a quite remarkable document. Saturn and the UAW, read the Preamble, "have long recognized the need for a new approach to Union/Management relations" and have agreed on "a cooperative problem-solving relationship" in a "renewed spirit of mutual respect and recognition of each other's stakes and equities."

From the outset, it continued, "Saturn has been, and is, a joint effort of both Union and Management."

And under the heading "Saturn Philosophy" was the following: "We believe that all people want to be involved in decisions that affect them, care about their jobs and each other, take pride in themselves and in their contributions, and want to share in the success of their efforts."

Given such heady language, it was no wonder I was humming hymns and thinking back to my starry-eyed student days.

★

When I arrived, Mike Bennett and Bob Boruff had been locked in intense negotiations on a new contract for almost a week. Bennett was the head of Spring Hill's UAW Local 1853 and chairman of its bargaining unit; Boruff was a GM vice-president of manufacturing and the top management man here at the plant.

I was scheduled to meet the two men together. This seemed to me an unlikely scenario under any circumstances, let alone in the middle of contract negotiations. But sure enough, at nine in the morning, they emerged from a meeting room full of grim-faced negotiators, grabbed some coffee, and sat down with me at a nearby desk.

"What about the negotiations?" I asked.

"They'll continue without us," said Boruff.

Bennett gave a thin smile: "We could do with a break."

He had disconcertingly pale gray eyes, matching his hair. The kind of man who would take your measure, file it away for future reference, and act accordingly. I'd been told he had a tough, sharp intellect and a sure grasp on the history of social theory. Not exactly your usual union man, though his credentials were impeccable. Before becoming the head of the Spring Hill local, he'd been a union leader in Flint, Michigan.

Beside him, Boruff had some of that bluff cordiality that is really cordial bluff—a corporate style at GM. Before joining Saturn, he'd run one of GM's most notoriously old-fashioned plants, Flint's Buick City facility. But he seemed a good deal less wary than most GM executives, who generally opt for defensive stonewalling over communication. Like Bennett's, his face was heavily lined for a man in his early fifties. These two were both a team and adversaries, and the conflicting roles had taken their toll.

"I did it the adversarial way, and we saw how that worked," said Bennett. "What I do now is more managerial than adversarial. In the old world, representation uses the bargaining process, and that's all. Here, the assembly-line work teams democratically elect representatives, and so on up through a series of levels, so that there's representation all the way to the top. We're equal partners in running the plant."

"*Equal* partners?"

"You bet. That's our competitive edge," said Boruff. "Everyone participates, and everyone is responsible. If there's conflict, we work it out.

We use the idea of conflict management as a constructive device. We see it as creative tension, leading to positive change."

There were a couple of leaps in logic that evaded me here, but I knew that this combination of psychology, democracy, and hard-headed business was the latest thing in the business world. Boruff was regularly invited to lecture to the top executives of Fortune 500 companies on the Saturn way of doing things. Business never argues with success. But of course I do.

"I still don't see exactly how this works," I persisted.

"Try thinking of it as an enterprise republic," said Bennett. I tried, but found myself thinking of Plato's Republic instead, with its strict divisions between peons and elite. "What we have here is a consensus decision-making process at every level."

"Consensus?" My voice took on the querulousness I hated hearing in it during endless dock meetings back home as my neighbors and I worked on the wording for a new moorage lease. The insistence on consensus decision-making—very much the Seattle political style—had been driving me somewhat crazy. And there were only fifteen of us there; there were ten thousand people at Saturn.

"Consensus?" I repeated. "That must take forever!"

Bennett nodded calmly. "True, you do spend more time on decision-making, but it also means that once you reach an agreement, you can implement it very fast and effectively. When you arrive at a decision, it sticks."

"It's kind of a Yogi Berra thing," added Boruff. "A decision is not a decision until it's implemented."

"Still," I insisted, "management and labor have major differences. Otherwise contract negotiations would be a breeze. Where's the consensus when management wants to pay less for more work and labor wants to be paid more for less work?"

"That's the essence of it," said Bennett, "letting go of that absolutism. I use what I call the seventy percent comfort rule."

"It works?"

That thin smile again. "Eventually."

Boruff nodded as he watched me wondering if a seventy percent comfort rule would work back home. "It's a whole different world from Frederick Taylor's time," he said.

"Ah yes, Henry Ford's favorite management consultant," I quipped, drawing a real grin from Bennett.

Maybe you had to have worked in Detroit to even remember the name of F. W. Taylor. I hadn't heard it since a student course on what was then still called "industrial psychology." Taylor, alias Speedy Fred, was the inventor of time-and-motion studies. He was the man behind old film clips of efficiency experts standing by the assembly line, stopwatches in hand, measuring workers' every movement to figure out how to get them to work faster. Or the assembly line speeding up in Charlie Chaplin's *Modern Times,* and the little man's desperate, futile attempts to keep up.

"That was the old-world paradigm," said Boruff, "the one that defined the adversarial relationship between management and labor. In the new paradigm, we're changing the whole way we organize work."

"And in the process of redefining work, we're also redefining management," added Bennett. "Bob here is doing his job very differently from when he was back in the old world."

That phrase "the old world" kept coming up. It meant the adversarial world of Detroit, and in particular the outmoded, benighted management style that pervades GM. And though neither Bennett nor Boruff went so far as to call Saturn "the new world," that was clearly what it was, as though they were Pilgrim Fathers set out to establish a new society.

They'd left behind the urban blight of Detroit and ventured six hundred miles south to the idyllic hills of rural Tennessee. Here, freed of the old restraints, they'd established their enterprise republic, and begun preaching their revolutionary message back to the old world. Only, the old world didn't want to know. As in history, so too here: the old world was downright dismayed by what it had given birth to.

The Saturn experiment had been so successful that it put the rest of GM in question, and what giant corporation was going to stand for that? While other Fortune 500 companies might be listening to Boruff's message that the status quo of adversarial labor-management relations would kill American competitiveness, his own parent company was not. And that rankled.

The shadow of Detroit loomed large over the gentle green hills of the new Jerusalem as Boruff began to pick his words carefully. "There's a feeling of ownership to a unique process here. But there's a lot of fear— let's call it apprehension—that we will perhaps not be allowed to continue with that degree of freedom, to be able to evaluate the best process for the company without dictates from a giant overseer."

In my mind, I glimpsed GM personified in the form of a black-leather-clad colossus towering over Spring Hill, whip in hand.

"It's a disappointment that the things we found successful for us are not embraced by General Motors," Boruff continued. "We were set up to think about doing business differently, and we've proved that it works, yet there's no real momentum on the part of GM to get over here and see it. Because this is part of our mission: to transfer this social process based on teamwork back to GM."

The man had just tiptoed through a minefield. All three of us knew that though nothing had blown up in his face, it could hardly be called a successful passage. In Detroit, he was a vice-president of GM; in Spring Hill, he was the top manager of Saturn. The two roles were in direct conflict, and it didn't seem to be a creative one.

★

Bryan took me walking through the plant. I'd toured many auto plants before, and physically this was not much different. That is, it was an assault on the senses: an enclosed, windowless world of harsh artificial light and hard concrete floors ringing with the discordant cacophony of industrial production.

Metal rang on metal. Stamping presses clanked, power tools whined, pulleys groaned, hoists clanged, welding robots whooshed, sparks crackled, lasers beeped, compressed air hissed, bolts banged into place, trolleys rumbled down the aisles, and all the while, conveyor belts carrying cars in one stage or another of production, from bare metal frames to fully painted bodies, clattered and clanketed beside us and behind us and even over our heads.

It had never been hard to understand the blank, vaguely hostile stares I'd get from people working on the line. They resented the visitor staring in wide-eyed ease as they labored. In their place, so would I. But here, those stares didn't exist. Partly, of course, this was because I was with "one of ours," a union man, but there was more to it than that. There was simply less here to be hostile about.

Between stops to chat with people on the line—Bryan had just gotten engaged to be married and everyone wanted to congratulate him—I figured out that what wasn't here was in some ways more important than what was. No time clocks, for example. No executive parking. No separate management dining. No uniforms beyond eye protectors and yellow Kevlar gloves to prevent burns and scrapes. And as stipulated in the Memorandum of Agreement, no layoffs except under "catastrophic conditions."

The workforce was divided into three giant groups rotating between day and night shifts of ten hours a shift, four shifts a week—a system devised and voted on by labor, not by management. It meant that the average Saturn employee had six consecutive days off at least once a month, and actually worked 180 days a year.

To a freelance writer whose income depends on her wits and who tends to work 365 days a year—well, maybe 350—working at Saturn was beginning to look rather attractive. And by the time we reached the open, airy cafeteria, more like a fern bar than a factory cafe, it even began to look healthy.

No junk food or sugar energy for Saturn workers. The soft drinks case had large sections of Evian water, fresh fruit juice, and sport drinks, and only a small section of soda pop. The rolls were fresh-baked, the quiche was light and delicate, and if there was ever anything battered and fried, it wasn't on the menu today.

We settled down at the same table as a team leader who unselfconsciously crossed himself and said a silent grace before starting on his salad of sprouts and beans. It seemed an incongruously small meal for such a large, muscular man.

"Is this your first visit to Spring Hill?" he asked. And when he heard it was, launched into a paean of praise for the good life in Tennessee.

"Part of the lure of the place for many of us who grew up in Detroit was the recognition of the value system we remembered as kids," he said. "The idea of open doors, open spaces, small-town values. No crime, no drugs. A good place to bring up kids. What we have here is the outdoor life, a pony in the back yard, weekend fishing trips with our sons. A sense of community, and no fear on the streets."

He was only in his mid-thirties. Detroit could have been no haven of peacefulness when he was a kid. But as he talked on, it occurred to me that this was a generic past, a mythic American childhood that he could now give his own children even if he himself had never experienced it—a middle-class semi-rural white lifestyle that he, an urban black, was now part of.

"A simpler, healthier lifestyle," as he put it, "with old-fashioned, traditional values."

Perhaps even a bit too traditional. After lunch, Bryan and I toured the two refurbished antebellum homes on the Saturn estate. They were perfect expressions of the longing for an idealized past, even though both homes claimed historical fame as places where Confederate generals were wined and dined before going into battle against the Union. Besides, as is the American way, the past had been reconstructed to fit the present. The original occupants would have been horrified at how both mansions looked now. They were all decked out for Christmas, and in addition to the trees and the wreaths and the silver stars, they were decorated throughout with photographs of Saturn workers and their families, silver-framed black faces smiling along with white over the mantels of the South's ornate marble fireplaces.

Upstairs in one of the mansions, I opened the French windows onto the narrow balcony and stared out through the pillars, Scarlett surveying her domain. I wandered through the bedrooms, bounced on the four-poster beds, tested the brass faucets in the marbled bathrooms. From one of the back bedrooms, I could just see the roofline of the plant a mile or so away.

I glanced at the ornately framed oil paintings on the walls, the usual bland landscapes and crinolined ladies and English hunting scenes.

Then came to an abrupt halt in front of the fireplace. A copy of El Greco's *Storm over Toledo* was hanging over it, the city shining high on the hill in the luminous light of the storm.

It wasn't a great copy, but I was stunned by it nevertheless. The mystic El Greco is one of my favorite painters, and his presence here was a strange collision of worlds, a reminder of the improbability of my own presence in the world of cars. It was like seeing an old friend from one world in a completely new context. "What are you doing here?" you ask, only to get the same question echoing back: "What are *you* doing here?"

★

At five in the afternoon, I started work, joining three other workers stationed around a huge rotating machine. Our job was to feed a robot.

Officially, we were preparing dashboard molds for foam injection. In fact, we were simply loading and unloading the machine for the robot, which injected the foam and then wiped its own nozzle as though it were wiping its nose—one of those infuriatingly human gestures that make you think, "Cute," and then hate yourself for having thought it.

This was one of the simplest tasks on the whole assembly line. Squirt some filler release into a hole. Lift a light plastic mold and place it on a protruding lip of the machine. Bang a board with your knee to drop three locks to hold the mold in place. Check the locks. Push a black button to bring the lip down into the right position for the next guy. Wait for the machine to rotate and present you with a new lip. And that was it. A ten-second job to be repeated ad infinitum.

At least there was plenty of time to talk. Dave, the blond, lanky man whose job this usually was, stood beside me, making sure I was "doing all right." We'd found a connection almost instantly. He used to be in the Coast Guard, part of the time on the 44-foot self-righting motor lifeboats; the past spring, I'd spent a week on those boats at the Motor Lifeboat School at the mouth of the Columbia River. As the machine clanked and rotated, and I shoved on molds and banged buttons, he told me how he'd left the Guard to go to work at the Buick City plant in Flint—he still had a crooked middle finger on his right hand from a conveyor belt accident there—only to get laid off in the early eighties. He'd been out of work for ten years until Saturn started up and he'd moved South.

"I've just turned forty," he said. "That means seventeen years to go."

"To what?"

"Retirement."

"Seventeen more years of . . . ?" I couldn't quite finish the sentence, not wanting to insult him. I couldn't imagine doing this job for more than an hour, let alone seventeen years.

He nodded. "You got it. Why do you think they pay me so well? They pay me to be bored."

Oh sure, working at Saturn had its good points. "It's fairly loose. We decide within the team when to take a break, determine our own vacations and schedules, do our own quality checks, swap jobs within the team. There's fourteen of us and we get on well with each other, but for all that, it's really just another job on the line."

He missed "the old world." What Boruff and Bennett meant by that phrase was their business. To Dave, it meant simply his life back in Michigan. "All my friends are still up there. I know people go on about living down here being basic American values and so on, but"—he shrugged—"the truth is I find it bland. Besides, the fishing's no good. Only bass. No steelhead, no salmon."

Soon he was asking me as many questions as I'd asked him, curious as to how a writer earns a living. We discovered that he and I had earned just about the same amount in the past year.

"But I don't have a pension and I can't retire," I pointed out.

"You don't need to," he said. "You're doing what you want to do."

Touché.

The team called a ten-minute break, and a sheet of paper detailing the latest status of the contract negotiations was distributed. There'd be a $2,000 ratification bonus, an annual college tuition grant for all Saturn workers and their family members, and extra bonuses based on quality and customer-satisfaction surveys. The sticking point was over post-retirement health-care benefits.

Dave and I sat down, broke open a couple of cans of Diet Seven-Up, and got into the issue of quality. I gave him my usual line about how when the average price of a new car is half the average annual income, the least anyone could expect is that it have no defects.

"If you worked on the line," he said, "you'd be a lot more forgiving."

"How so?"

"Say there's a rattle or a loose wire. I'd think maybe the guy on the line was hung over that day, or maybe he had an argument with his wife, or trouble with the kids. His mind was elsewhere. You see how it is: you can't keep your mind long on this kind of work. You'd be inhuman not to wander off. And that's when mistakes creep in."

"Still, there's fewer of them nowadays. American cars are much better made. How come that happened? Less drugs and alcohol? Higher awareness of quality?"

"Nah. That's all management b.s. It's because we're afraid for our jobs. Back in the early eighties we weren't afraid for them. It never occurred to us we could be laid off. You got a union card and the job was yours for life, so there was no reason to work hard or make sure quality was high. Now we know what can happen." And with a half-grin, half-grimace: "Plus I've got a dozen team members who are going to get on my case if I don't do my job properly because that'll hold us up as a team and make life difficult for them."

"But what about the 'Saturn difference'?"

He shrugged. "Once, I'd have agreed. That's when our paychecks used to read 'Saturn, a subsidiary of GM.' Now they simply say 'GM.' Just so's you know who's really in charge."

The light was dimming fast on the new Jerusalem. Labor might be equal partners in running the plant, but the profits went to GM. "Employees sharing in the success of their efforts" did not mean actual shares, but old-fashioned bonuses based on performance, even if quality had replaced quantity as the prime criterion. And though the conditions of employment at Saturn were vastly better than at any other plant in America's hidebound auto industry, the day-to-day, hour-to-hour experience on the line was still a clanking monotony.

Unless, of course, the job was so complex that there was no time to register the monotony. Two hours later, I left Dave and moved from one of the simplest jobs on the line to one of the most complicated: assembling the whole instrument panel. Steering wheel, indicator and wiper wands, gauges, dashboard liner, the lot.

Audrey, the woman whose task it was to teach me this job, had a tough challenge ahead of her.

I guessed she was in her mid-thirties. Despite a mass of long brown curly hair, she had a boyish way to her, maybe because of the leather builder's apron she was wearing, its pockets so full of connectors and screws and bolts that it took me a while to realize she was six months pregnant.

"Is this your first?" I asked.

She burst out laughing. "Honey, I'm forty-three years old. And a grandmother. I married again not long ago, and"—she spread her arms wide and stared at her belly—"just look what happened. This sure is the last thing I ever expected."

"How long will you go on working?"

She laughed again. "Do you know how much kids cost? I'm staying right here till the day I pop."

She hadn't stopped working for a moment as we talked. She couldn't. The line was rolling, and it was either keep up or bring everything to a halt. We were standing *on* the line, a wide conveyor belt rumbling past an array of shelves piled high with parts, and beneath an overhead rack dangling power tools and bins of screws. On the line with us, every six feet or so, was a workstand holding an empty dashboard shell, placed upside down on the stand so that it was easy to work on. Audrey's job was to make it into a complete instrument panel.

For the first few moments, standing on the moving belt was almost childishly fun. The world was reversed: you stood still and it went past you. Your mind knew it was you moving, not the world, but your senses told you otherwise. And all the time, the belt vibrated gently underfoot; if it weren't for the noise, it might even have been pleasantly sexy.

"Watch your head," Audrey said, and I ducked as a power wrench came dangling past my right ear. Followed by another. And yet another. Even though I reminded myself that it was me moving, not them, every time I looked up they seemed to be aiming for my brains with a certain inexorable malevolence.

I spent the first half-hour watching Audrey and figuring out how to stay out of the way. So far as I could make out, she had a total of some fifty separate procedures to complete in a logic-defying sequence of about three minutes. Each step had to be performed in perfect timing, so that the right parts and tools were at hand exactly when she needed them. And to add to the pressure, this job was what they called a "show-stopper."

Farther on down the line, the completed instrument panel would be lowered into the "smile joint"—a large lazy U going from side to side of the car's frame. If it didn't fit, the line would stop, and the whole plant would start running behind. "You can't go back and do it again," Audrey said. "You got to do it perfect the first time."

I knew I'd never be able to do this job. Yet Audrey seemed convinced that I was educable. She talked each movement out loud as she worked, with me following her around like a pet dog. Somehow, she convinced me to do a bit here and a bit there, until within an hour, I had the beginning of it down pat:

Walk six stands down the line, past other team members at different stages of the job, and read the manifest hanging on the dashboard shell. Pick up different parts from the shelves alongside the line, depending on whether this is to be a sedan or a wagon, an automatic or a manual shift. Jam a leather sheath over the sharp metal edge to the side of the module. Ease the parts into place. Snap-connect electrical wires: gray to the right, blue to the middle, white to the left.

So far so good. I was feeling quite proud of myself. Trouble was, this was only the beginning of the beginning.

The rest began to blur: Snap-connect a black fastener, then a yellow one. Don't delay. If you go too slow, the line will take you past the parts you need, and you'll have to start running back and forth for them. Pick up the steering shaft from a shelf and ease its thirty-pound weight down through the center of the module. Arrange the wires to run over the top of the shaft. Slip on and snap a green fastener . . .

Or were those last two steps the other way round? "Here," said Audrey, redoing my work.

Okay, now pick up two bronze-colored bolts and screws, two black bolts, a circular piece, and two silver bolts from those big bins alongside the line. Insert the silver bolts. Fine. Place the bronze-colored ones in one place, the black ones in another. Great. Pull down a power wrench from the overhead line . . .

I grabbed for it and missed. It began to recede from me. I stretched and yanked it down just in time to tighten the bolts. I had no idea of what I was bolting to what, or why. Neither, it turned out, did Audrey.

Right, you've got those bolts nice and tight. Now pick different bronze-colored bolts from another bin. No, not alongside the line—right here, hanging overhead. Fine. Insert them and tighten them by hand for now. What about the wrench? Not there yet, that comes soon. First, thread the electrical wires through the back of the module and out through this flap, then loop them over and under the shaft like so, and then . . .

Then what? I couldn't remember. And I was only a third of the way through the job.

"Don't worry," said Audrey. "It takes most people four days to learn this job. You're doing real good."

That was sweet of her, but it didn't feel real good to me. My attention strayed for a moment, I lost a beat, and suddenly the power tools and screw bins were bearing down on me way before I was ready for them. I worked as fast as I could, one eye on my hands, the other on the dangling wrench going past. I swore, lunged for it, and yanked at the cord as though if I pulled hard enough I could pull back the whole line and slow things down to my pace. I remembered Charlie's desperation in *Modern Times*, and suddenly there was nothing remotely funny about it. I dropped a bolt, reached for the wrong wrench, and watched pathetically as Audrey stepped in and put everything to rights. I hadn't felt quite this incompetent since I was a kid trying to thread a sewing machine at school. I never did master that.

The Saturn people were crazy to let me even try this job. I could already see the news reports. "Saturn Cars Recalled," the headline would read. "Instrument panel problems have led to the recall of two hundred Saturn cars after customers complained that the windshield wiper wands controlled the lights. In some cars, the headlamp wand turned on the air-conditioning. In others, it came off in drivers' hands. The problem first came to light when a steering wheel shaft fell into a driver's lap. Fortunately, the car was not in motion at the time, since the ignition was incorrectly wired."

"Try not to get behind," said Audrey, "because that's when mistakes happen."

"Umh," I said. And gave a silent thanks to the person checking quality at the end of this section.

Every time I thought I had the hang of it all, another two steps somehow reversed themselves in my mind, or one slipped out of existence altogether. My ears were ringing, my mind was reeling, and my hands had never felt clumsier. I began to fumble the screws, inserting them at an angle so that they wouldn't tighten properly and had to be taken out and inserted anew. Audrey was working as hard as I was by now; we stood shoulder to shoulder, me fouling things up, her fixing them.

And suddenly it was ten o'clock, and there was a half-hour break for lunch. Ten at night, that is. By now, I was squinting to stop from seeing double. I was convinced that if I could just work through to the end of the shift, I'd get this job down pat. But as the line came to a halt and everything stopped moving, some remote part of my brain managed to signal a weak but just decipherable message that the pressure was getting to me. It was time to call it quits before I damaged a car, or myself, or worse still, somebody else.

"Don't you want some lunch before you go?" said Audrey. But I was too exhausted to even look at food. I needed fresh air. And solitude. And silence. I made my excuses, stuffed my yellow Kevlar gloves into my pocket as a memento, got lost twice trying to find the way out, and finally emerged into the parking lot.

Never had a parking lot seemed so beautiful: so quiet, so peaceful, so serene. Even the buzzing yellow of the sodium vapor lights seemed soothing. Behind me, the plant hummed gently, its skylights glowing into the night. Midshift, I was the only person out here, and I had a flash of guilt mixed with giddy freedom, the kind that comes from play-ing hooky.

I found the truck, climbed in, made to start it up. Then stopped, hand in midair, and sat staring at the instrument panel. Something was wrong. It took a moment to figure it out: I'd spent the past few hours working on upside-down instrument panels, and now I was seeing this one the right way up.

I reached out and examined it for its component parts, thinking of the man or the woman who'd put it together, and appreciating the way it had been done. This thing I usually took so for granted that I'd never before paid a moment's attention to it, was now an astounding piece of man-made—woman-made—complexity.

I started the truck and drove slowly out of the lot, wondering how long I'd keep this awareness that cars are not merely machines, but things put together by human beings, products of real men and real women doing the kind of work that would drive most people crazy. Not long enough, for sure.

Chapter Seventeen

Another few days and the whole country would practically shut down. It seemed so unlikely that the holiday was already here. The radio told me it was. The lights on storefronts and house porches told me it was. The carols tinkling away in truck stops and diners and motel lobbies told me it was. Everywhere I went, people wished me a merry Christmas, and I wished them one back, wishing at the same time that they would stop trying to be so very merry. I wondered if there was a road equivalent of jet lag. The truck and I had gotten as far as Tennessee, but somehow I was still back in Texas, and it was still November, and my father hadn't died yet.

All the things I usually did around Christmas had remained undone. I'd canceled the party I usually gave for the caroling kayakers, who'd come gliding over the lake to my houseboat, Santa Claus in the lead kayak and reindeer-horned and elfin-hatted helpers paddling behind. The lights and candles I usually placed around the raft—including Hanukkah candles when the dates coincided—would remain unlit. It hadn't occurred to me to send cards. And though I'd been picking up stocking-stuffer bits and pieces ever since I'd left home—cowboy-boot candles, chili-pepper candies, cactus earrings, "rattlesnake eggs" bubble gum—I hadn't even thought about the serious business of proper gifts.

I'd originally planned to take a two-week break back home over Christmas. If I was lucky and could get on a plane, I could make it. But there was one more stop I wanted to squeeze in first. Three hundred miles to the north, on the outskirts of Cincinnati, was the headquarters of O'Gara-Hess and Eisenhardt. O'Gara for short. I'd been curious about them for years, but right now what they offered seemed to be just what I needed. Their specialty was armoring. I called and confirmed that I'd be there the day after next. Maybe I'd get the truck armored.

It was early afternoon by the time I headed out of Spring Hill, so I stopped for the night just a hundred miles north in Bowling Green, Kentucky, to pay my respects at a national gearhead shrine: the Corvette Museum. It was, I'd been told, a stunning design. And I'd been told correctly.

The basic design was starkly simple: an upturned yellow bowl with a red spike sticking through it, and a low black rectangle alongside. I could see it from miles away as I drove in on the interstate, and the closer I got, the worse it looked. Loud and obvious, tacky and flashy, this was the perfect building for the Vette.

The Vette was not always quite the muscle car it's reputed to be. In fact when it was introduced back in 1953, though it looked the part—racy and radical—its handling and performance were atrocious. So Chevy brought in Zora Arkus-Duntov to make it go as fast as it looked. Belgian-born of Russian parents, Zora would die of comfortable old age in 1996, renowned as the Father of the Corvette. The small-block V8 engine that he designed for the car had earned him that title. It had also earned him the singular honor of having his ashes displayed in the museum.

Zora's ashes lay in an eye-level display case right in the middle of the main gallery. They were inside a gold box, and around the box were assorted Zora memorabilia, including his driving shoes and driving gloves, a battered yellow crash helmet, and a bottle of Mumm's in an improbably pristine state, still corked.

I wondered if other visitors were disappointed that the gold box was closed. Surely it should have been open, the ashes spilling over the sides and cascading down to the very edge of the glass case so that you could stick your nose up against them and hope for a whiff of engineering greatness. I realized this was perhaps not in the best of taste, but if your ashes were going to be immortalized, or at least museumized, it seemed they should be on full display.

Besides, nobody could accuse the National Corvette Museum of a surfeit of good taste. Its ranks of distinguished Vettes included the 1959 racer called the Purple People Eater, the 880-horsepower Callaway Sledgehammer, and the 1969 L-88 Rebel, the whole of which, from front to rear, was painted in the Confederate flag. The only one that aroused a glimmer of yearning in me was a silver-blue 1959 convertible with recessed gauges, its curves downright delicate compared to the broad-stroke mass of modern Vettes. As European, that is, as the Vette would ever get.

It was no use. No matter what passport I carried, I'd never muster any real enthusiasm for the most renowned of American cars. It seemed to me all muscle and not much brain, a kind of mechanical Charles Atlas or Sly Stallone. And unless you considered Stallone the American equivalent of Laurence Olivier, even to think of the Corvette in such terms was to commit automotive heresy. If the gearhead community had the equivalent of a House Un-American Activities Committee, they'd have me up before it in a flash. Turn up your nose at the Vette? That's worse than voting for Ralph Nader. Send that woman back where she came from!

I took refuge the next morning on the country roads of Kentucky, and America welcomed me back again. Driving east on Route 1297, which traced a gentle roller-coaster over hilly farmland, I felt quite at home. Here and there, children playing in their yards stopped to watch as I went by, and waved hello. Even the mailman waved hello. I was think-ing how good it would be to live here when I turned north onto 31E. And into Abraham Lincoln's childhood.

The small brown sign saying "Abraham Lincoln Birthplace National Historic Site" was so discreet that if you were in a hurry you'd never notice it. I did a double take. I hadn't realized that the defender of the Union was born in Kentucky. The modest size of the sign seemed to indicate that many people around here would much rather he hadn't been.

A narrow driveway took me into a landscaped two-acre site with an empty parking lot in the middle. A small wooden building pronounced itself the visitors' center. An even smaller one was a gift shop. That left only one other building here: a faux-classical marble and granite box on top of a hill with a broad flight of steps leading up to it. It looked like a cross between a Masonic temple and a post office.

I frowned. This couldn't be it. Didn't all the history books talk of a log cabin?

I knew there'd be a museum inside the building, with photographs and documents and bite-sized biographical snippets on the walls. There'd be bits and pieces of Lincoln's life too, just as the Henry Ford Museum in Detroit had what it claimed to be bits and pieces of his death: the chair he was sitting in that night at the theater, the blanket that covered his knees, the program he'd been holding. I'd seen them there the last time I'd been to Detroit, alongside a glass vial labeled as holding Thomas Edison's dying breath—all part of Henry Ford's private cabinet of wonders. I didn't want to play the voyeur on Lincoln's birth now any more than I'd wanted to play it on his death then.

But at the foot of the steps, a plaque set into the retaining wall informed me that there were fifty-six steps here, one for every year of Lincoln's life. I liked the idea of a man's life as a flight of steps. It seemed ungracious, knowing this, not to ascend them.

I placed each foot very firmly and deliberately on the wide, pale granite, and as I went up, each step began to gain the weight and heft of a year. By the time I reached the top, my feet had the sense of a life well lived. I stood there, looking back down, wondering at how strange it was that the flight of steps hadn't seemed too short. Maybe that's why they use stone in graveyards: stone makes things permanent, unchangeable. You have no alternative but to accept.

A damp wind had come up, and I shivered, turned under the columned portico, and pushed open the heavy ornamental door. And found myself staring at the log cabin.

About sixteen by eighteen feet, it took up nearly the whole of the inside of the building, crude logs in sharp contrast to the expensive, polished stone around them. There was just enough pale light filtering in from windows high in the marble walls to see the lopsided doorway, the single small window opening, unglassed, the shingled roof, the rough clay chimney. Even to an eye untutored in woodwork, it was a peculiarly inept effort. I've stayed at one time or another in many log cabins, but the simplest of them had been a palace compared to this. I leaned over the velveteen rope barring the doorway to see, laid on top of the marble slabs, a dirt floor.

I stood blinking in the gray light, thinking how Lincoln would have hated this. At least I hoped he would have hated it. Imagined him giving orders to tear down all that damned fancy stone and let the cabin be . . .

A shadow detached itself from a marbled corner and I gave a start. "Sorry," said a park ranger, "didn't mean to frighten you. Just wondering if you needed any explanation."

"Well . . . Yes . . . I mean, what happened here? Was this building built around the log cabin, or what?"

"This *memorial*," he corrected me, and launched into his standard presentation. I was, he told me, on the site of Sinking Spring Farm, where Lincoln spent the first two years of his life. The spring itself, well and truly sunken by now, was off to the right at the bottom of the steps. As was the stump of the Boundary Oak, the sapling that started life along with Lincoln, and had to be cut down, dead, in 1976.

"But this *is* the original log cabin?"

"More or less the original."

"How much more and how much less?"

"Well, you'd probably have to say it was a reconstruction. Cabins like this don't last that long, you know." And he gazed at it with the eye of a man thinking how much better a job he could have done.

I gazed along with him. "It seems unlikely that the original was up here on the hill when they had to carry water from the spring."

He nodded judiciously. "I think you might say that when they built the memorial back in 1909, they weren't as concerned with historical accuracy as we are now."

"But he *was* born here?"

He cracked a smile. "Oh yes, you can rely on that. Most people think he was from Illinois, but he spent the first seven years of his life in Kentucky—right here at Sinking Spring, then on another farm just up the road a ways."

I was rather glad that the South had a claim to Abraham Lincoln, and celebrated the fact at a diner in Hodgenville, a couple of miles on, with a lunch of pot roast, collard greens, and mashed potatoes with lots of gravy. Together with an extra helping of greens and a big portion of apple pie, it cost me five dollars even.

"You take care now, it's coming on rain," said the waitress as I left, and as though to make her point, a few drops spotted the windshield as I drove on up 31E to "Abraham Lincoln's Boyhood Home" at Knob Creek, a much fancier and suspiciously spiffy log cabin, sans marble shrine and sans the blessing of the National Park Service. Very much, in fact, a private enterprise piece of history. Bunting was strung up between the cabin and the large modern house next to it. Behind the cabin was a large radar dish; in front of it, a banner advertised "Lincoln memorabilia." I passed, and two miles farther, came to a sign for "Site of Abraham Lincoln's first school," now occupied by an old one-room clapboard schoolhouse rotting on its foundations.

For a moment I was tempted to keep following the path of Lincoln's life, up into Indiana and then over to Illinois, but by now the rain was pelting down just like the waitress said it would, and I still had a long way to go if I was to get a good night's sleep and be at O'Gara the next morning. When I reached the Blue Grass Parkway I bade farewell to Lincoln, drove east to Lexington, then took I-75 north. By nightfall, I was crossing the Ohio River into Cincinnati.

★

"Treat me as you would a really important client," I'd said to O'Gara's sales manager on the phone. "Just call me Madonna."

He'd picked up on it instantly. "It'll be an honor to have you visit us, Madonna. As you can imagine, Mr. O'Gara is deeply disappointed that he'll be overseas and won't be here to receive you personally. But he asked me to assure you that as the oldest and largest armoring company in the world, we'll give your security needs our very top priority."

"Good," I'd said. "I like all my needs to have top priority."

I hadn't planned to play Madonna, but when you enter the world of security, the imagination begins to take over. Perhaps I was picking up

on the James Bondishness of it all, as though I were about to come face
to face with Q and his toys. I imagined cars with scythes coming out of
their wheels at the press of a button. Missile launchers sprouting from
the headlights. Rockets to power a quick getaway. No question of my
being Bond, of course, but Madonna would be a match for him any day.
I wondered how 007 would deal with her. The question engaged me all
the way through Cincinnati and up to Fairfield on its northern outskirts.
Sean Connery would have been up to the job, for sure. Pierce Brosnan
wouldn't have a clue.

At first glance, O'Gara was somewhat disappointing. The building
looked so innocuous it could have been just another insurance or soft-
ware company, like its neighbors. But then what had I expected? A
barbed-wire perimeter? A moat? Perhaps not, but at least something
that would indicate that this was where they had armored cars for every
United States president since FDR, as well as over sixty other heads of
state.

Of course it occurred to me that there was one glaring exception in
their protection of every American president, though admittedly
through no fault of theirs. That day in Dealey Plaza was the last time
any president drove in an open convertible. I suspected it was also the
day that O'Gara's business began to grow. And as kidnappings and
drive-by shootings had become facts of corporate and criminal life in
the eighties, it had boomed. Not only presidents and sultans, but also
CEOs, rock stars, all manner of public figures and a lot of would-be private ones—everyone who was anyone worth threatening—sought the
protection of O'Gara. Now so would I.

Dan Heimbrock, the sales manager, had prepared the way well. The
receptionist fluttered and all but curtsied. I was ushered in by several
solicitous young men, and could almost hear the buzz going around the
place:

"Madonna's here."

"You're kidding."

"No, really."

"Hey, d'you hear that? Madonna's here."

I raised my chin high, walked taller, and glided into Dan's office, spreading myself over the best chair in the place before graciously condescending to accept some coffee. I wished I'd worn something more outrageous than my usual leggings and boots. High-heeled boots, at least. I dug a lipstick out of my purse and applied an extra thick layer. It seemed to have the desired effect.

The coffee served and the fuss made, everyone else disappeared. "Alone at last," I said.

Dan grinned almost bashfully. He wasn't nearly as old as I'd expected; in his mid-thirties, perhaps, with the kind of regular blond good looks that sales managers always seem to have, no matter what they're selling.

"I'm going to have to ask you some questions, Madonna, and I hope they don't seem too intrusive. Normally of course we'd deal with your security people. It's unusual that a public figure of your caliber would take such a personal interest."

"I do believe in a hands-on approach," I said, giving him a seductive glance under lowered eyelashes.

He cleared his throat. "Ah . . . yes. Your people tell me that your security situation has become of greater concern recently. We will of course perform a complete threat analysis, but first I'd like to hear from you, if I may, exactly what those threats are."

I shrugged. Normally I wouldn't even bother with such things, I said. Of course there were always the usual nuisances—nutty letters from outraged saviors of the nation's morality, and equally nutty letters from impassioned adorers who wanted to make me theirs in quite alarming ways. I waved my hand dismissively. I didn't take those seriously. Dan made as though to disagree, but I silenced him with a stern look, and continued.

Two things had changed, I said. First, I now had a child, and was getting kidnap threats. This was intolerable. And second, I was especially concerned since I was about to continue my series of movies on dictator women of the world. The new one would involve location scenes in the Philippines, where I'd heard that the security situation was very bad. The movie, a musical, was to be called *Imelda*.

To my surprise, Dan managed not to crack a smile. He simply nodded understandingly. But then maybe I shouldn't have been surprised. A good sales manager is always playing a role. "Since this involves overseas," he said, "let me call in our international analyst to sit in with us, if that's all right with you."

I granted my permission, and meanwhile took a quick look at O'Gara's shiny prospectus, which described its services as "the safest way to travel through today's dangerous world." I'd traveled some ten thousand miles to get here, and it hadn't seemed that dangerous to me. But of course I hadn't been Madonna then.

There were six levels of protection against that world out there. Level One would merely fend off a smash-and-grab attempt on the car. Forget that. "Ballistic protection" began at Level Two, meaning handguns and anything up to an Uzi. That was more like it. Level Three took the "maximum allowable threat" up to high-velocity handguns, including .44 Magnums, and Level Four, up to military assault rifles. Now we were getting serious. By Level Five, someone could fire military penetrating rounds at my car and not get through. But Level Six was best: with that, I got blast protection as well as defense against chemical attack. Level Six was for presidents. I thought it would do just fine for me too.

The international analyst arrived, suitably primed as to whom he was about to meet. "David Zimov," he said softly, and bowed over my hand. I rewarded him with a star-power smile. There was something perhaps Russian or Asian in his features, delicate and dark, and he looked even younger than Dan. The voice betrayed just a hint of Harvard, though when I asked, he told me he had a doctorate from the London School of Economics in international history and developmental economics. Not exactly the kind of person I'd expected to find selling cars, even armored ones.

He seemed to know his stuff all right. Security conditions varied from country to country, he explained, and I was quite right: the Philippines was one of the highest-threat countries in the world for someone of my caliber. He rattled off a series of bombing, assault, carjacking, and kidnapping numbers. Only twenty percent of major terrorist incidents in the world were directed against diplomatic, governmental, or military targets, he said. The other targets were all people from the business world and the private sector. Los Angeles, it seemed, was innocent by comparison.

"We'd probably suggest a good sporty sedan like a Mercedes or an Audi for when you're at home in California, protected to Level Two."

"That's not much fun," I said. "Only Level Two? What about a Porsche 911 to Level Six?"

"We know you'd prefer a sportier car for your personal use, but I'm afraid you wouldn't be satisfied with an armored Porsche. Even a lightly armored one with the high-tech materials we use here—composites like Kevlar and new classified ceramics developed in the military—is going to be carrying so much weight that it would be no fun to drive. It just wouldn't do what you'd want it to do."

I gave an exasperated sigh. "Just like a man."

David suppressed a smile and carried on. "If you're going to be attacked in LA, the probability is it will be with a handgun. Level Two is perfect for that, and you'd hardly even notice any difference in the handling. But for the Philippines, your Ford Expedition protected to Level Four would be a very good idea. I assume you'd have a driver there?" I nodded. "Good. We'd want to put him through our security training, of course. We have an excellent staff of former FBI officers and government security agents in our driving program. In the Philippines, you see, you have professional kidnappers, plus insurgents, looking especially for people who will put them in the news. People like yourself, Madonna. They would probably use military assault rifles, something like an AK47 with muzzle velocities exceeding twenty-three hundred feet per second."

"That's fast?"

"It is compared to a handgun, say a 9-mm automatic with muzzle velocities of about thirteen hundred feet per second. When the bullets go slower, you see, they're much easier to stop."

"Ah." He seemed to have an impressive grasp of lethal detail for someone with a doctorate from the London School of Economics. "Did you learn all this at LSE?"

"Let's call it on-the-job training," he said with just the hint of a smile.

I raised my eyebrows. "How very discreet."

Dan saw his chance. "Precisely," he said. "Discretion is exactly what we offer at O'Gara. Madonna going down the street in an obviously armored vehicle would attract more attention than you'd want. With our cars, you need a trained eye to tell the difference, and then only at close range."

"How?"

"Up close, you can see that the glass is thicker, and the steel frame intrudes an inch or two into the window space, closing all ballistic gaps."

"Which are . . . ?"

"Places where a bullet can get through," said David drily.

But I was only half listening. I'd been flicking through the prospectus as we spoke, and had just come to a double-page spread illustrating all the armoring options. "Gun ports!" I said. "Tear-gas dispensers! I have to have those!"

There was an odd silence.

"Come now, gentlemen, you surely don't think Madonna would accept any half-measures."

David stepped up to the plate. "Well actually, despite your fame, we really don't recommend going to such levels. Not in this country, at any rate. Things like tear-gas and gun ports are not liked by the authorities in this country. Which is to say, they're not legal. And elsewhere, you do have to consider if you want to escape or fight a pitched battle, especially if you have your child with you in the vehicle."

"Hm." I could see that this appeal to maternal protectiveness might work even on Madonna, however appealing the idea of the car as an armed fortress. But then my eye lighted on the reinforced bumpers that could ram through roadblocks and anything else in your way. I loved the idea. I definitely wanted ram bumpers.

Dan looked quite alarmed at my enthusiasm for extremes. "Such options are really for professional assassination attempts, which are usually political," he said. "We would expect attempts against you to be amateur by comparison . . ."

He saw the look on my face: you do not insult Madonna by telling her she's not worth a proper assassination.

"We do need to take these death threats against you very seriously, however, so we would definitely recommend a remote bomb scan on both vehicles. You operate it like a garage door opener, from up to a hundred yards away, and if there's nothing present, it will start the car. Any bomb would need an ignition circuit to set it off, and that's almost always rigged off the car's own electrical system."

I nodded. "Where were you guys when I needed you?" I said quietly.

Dan looked worried. "When was that, Madonna?"

But I'd slipped out of role. The world of James Bond had just edged over into my own real world. I knew that Madonna must indeed have received plenty of death threats, and suddenly I sympathized with her, because I'd received them too.

It only happened twice, and both times were years ago, but no matter how far you push the memory to the back of your mind, you can't ever really forget those disembodied words over the phone line:

"We know where you are."

"We know how to deal with our enemies."

"You change your tune or you die."

Tired Hollywood clichés, except when you hear them in real life directed at you.

The first time, they came from far-right nationalists in Israel; the second time, from far-left anarchists in New York's East Village. Both times, I tried to laugh them off as a compliment. They were a backhanded testament to the power of words. Any good political reporter would get such threats, I reasoned. And I had to be doing something right to receive them from opposite ends of the fanatical spectrum.

But it was unsettling, to say the least, to know that some complete stranger wished me dead. Perhaps even to the point of acting on that desire. Friends tried to reassure me that the threats weren't worth taking seriously. They were probably right, but I'd have preferred certainty. Both times, I'd called the police. Ten thousand miles and ten years apart, they'd reacted the same way: "Let us know if anything happens." This had not been comforting. For weeks, I'd walked down the street in a state of hyper-awareness, carried Mace in my pocket, opened unidentified mail with extreme caution. And checked the underside of my car before I started it up. I could have done with a remote bomb scan then.

★

We went for lunch to the White House restaurant nearby. It was indeed a white house, and had a parking lot full of salmon pink Cadillacs. "The Mary Kay Christmas lunch," said the maître d'. I peered in to the main dining room, and got a distinct whiff of gardenias. Dan and David steered me toward the bar as an evasion procedure, and for the next hour, the closest we came to the world of cosmetics was an occasional high titter of laughter as we hunched close, exploring levels of threat.

Somehow the subject didn't affect my appetite, and I'd polished off a good steak by the time I asked David exactly what he did for the company. "I do the international strategic planning, competitor assessment, and new international market development," he said.

"Meaning?"

"Meaning I spend my time assessing reports on political and social unrest, analyzing rebel movements, tracing patterns of terrorism, and so on. Particularly in Latin America, Asia, and the Middle East."

"That's a very high-powered analyst to have on the team of an armored-car company."

He gave the kind of enigmatic smile I'd seen before on people who work in intelligence, but said nothing.

"In fact it sounds very close to the work of a CIA analyst."

He studied his drink, which I noticed he'd barely sipped.

"You wouldn't be above fomenting a little unrest to improve business, would you?"

He pushed his plate away, steak half eaten, and gave me the kind of reproving look that said, "That's not funny." By now I wasn't even sure if I'd intended it to be.

Ladylike applause filtered through from the main dining room as I tried another tack. "Beyond the American presidents, you haven't mentioned exactly who your clients are."

Dan intervened. "As we said before, this business is really all about discretion. Obviously we can't divulge our client list. I think you can understand that many of our political customers have to deal with particularly dangerous situations at home . . ."

"You mean that you're helping totalitarian regimes stay in power?"

He gave a weak smile. "We're running a business," he said. "We don't make political judgments."

"Just political assessments?"

"Exactly."

In fact, he pointed out, O'Gara's growth had come mainly from the private sector, where international security was in increasingly high demand. He mentioned a growth rate of ten percent a year. Intelligence and security were no longer the domain of governments and military; they were being privatized. That was why O'Gara was about to merge with New York's Kroll Associates, a global detective agency specializing in corporate clients, and why it was now offering "integrated security services," including site protection, satellite communications, background checks, and security agent training. "Our security service group is headed by Ted Price, who was the CIA chief of operations in the eighties. And William Sessions, the former head of the FBI, is an adviser and a board member."

I ordered a brandy. Play-acting Madonna, I'd waltzed right into the underside of fame and business at the end of the twentieth century. Political insecurity was once considered bad for business; now it *was* business. And quarter-million-dollar "protected cars" were an essential deductible expense.

High voices laughed and giggled as the Mary Kay party began to break up next door. A heavily made-up woman peeked into the bar. "Oh my, girls, there's a whole other world in here!" she exclaimed.

Dan grimaced. "Let's go," he said. "They should have an Expedition ready for you to drive by now."

They did. A black one, "armored to defeat a Level Four threat." I waited with Dan while they maneuvered it out of the workshop, which was the size of a couple of ballrooms and held about fifty cars in one stage or another of the armoring process: Rolls Royces and Mercedes-

Benzes, Cadillacs and Town Cars, Suburbans and Expeditions and other large sport-utes.

Off to one side were four full-camouflage Hummers. These were being "up-armored," Dan explained. "We do a lot of that for various military forces, including the United States military."

"Aren't they already armored?"

"Not like we do it. We mine-proof them and install armor-piercing protection for special details such as peace-keeping in Bosnia."

It was odd to think that the military itself might need extra protection; somehow I'd assumed they were the protectors, not the protectees. For a moment, there was a certain pleasure in knowing that at least a few privates and sergeants would get the same high-tech security as sultans and CEOs, but that was only fleeting. The sultans and CEOs were protecting themselves against the possible; the privates and sergeants would use up-armored Hummers only to drive into highly probable danger.

My own Expedition seemed innocently friendly compared to the one I was about to drive. The knowledge that it was armored made it loom menacingly, as did the color. "All yours," said Dan.

I made to open the driver's door, but it seemed unwilling. "There's something wrong with this door."

"Check the glass."

I peered close. It looked well over an inch thick. "An inch and three-quarters," said Dan. "That's what makes it so heavy."

"How thick is the glass at Level Six?"

"Three inches."

No wonder dignitaries always had their doors opened for them. It wasn't just a matter of courtesy, but the stark fact that you'd need regular workouts at the gym to make opening or closing such doors look remotely normal.

I climbed in, switched on the ignition, and pressed the power button for the window. There was a loud groaning sound as it went down. "Hydraulic mechanism," said Dan, "to deal with the weight." It began to dawn on me that any relation between this Expedition and mine was tenuous at best. This one was well on its way to becoming a tank.

I peered through the windshield. It was lower and narrower than on mine, as were the side windows. All around the glass was an inch-and-a-half-wide ledge of upholstery-covered steel; all ballistic gaps were well and truly closed. I should have felt secure and protected, but the association with a tank only made me feel more vulnerable instead of less. I'd never understood how soldiers could volunteer for the tank corps. Did so much steel around them give them the illusion of safety? Couldn't they imagine being burned to death inside a metal coffin?

I shifted into Drive and turned onto the road, feeling a bit easier now that I was at the controls. The truck was heavy, no doubt of that, yet they'd compensated for it pretty well. They'd reinforced the suspension, souped up the engine, installed larger brakes. So long as I just kept rolling, I could almost forget that I was driving an armored vehicle.

Almost, but not quite. Those layers of armor made themselves felt in subtle ways. It was the same truck I'd been driving around the country for the past few months, yet with an underlying layer of unfamiliarity. I felt it in the extra time it took to accelerate, the engine pulling at the added ton and a half of weight. I felt it even more in the longer distance I needed to brake. And I felt it most of all in the corners. I would hate to have to attempt a slalom course in this truck. To drive it with any degree of real confidence, I'd definitely need a few days' training with those former government security agents.

"Insulate, insulate . . ." The refrain of Tom Wolfe's *Bonfire of the Vanities* haunted me as I steered warily through the newly landscaped industrial suburbs of Fairfield, Ohio. The way to survive in "today's dangerous world." Quite literally insulated in multiple layers of composite plastics and classified ceramics and bombproof glass.

When I got back into my own Expedition an hour later, it felt very light and malleable. And peculiarly vulnerable. There was a steady rain, and it was five in the afternoon. I checked the map. Cincinnati to Detroit, 268 miles. I could make Detroit that evening if I wanted.

I turned on the radio, checked the news, and heard that Saddam Hussein's oldest son, his heir apparent, had been shot while driving his Porsche in Baghdad. I felt like turning back to find David Zimov and ask him again if he was drumming up business. The coincidence was suspiciously perfect. But then any kind of contact with this business makes you vulnerable to conspiracy thinking. Certainly, if Saddam Junior lived, he'd be driving armor from now on. His Porsche days were over.

And suddenly I wanted to make Detroit that evening very badly. There were twelve days to go to the start of the auto show: just time to seek the security of home for the holidays. I drove steadily north through a dark and wet Ohio—Dayton, Lima, Toledo—made Detroit Metro by ten, presented my frequent-flyer card, and talked my way onto a red-eye to Seattle.

Chapter Eighteen

Two weeks later, I stood waiting for a crash. The 10,544th vehicle to undergo the ultimate test at Ford's Dearborn Proving Grounds was a prototype truck, part preproduction and part hand-made, that had cost a quarter-million dollars to build. It was about to be dragged at high speed down a 520-foot tunnel. At the last moment, just after it emerged from the tunnel into a hangar, it would be released from its hydraulic cables like a slingshot, and slam into a one-million-pound slab of concrete at precisely 31 miles an hour.

I shouldn't even have been here. I should have been back in downtown Detroit, at the third press day of the auto show, being wined and dined and made to feel that I was God's gift to journalism. But nothing, these days, seemed to be going according to plan.

I'd thought my days back home would be a much-needed time out, but right after Christmas, Seattle got socked by a foot of snow. This was a huge snowstorm by Pacific Northwest standards, and the once-in-a-century storm according to the local television news, which wasn't quite true; once-in-a-half-century was impressive enough. We lit the wood stoves and hunkered down as the temperature kept falling and the snow froze solid. The houseboats sank a couple of inches under the weight. And sank deeper still the next day when another eight inches of heavy, wet slush came down, and then froze on top of what was already there. Across the lake, two houseboats went under. There was nothing to do but start scraping the ice off our roofs and decks with brooms, shovels, oars, boathooks—anything that might reach. It took a full night and a day to achieve buoyancy again, with occasional leaps to the dock for safety as huge blocks of the stuff came loose and went crashing into the water.

On New Year's Day, just as the temperature began to rise in Seattle, I'd flown back east to Detroit, where the mercury instantly began to plummet. Both the snow and the freeze made Seattle's weather look like spring. The wind came howling down from Canada and whipped off the frozen Detroit River. Wind chill was way below zero Fahrenheit, the underground parking lot in the downtown concrete cube known as Cobo Hall was full, and on the ten-minute walk from the nearest open lot to the hall—it was too cold to run—I wondered exactly how long it would take for frostbite to set in.

I'd forgotten that such weather is normal for Detroit in early January. My memory, in fact, had been playing me false all round. From a distance, the press days of the North American International Detroit Auto Show—an oxymoronic mouthful if ever there was one—offered a non-stop week-long shmoozefest. Automakers threw Motown parties and Mardi Gras parties, black-tie parties and indoor tailgate parties complete with bales of hay and cowboy rope tricks. From the Rattlesnake Club to the Detroit Club, from Greektown to Motown, they laid on a movable feast of hype and glitz, oiled by bountiful supplies of fine liquor and gourmet food. After months on the road, this was exactly what I'd thought I needed: the red-carpet treatment.

The red carpet had been laid out for me, all right. Trouble was, it had also been laid out for five thousand, nine hundred and ninety-nine other "members of the press." Press credentials had been handed out like candy to kids at Halloween, and the show organizers bandied the six thousand figure around as though it could attest to the importance of the show. Which in everyone's mind but mine, it apparently did.

I'd forgotten about the "unveilings" of new models, staged to grab the standard fifteen seconds of limelight on the six o'clock news. Forgotten what it was like to play the audience as Chrysler's top executives sat on a Broadway set and bandied doggerel verse with Kermit the Frog. Or watch Nissan put on a mini-musical with Ken and Barbie as the stars. Or a magician doing an elaborate disappearing act with a Corvette—all, literally, smoke and mirrors.

"These aren't press conferences," I complained. "They're photo ops."

"But they're fun," a colleague said.

"I'd think so if I was ten years old."

I'd forgotten what it was like to see my colleagues applaud such "press conferences." Or to listen to them cheer screenings of new television commercials. Or watch them lob soft questions at the men who ran Detroit, angling for advertising dollars for their magazines and television programs.

But who was I kidding? Glitz and glamour, hype and buzz, and I was part of it. All geared up in full makeup and telegenic red. Never turn down an invitation for sex or a television appearance, Gore Vidal once said. Ever the selective listener, I followed the second part of his advice, and became part of the system whereby journalists interview journalists. Always good for a provocative sound bite, even as I was disgusted at how easily I could produce them. The makeup coated my face uncomfortably; the flashy jacket robbed me of a journalist's best asset, the ability to blend in. I had become part of the show.

By the end of the second day, after the twenty-fourth press conference, my head was ringing. Teamsters were still hammering throughout Cobo Hall, putting the finishing touches to displays before the formal opening in three days' time. Fantasy "concept" cars revolved on turntables, comic-book visions of the future. Huge trucks tilted at impossible angles high overhead, gleaming and glinting like metallic idols. Everywhere you looked, sheet metal shone in red and yellow and purple and chartreuse—any color that would grab attention.

In the bathrooms, skimpily clad showgirls shivered under their pancake makeup and practiced their routines: "One and two and three, four, five . . . Forward two and right for three, then kick and toe and . . ." Others mouthed their spiels into pretend microphones in front of the mirrors, practicing high-tech torque talk in the blank low-tech accent of incomprehension.

The video screens at every stand had been hooked up and were now blaring full volume, each competing with its neighbor so that Buick played backup to Honda, Saab to Toyota. They flashed and pulsed to variations of the same music: an urgent, throbbing rhythm intended to set the blood racing, make you forget that you were in downtown Detroit and it was zero degrees outside, and set you to fantasizing about driving a drop-dead roadster down a twisting mountain road into the sunset, all mundane responsibilities left behind as you headed into the twilight of the great American automotive myth, where the roads are always empty and there are no kids arguing in the back seat and the whole of the continent and life lies before you, beyond the next hill, around the next bend, over the rainbow.

I stood up on the second floor of the Chrysler hospitality center, a square tower right in the middle of the whole shebang, and talked into yet another television camera.

"The problem here," I heard myself saying, "is that there's too much sheet metal in the world." I swept my arm demonstratively across the gleaming vista. "Who needs all these new cars?"

The reporter flinched. I could practically see the word *sponsors* flash through his brain in bright red warning lights of alarm. And I realized I was suffering from a bad case of absence of illusion.

It wasn't just that I was tired of the nonstop flow of sales figures and projections. Nor even that I was bored with talk of twenty extra horsepower here and fifteen extra pound feet of torque there. As the whine of power tools echoed through the big hall and ricocheted off the concrete beams high above, as bad music blared and every sales pitch tried to outdecibel the next, I couldn't quite believe that I had driven several months and thousands of miles in the fond imagining that this was the perfect goal.

I wanted reality—a final crescendo unmediated by public relations whizzes and market research surveys, unfiltered by Hennessy cognac and oysters Rockefeller and Cuban cigars bought just over the river in Canada.

I wanted, in short, to end my book with a bang.

★

The crash barrier at the Dearborn Proving Grounds was the most expensive concrete slab in the world. Three and a half million dollars, to be precise.

It was ten feet high, twenty feet wide, and another twenty feet deep, and was fronted by an eight-inch-thick panel of steel covered by a grid of thin plywood squares. Embedded in this steel panel were forty-seven piezo-electric load cells—tiny crystals that give off an electric charge under pressure. Each one would render up three measurements, creating a network of a hundred and forty-one parameters just for the frontal impact of each crash.

I'd spent the past hour watching the engineers ready the prototype truck up the other end of the tunnel. It was a new version of the F150 pickup, in a shade of azure blue not yet on the market, and which I liked a lot. In fact I took a very personal interest in this truck, since from the windshield forward, it was identical to the Expedition. So far as I was concerned, this was my vehicle they were preparing to crash.

"Do you ever feel scared to get into a vehicle again?" I asked Risa Scherer, the crash engineer who was showing me around.

She smiled. "We crash four vehicles a day here. I guess you could say we're used to it."

For someone whose business was creating havoc, Risa seemed surprisingly normal. She was in her early thirties, with shoulder-length dark curls and a round, open face. In her white coat, she could have been a doctor or a laboratory researcher. "What made you become a crash engineer?" I asked, fascinated by the very idea of such a profession.

"You mean do I enjoy my work?"

No fooling her.

"Yes, I do enjoy it. Do I take some particular delight in it, like kids crashing toy cars?"

She'd read me perfectly.

"No, I don't. I know there's a theory that we're acting out unconscious desires, like potential arsonists becoming firemen, but I don't think that's true of either firemen or crash engineers. Sure we develop kind of a sick sense of humor. That's the way you cope. But in fact this bunch of people are more committed to the idea of improving safety than practically anyone else around. Except perhaps for emergency-room surgeons."

We'd watched as technicians applied the circular black and white decals used for precision photography. Cameras at the crash site would focus on the specific stress points indicated by the decals, which were unnervingly similar to the universal symbol for nuclear radiation.

Behind us, a long double line of cars waited to be crashed. One was a police car, lights and all, and I told Risa how I'd once indulged in the stock Hollywood cop-chase fantasy by driving one of those on the test track here at Dearborn, lights flashing and sirens wailing and howling over the protests of the test driver beside me. She'd grinned: "I'm glad you did that. That's exactly what I've always wanted to do."

Many of the cars waiting to meet their fate had had their paint "fogged" to reduce the glare for the cameras. I liked the effect—a kind of matte marbleized look. But the tires were all painted a sickeningly bright orange, and the undersides were an unexpected jumble of pastels. Powder pink and light green, robin's egg blue and primrose yellow picked out oil pans, exhausts, axles, all the separate components of the cars' underbodies, as though a pale child had daubed them in an ineffectual attempt to prettify the mechanical. "It's so that we can identify which part is which, post-crash," said Risa.

"Why pastels?"

She'd shrugged. "Whatever colors are on bulk discount."

If the F150's orange tires were a bad match for the azure blue, I was the only one who was bothered by it. The technicians had been otherwise occupied, hooking up the crash dummies inside the truck: a fiftieth percentile male and a fiftieth percentile female—as average, that is, as could be. She was in the driver's seat. Both, I was pleased to see, were wearing seat belts, thus displaying a far greater desire for life than thirty-five percent of the humans they were substituting for. Chamois cloth had been placed over their faces and dusted with colored chalk—the upper part of her face blue, the lower part red, and the colors reversed for him. They might have been prisoners about to be executed, with cruelly clownlike blindfolds.

Thick bundles of cables snaked out from their backs like reverse umbilical cords, linking them to large black data boxes set in the bed of the truck. The dummies and the car had been wired to provide a hundred and sixty channels of data, making this a fairly complex test. The maximum was just over three hundred, though most tests used only a hundred or so. Add these on-board data channels to the array of cameras and cells at the crash barrier, and you had over five hundred data channels available for any one test.

This, in short, was where you really found out what happened in a crash. As I was now about to do.

Above the exit from the tunnel, a red light had begun to flash. "Time to take cover," said Risa, and led me behind a plexiglass shield some thirty feet from the barrier, where four other engineers were already standing in a huddle.

That flashing red light was making me nervous. The shield seemed awfully flimsy. "Are you sure this is strong enough?" I asked.

I caught an exchange of amused looks. "Always has been," said the chief engineer, "but it'd be just our luck to find out it's not with you here."

A deep, foghorn-like siren started sounding in monotonous bursts, like the emergency alarm in a nuclear reactor on the verge of meltdown. It provoked exactly the same reaction in me—a sickening sense of impending doom.

Checking out test crashes had seemed a good idea just the day before, but right now, it was beginning to seem like a terrible one. The sick feeling in my stomach started to reach up into my throat, and I swallowed hard, trying to suppress it.

Somebody in the control room above the barrier began to count down over a loudspeaker. "Ten, nine, eight . . ."

The voice had the same effect as music in a Hitchcock movie, building up to blood and terror. But this was worse. This was real. Something terrible was about to happen, and I knew I wanted to be anywhere but here. What I'd come to see was suddenly the last thing on earth I wanted to see.

"Six, five, four . . ."

My heart was beating very hard and very fast. A faint sweat broke out on my chest. My hands felt clammy.

"Two, one, launch . . ."

Suddenly the whole place turned bright white. Giant banks of camera lights had burst into life with the force of a million flashbulbs, giving everything a sharp-edged hyper-reality. The sudden whiteness seared my eyes. It jolted my brain, shocked it into a freeze-frame of fear.

"It's coming," somebody said. I began to look away, then forced myself to look back, powerless to stop what was about to happen.

In that split second, I wanted to cry. But there wasn't time. I glimpsed the truck hurtling out of the tunnel. Steeled myself for the impact, every muscle rigid, every nerve straining . . .

And then it was over.

That was it.

There was before, and there was after, but there was no during. It had happened so fast my eye hadn't been able to register it. My whole body had flinched, but I'd seen nothing. Or rather, what I'd seen was a sound.

It wasn't as loud as I'd thought it would be. Not at all the big bang I'd expected, but something else entirely: a peculiarly muted *ba,* a sound that had maybe started out as a loud bang but then been cut short. As though the world, shocked by the impact, had shut down into absolute silence.

There'd been no explosive quality to that sound. It didn't reverberate. That is, whatever reverberation there was had been absorbed by the million pounds of concrete, so that there was barely an echo in the vast hangar. Just a weird finality. And the knowledge that death could come with neither a bang nor a whimper, but a flat, toneless retort.

For a moment, nobody moved. That sound had stopped everything. My breath had caught somewhere just below my throat, and stuck there. My whole body seemed to simply stop living. No sound, no movement, no breath, no eyeblink, no heartbeat. Just a horrible flat absence.

And then the bank of bright white camera lights went out, and everything was darkness by contrast, and the world suddenly felt very cold. I shivered, and with the shiver, life returned and I began to breathe again.

But there had been a hiatus, an interruption, in the flow of life. This was clear. A cold split second of nothingness.

I blinked. "The impact is over in literally the blink of an eyelid, one-tenth of a second," said the chief engineer. "The whole event, including the rebound, is over in less than a quarter of a second."

One moment—one-tenth of a second—there'd been a prototype of a brand-new truck. The next, the truck was two feet shorter, its front end a mangled maze of twisted metal. There seemed to be no connecting moment between the two images. Time has been divided, and with it, experience.

We crept out from behind the plexiglass shield like survivors, slightly shell-shocked. At least I was. The truck's hood was twisted and tortured in on itself. All around the barrier, the floor was littered with shards of plastic and glass from the headlights, wood shavings from the plywood facing, and a swarm of tiny lead pellets that had been used for ballast inside the truck. The pellets worked their way into the soles of our shoes and made the going slippery, forcing us to walk with arms out for balance, as though we were on a sheet of ice.

The truck's windows were unbroken, I noticed; there was a crack in the windshield, but it had stayed intact. As had the passenger cabin. While the front of the truck was satisfyingly mangled, the rest looked peculiarly normal. The crush had been absorbed entirely by the engine compartment, just as the engineers had intended. I suppressed a tinge of disappointment.

The dummies had not done quite so well. They'd been shaken out of their perfect upright postures. He was hanging askew on his shoulder belt. She'd ended up with her head on his shoulder, which was kind of touching until I remembered they were just dummies. The air bags had exploded, of course, and were hanging limp like used condoms. Each one bore the imprint of the dummies' chalked faces—red and blue, blue and red—secular shrouds of Turin in ghostly kindergarten colors.

"Don't get too close, and don't touch anything," warned Risa, as though I were at the site of a crime scene and might disturb the evidence.

Engineers gathered around the truck like emergency-room doctors around a trauma victim, each one examining his or her particular piece of evidence. "Looks like another good one," said the chief engineer cheerily.

I stared at the dummies through the driver's window. It seemed unnatural that they could survive a 31-mph impact in such good shape, as though I'd expected them to cut and bleed, bruise and mangle. Their injuries were all electronic, of course—measurements on data channels, impulses carried down cables to be fed into computers, correlated, and spat out as human equivalents. Virtual injuries. That was good, I told myself: sensible, even humane. Yet some part of me had been hoping for something more dramatic. And again, I was both surprised and disgusted at my own appetite for blood.

The video monitors scattered around the hangar came to life with slow-motion replays of the crash, camera by camera. The cameras were digital—one thousand frames per second, as against a mere twenty-four frames a second in movie cameras. There'd been twenty-five of them in all, both on board and at the impact site, and even in a trench below the impact site. And now, one after the other, they replayed the crash, the clips looping together to show it from every possible angle. Each time the crash was over, the film flash-cut back to just before the moment of impact, and it happened again, angle adding on angle to create a long, *Rashomon*-like tale of every driver's nightmare.

I watched in fascination as the dummies lurched forward and then back, arms and legs waving, heads lolling like rag dolls. The air bags inflated and deflated like soft billowy cushions instead of the explosive devices they truly were. Shards of plastic and glass drifted through the air like snowflakes. The rear end of the truck lifted off the floor, and the whole truck bounced three feet back from the barrier, as though recoiling from the horror of impact.

An event that was so fast the eye couldn't see it now became endless, almost the visual equivalent of a Gregorian chant, with the ultimate disharmony of violent impact rendered harmonious by slowness. Each time the film looped through, I saw more. Saw the way the dummies' arms were thrown upward, as if trying to ward off the inevitable. Saw metal slowly crumpling like paper. Saw the rear wheels rise off the ground as if filled with helium, then come down to earth again with a soft squish.

I turned to see that the engineers had stopped to watch the monitors too, the same fascination on their faces as I knew was on mine. And they saw them every day.

Unbidden and unwanted, a scene in the movie of *Crash* came to mind: the one where the crash junkies sit side by side on a sofa watching slow-motion test-crash videos, each with his or her hand in the groin of the next. I'd originally thought it just another of the many scenes that turned Ballard's satire into mere farce. But then why did I think of it now?

I turned away, embarrassed by my own memory. Eroticizing horror was one way of dealing with it, perhaps. A dumbly literal acting out of the old Freudian assertion of Eros over Thanatos. Perhaps that's the attraction of horror movies. But was what I'd been doing any more acceptable? Was there that much difference between watching horror made erotic, and watching it made graceful? Either way, all that was needed was the artifice of the replay. That one split second of impact was stretched into the timelessness of slow motion, dissolved in the flash-cut jumping back and forth, lost in the continuously repeating loop. Staring at the monitors, you could make reality safe.

★

We left the technicians to their task of deconstructing the crash, and Risa walked me through the rest of the Automotive Safety Center. That is, through a series of torture labs for one part or another of the human body. Just as a car can be broken apart for analysis into its separate components, so too can a body. And these rooms were where each humanoid component met its crash-specified metallic one.

In one, the "Interior Head-Impact Facility," a dummy head was mounted on the end of a mechanical battering ram; once a minute, it rammed into a dashboard with a short, blunt thump. The far side of a partition, more heads were being shot around inside a sedan; they bounced from side to side, from seatback to roof, like badly made over-sized tennis balls, *thwunk thwunk thwunk.* A few rooms down, an arm flailed over and over against a roof, as if helplessly trying to beat off an attacker. A leg banged sideways against a door. A knee against a steering wheel.

With every retort of limb against metal, I flinched. "Stop!" I wanted to shout. "This is inhuman." Stopped only by the realization that this was precisely the point.

"I don't think I can take much more of this," I said.

Risa smiled sweetly. "It can be hard on the nerves, I know. Come on, I'll take you to see the dummies."

They had their own room. Brightly lit, with bare white walls, it had something of an old-fashioned insane asylum about it, the kind where everyone is so heavily sedated that they slump in their chairs, heads nodding. Seated in rows on metal bleachers, legs splayed, arms akimbo, the dummies looked helplessly, vulnerably human. A few were in wheelchairs, which made them all the more unnerving.

There was a whole tribe of them here—a hundred and fifty-nine in all—each one defined by the laws of averages, of bell curves and norms. The adults ranged in size from tiny fifth percentile females to hulking ninety-fifth percentile males. Two of the females were pregnant. And then there were the kids: six-month-old infants, twelve- and eighteen-month-olds, three-year-olds, six-year-olds. There seemed to be no rhyme or reason in who sat next to whom—or what, I reminded myself, sat next to what—so that something in me wanted to rearrange them, seat the kids next to mothers, the mothers next to fathers, and play happy families in the face of death.

They had names, these dummies, which was disconcerting. There was Sid, for instance, and his relation, Bio-Sid. It took a while to realize that there were many Sids, and that the name was short not for Sidney, but for Side-Impact Dummy. Bio-Sid was a Bio-Fidelic Side-Impact Dummy. The six-month-old was called Crabby, which many parents might empathize with, but in fact it was spelled CRABI, for Child Restraint Air Bag Interaction. Adult frontal-impact dummies had not done so well in the naming game; they were known as Hybrid IIIs. Hybrids I and II, it seemed, had been rudely discontinued.

Their wires and cables were stuffed into plastic shopping bags slung around their necks. "All their earthly possessions," I thought, like in those photos of refugee kids in World War Two, in transit with bags slung over their necks and shoulders, along with their name tags. Even their clothing seemed to have come from some charity organization forced by emergency into random distribution. Heavy black army-surplus shoes stuck out from the end of stick-like legs on the adults; the kids were barefoot, or wore cheap plastic sandals. And all had red or blue shirts of one kind or another, often thermal underwear. "K-Mart's best," Risa assured me.

But the most disturbing thing about them was their faces. They were beautiful. Delicately sculpted in latex and balanced over long necks, they had the smooth mask-like quality of an ancient Egyptian sculpture of Queen Nefertiti. Their blank-eyed gaze had that same serene other-worldliness. Yet behind each face, there was nothing. Or rather, there was metal and wires. The back of each head lay nakedly revealed as the piece of mechanics it was. And staring at these faces, I saw Peter Weller's face in *Robocop:* the beautiful human mask in front, the steely robotic mechanism behind. For the first time since I'd entered the room, I smiled, realizing that Hollywood had stolen a sci-fi image from a Detroit dummy.

"May I touch them?" I asked.

"Sure," said Risa.

I reached very gingerly toward the upturned palm of a fiftieth per-centile female, as though I might insult her by touching her uninvited. My forefinger made contact with the latex surface, oddly cold and almost clammy. I stroked it gently: a strange feeling, so like human skin and at the same time so unlike it.

Tentatively at first, I held the hand in mine. Dummy hand lay limp in human hand, one palm smooth, the other lined. I thought of the old story of the gypsy woman reading a man's hand and, seeing no lines there, knowing that he was about to die. "Poor dummy," I thought, and began to caress the smooth, cold skin, aware even as I was doing it of how very strange it was to reach out and caress a hand without eliciting any response. There was something almost voyeuristic about it.

But now that I knew what a dummy's hand felt like, I wanted to know more. On a nearby table were a few heads being worked on by a technician. I picked one up, and nearly dropped it, surprised by the weight.

The technician nodded. "The average weight of a human head," he said. "Ten pounds." My own head suddenly felt very heavy on my neck.

Beneath the latex was a thick steel frame with a hollow bore in the center of it, for all the instrumentation. It looked just the size of my hand. I cradled the head carefully in my left arm and worked my right hand up into that steel cavity, the sense of transgression growing all the time. It seemed almost obscene to be able to do this, to reach inside a human head. I raised my hand, heavy with the ten-pound weight, and stared at the face impaled on it. It stared blankly off into the distance, totally impervious to the fact that my hand was inside it. Of course it was, I reminded myself. It was just a dummy.

And suddenly I had an extraordinary desire to know what it was like to be a dummy.

I knew it would feel like nothing. What else could it feel like? A dummy had no feelings, just pressure cells that worked only if all the cables were hooked up. But the surreal presence of those silent, serried rows of latex-covered humanoids had induced an odd split between what I knew and what I imagined I could know.

A fiftieth percentile male torso—no head, no limbs—had been propped up on a workbench, shirtless. The latex chest casing had a big zip up the front. I tugged at the top of the zip and peered inside. The casing sat like a snug vest over a perfectly symmetrical steel cage, a dummy equivalent of human ribs. I tugged a bit more at the zip. There ought to be room for me inside a fiftieth percentile male, I reasoned.

Risa and the technician saw what I was about to do. I caught a glimpse of the looks on their faces, and realized I had crossed some line. They weren't sure whether to be amused or sickened. This was weird, their faces said. And from people whose work was crashing cars, I knew it had to be truly weird.

I'd always thought of latex as soft and pliable, but this was extraordinarily stiff, and far thicker than I'd realized. A good half-inch thick, at least, like a bulletproof vest. I had to pull hard on the zip, climbing up onto a chair for leverage and working at it with both hands. It made a tearing noise as I worked it down.

And suddenly it was as though I was unzipping my father's chest, tearing into the flesh and making the long vertical incision of open-heart surgery. I knew for sure now that this was sick, that Risa and her colleague were right to be grossed out. This was weird and irrational and totally inappropriate. And I didn't care. I got the zip undone all the way and set about pulling back the latex so that I could get it off the steel cage, my arms straining with the effort. Had the doctor strained this way, pulling the ribs away from Jessel's chest cavity, exposing the sick heart inside? My vision went blurry and my heart started to pound, but I couldn't stop. I had to get inside this dummy. Get inside the chest casing. Make my heart its heart.

What does it feel like to be a dummy? An idiot question. Or was it? The dummies were supposed to represent us. They were our stand-ins. They took the punishment for us. If I knew there could be no answer, so what? It was like asking what's the sound of one hand clapping—a Zen-like paradox, absurdly sensible. Or perhaps just reasonably absurd.

I worked my right hand through the armhole and eased the casing up onto my shoulder. It hung heavy there, and I stumbled under the weight of it. Risa was looking nervous now, fearful that I'd bend the latex too far and damage it. I knew she'd stop me if she could, but she seemed to realize that something else was going on here.

I struggled to get my left arm through the other side. Neither Risa nor the technician stepped forward to help me. This was a private matter, and they seemed to know it. But the thick latex casing allowed no room for a human arm to slip into place. It had no flexibility. Like Jessel's heart towards the end.

My left shoulder wrenched, flashed with pain, and then I was in. Encased. I had arrived at where I'd wanted to be: virtual flesh weighing down on human flesh. I was inside a dummy.

I zipped up the casing, and closed my eyes. It pressed hard against my chest. When I breathed in, it crushed my ribs. I might as well have been strapped about by steel.

I fought off claustrophobia. Struggled for breath. Imagined myself strapped into the driver's seat, the chamois cloth placed over my face, wires snaking into every joint, cables working their way inside my head. Imagined the countdown, the siren, the hurtling down that long dark tunnel . . .

"Get me out of here," I heard myself saying. Risa and the technician helped, gently prying apart the latex, easing it off my shoulders. I felt very small and fragile without the casing around me.

"Did you find out what you wanted to know?" Risa asked.

Chapter Nineteen

My journey was done; I was home free. I could put away my notebook and laptop, take it easy, relax. Maybe open a bottle of champagne and celebrate. But it's hard to delight in champagne after watching cars crash. And while I may have been home free, I wasn't home.

This simple fact took me by surprise. All along, I had been so focused on getting to Detroit that I hadn't given a moment's thought to how I was going to get home again. I'd achieved my goal, but not my end. And suddenly I wanted that end very badly. I wanted not to have to move anywhere for a long time. Wanted to be where I could settle in and let the rhythm of the road dissolve in my veins. To be sheltered. Safe. Still.

I dug out the Rand McNally road atlas from the back of the truck. Detroit to Seattle: 2,393 miles.

"Stay a while longer," said the friend I'd been staying with. "There's more bad weather coming in. You don't want to drive cross-country through a midwinter storm."

"Why drive at all?" said another. "Fly, and send all your stuff cargo."

But it semed dishonest, somehow, to fly—a kind of cop-out. I couldn't imagine emptying the back of the truck and walking away from it, as though the accumulation of five months and eleven thousand miles could be cleared out, packed up, and shipped off just like that. The Expedition had stayed with me all the way; the least I could do was stay with it to the end, and bring it full circle.

Besides, I wasn't ready for the abrupt dislocation of airplane travel. A few days of being in transit would be the ideal way to wind down. Confined by weather to the interstate, there'd be nothing to do but put the truck on cruise control, follow the thick blue line on the map, sit back and quietly think. It would be a space between the journey and real life, as it were. A place in time to assimilate all that had happened, before the demands of everyday life took hold again.

Had I found what I was looking for? I still wasn't sure. Still replayed in my head the sound of two and a half tons of metal crashing into a million pounds of concrete. I'd heard it twice more that day at Dearborn, but hadn't yet pinned it down. And it seemed terribly important to get it right, to find the words that would perfectly express the flat finality of it. I wanted to be able to say, "This is exactly what a crash sounds like." As though if I could define that sound, I could own it, make it mine, and by doing so, exorcise it.

I knew that the long drive home would itself be a kind of exorcism: one last intense dose of motion, the better to be still when it ended. The weather didn't bother me. If there really was more of it on the way, I reckoned I could handle it. A few years back, I'd spent two days at a winter driving school, racing round a track carved into a snowfield just outside Steamboat Springs, Colorado, and learning high-speed control in the middle of a blizzard. That had been in a regular sedan. Now I had four-wheel-drive, antilock brakes, knowledge and experience and a two-and-a-half-ton truck. And the built-in drama of the long-distance push: "Lone woman races ahead of storm system, intrepid, determined, following the homing instinct through rain and wind and hail and snow, completing her appointed round . . ." The image cheered me. I was full, once again, of brave insouciance.

"An Arctic front headed our way," the newscaster warned on Tuesday night. "We're calling for heavy snow and high winds. This one could be the worst of the season." He seemed to think this was reason not to travel. To me, it was a red flag with a very different meaning: get out quick, before I got stuck. Leave before dawn the next morning, drive like mad for three days, and be home by Friday night.

I'd driven cross-country in three days once before, the spring after I'd moved to Seattle. Having fulfilled a prior commitment to teach one more semester back East, I couldn't wait to get back to my new life out

West. True, that had been in May: the days long and the weather mild. But it seemed I could at least match my own record, especially since that would get me home for the weekend. Not that I had a nine-to-five job and the weekends were my one private time. Nor that I'd told kids and husband that I'd be home by then, or promised to be at a soccer game or a school play. None of the above, and yet the idea of "home for the weekend" glowed comfortingly on the far side of the continent.

Getting up at five on Wednesday morning was no problem; I've never slept well the night before a trip. I packed up the truck in the solitary darkness, the cold so crisp it seemed to ring in my ears. Gobs of frozen slush hung off the underside just as the Bonneville salt had hung off it months before. It caked the wheel wells and the running boards, streaked the metal of the upper body. No point in trying to get it all off now; it'd look just as bad after an hour or two on the highway. I cleaned off the headlights and brake lights, patted the hood, made a silent vow to take the truck twice through the car wash when I got back, and pointed its nose westward for a straight-line dash home.

There were just a few other cars about as I drove through the icy brown slush of Detroit and onto I-94. We were the day's small avant-garde, getting a head start on the rest of the world. Rand McNally lay beside me on the passenger seat, the unwieldy book dog-eared so that I could flip the pages from state to state as I went. No need for larger-scale state maps now. I'd folded them up and stacked them away somewhere in the back of the truck. All I was going to do from here on in was make my way across the pages of the road atlas.

The storm hit before I'd even gotten clear across Michigan. It had been forecast for the early afternoon, but the weathermen had missed by a few hours, and in the wrong direction. By the time I turned south to join I-80 outside Gary, Indiana, the snow had begun, so had Central Time, and so had the rush hour.

I crawled along, as anxious as all the commuters around me. They were losing an hour of work; I was losing an hour of home. I leaned forward over the wheel and peered through the gray snow mist, trying to figure out how long this jam would last. Even as I did it, I knew this was pointless. Visibility was down to less than half a mile, the snow was coming down wet and heavy, and no matter what I might see, I wasn't going to start messing around on back roads in this weather. "Bad timing," said a forecaster on a radio station out of Gary. "A slushy commute to work, and with the mercury falling as the front moves in, it will freeze by the afternoon, making for a truly horrendous evening commute." I had no intention of being around for that.

Go slow and steady, I told myself. Four-wheel-drive all the way. Stop if it gets too bad. You can always hole up in a motel for a day or two. You have your laptop. You have books. You have plenty to think about. Isn't that why you're on the road in the first place? To think? A delay would actually be welcome.

And having thus assured myself that I was capable of being sensible, felt free not to be.

South of Chicago, the snow let up for a while. The radio told me it was only a temporary respite, but that was okay: I'd be long gone by the time it started again. And if the road ahead was clear, I could make up the lost time, get well west of the storm system, and bunk down for the night once I was sure I was beyond its reach.

I was heading for the Mississippi now, "Morning Edition" playing over and over on the radio as I passed from one public radio station's reach to the next, so that the broadcast seemed to be on continuous rewind. The sky still hung low and gray over the earth, but there hadn't been any new snow for a couple of hours. I came down the low hill toward the river. It was nothing like I remembered it. Memory had endowed it with the breadth and grandeur that the boundary between East and Midwest should surely have. But today the river was a grayish white, packed with ice floes; if you didn't know it was there, your eye could imagine it was just a valley, snowed in like the low hills either side.

I drove over the bridge and into Iowa, and just as my spirits began to pick up, saw the first exit sign: Exit 306. That meant 306 miles to go to Nebraska. Mile upon mile of straight, flat highway.

I'd forgotten the exhausting length of the Plains states. Had been betrayed by Messrs. Rand and McNally into thinking them far smaller than they were. Squashed into one page, maximum two, the states had been cut down to size. I could see each one at a glance, and it seemed I could zip right across the page in a couple of hours at the outside. Just follow that blue interstate line, the road atlas's yellow brick road. So simple, so easy, except that the real road was made of snow- and ice-covered concrete and asphalt.

And now the tyranny of miles began to assert itself. The interstate syndrome took over. Driving was reduced to computation—time, speed, and distance in constant calibration—as though if I could account for every mile and every minute, I'd get there faster. I was playing games with time as though I could reshape it to my purpose. As though I could literally make time.

The numbers weighed heavy in my consciousness. Their presence couldn't be ignored. Each exit sign blared the number of miles remaining in the state. They taunted me with the knowledge of how far I had yet to go. If I could only get a good start. Get a healthy chunk behind me on this first day. Reach Omaha, Nebraska, then relax. Then I could take it easy the second day and the third. Then I'd know I had it in the bag.

I stuck at a steady sixty miles an hour, the same speed as the big semis whose tracks I was following, and by mid-afternoon came near Iowa City. My head had begun to ache with numbers, my eyes with the constant vision of grayish whiteness. I thought of stopping. A friend's mother lived nearby; I could call from the next truck stop and beg shelter for the night. But that would mean committing myself to a four-day drive instead of a three-day one. I wasn't ready to do that yet, and I was too tired to stop and ask myself why. Besides, it would be silly to stop in daylight. There was still an hour and a half of it left. If I got a second wind and drove an hour or two into the dark, I could make it over the Missouri to Nebraska. Then I'd be right by the center fold of the full United States route map. Close enough to persuade myself that I was back West.

I counted down the exits. Past Iowa City at 245 and 244, and daylight began to fade. An hour later it was dark, and the snow began again: the going slow, visibility down. I hunched forward over the wheel as though the few inches' difference would let my eyes penetrate the murk. Another hour, and I was still a hundred and fifty miles short of Omaha.

I gave up, turned off near Des Moines at Exit 131, and sought refuge in a motel. I'd driven 619 miles from Detroit. Not nearly as far as I'd wanted.

Everything in me ached. Shoulders, back, thighs, arms, head. I found a freshly plowed parking spot and limped into the lobby, willing to pay whatever they asked, which turned out to be their normal rate. Dumped my overnight case on one of the two double beds, soaked a good half-hour in the tub, went downstairs and got a soggy hamburger and pale lettuce in the fake wood-paneled restaurant, then went back upstairs and stood staring moodily out at the snow, wondering if I was trapped in this overheated motel room with its pilled brown carpet. The snow was coming down with an ominous steadiness, molding the Expedition and the other vehicles in the parking lot into soft mounds. An occasional car went by on the road, its wheels swishing against the white buildup, but other than that, there was no sound. If the interstate was still open, I couldn't hear it.

I wished I could think the snow beautiful. Wished I still had that delight in it I remembered as a kid. The delight the third-graders had written about in their last bunch of letters, which had been waiting for me when I'd gone home for Christmas.

A swarm of origami snowflakes had poured out of the packet as I'd opened it, followed by snapshots. Nancy had taken photos of each child separately, and I studied the shy, gap-toothed smiles, putting faces together with names, amazed at so much life where I felt mired in death.

> Hi it's me Alberto and guess what we had a big blizrd and
> at my house all the lights went out and outside I made an
> igleu and we distrored it and bilt another igleu.

They wrote about snowmen and snowballs and snow forts. Bianca had made a snow heart. Kristin had had a hard time in the snow:

> Yesterday it was a snow day and I played in the snow and
> when I came in I had hotchocolate. When I was playing
> some snow in the trees fell right on the tip top of my head so
> now I got a very big bruise on my head.

They were full of news and plans. Hans had found a puppy shivering under the porch; he'd taken it in and named it Sam. Danny and Colt had been running a toy car derby; Danny had won. Heather was going to Disneyland for Christmas, Alberto to Mexico, Kristin to Los Angeles. Jorge's family had been planning to go to Detroit, where a great-uncle of his father's had painted murals. "His nem Diego Rivera." But the trip had been postponed, for which I was sorry: I'd have stayed in Detroit for a chance to stand with Jorge in the Institute of Arts, looking at Rivera's magnificent frescoes of autoworkers with muscles bulging out of rolled-up shirtsleeves, still wearing their fedoras as they strained to feed the gleaming machines of production.

And then there was what would evidently be the last letter from Kameron, she who liked to eat snow and went to visit her father for her birthday:

> My grandma is in the hospital. I think my grandma is not
> going to make it. I am very sad for my grandma. I am going
> to my dads house for a long time.

Sure enough, Nancy wrote that Kameron was leaving. Martin had been moved into another class, and I missed him; I'd enjoyed his flow of questions. There were two newcomers: Karla, who wrote a five-page letter in a language all her own, neither Spanish nor English but an eager imitation of the act of communication rather than the content of it, and David, who had "a new baby brothre" who'd been baptized in a snowstorm "and a snowflak fell on his head and my dad said it was a good sin."

A sign, of course, not a sin, but either way, it was indeed a good one. And now as I stood by the window in this stuffy motel room and stared at snow falling with what seemed to me malign persistence, I wondered if it had been snowing that night many years ago when my father had baptized a child.

I'd heard about it for the first time just after the funeral. "I have something to tell you that Jessel confided in me," said a colleague with whom he'd worked on an interfaith committee. "He wanted to know if he was right in what he did, and though I assured him he was, I'm not sure he ever accepted it. But it's something I think you would like to know about him."

I was still a child at the time. He'd gone out on another of those many middle-of-the-night emergency calls, to deliver a baby. The infant was born with the umbilical cord wrapped around its neck, half-dead; my father called for an ambulance and did what he could meanwhile, but the weather was bad and there was no way the ambulance would get there in time. The parents, believing Catholics, were distraught: not only was their newborn about to die, but he would die unbaptized. So my father, a God-fearing, observant Jew, made the sign of the cross over the baby, said the appropriate words, concluded with "In the name of the Father, and of the Son, and of the Holy Ghost, Amen," and stayed and watched with them until the ambulance came, too late.

It was the quintessential Jessel story. That spontaneous act of kindness and generosity would haunt him the rest of his life, wondering if he hadn't committed the ultimate transgression not only against his own faith, but against that of others. He had betrayed his faith for a much greater one—in humanity instead of in a jealous God—and then questioned his own humanity for the rest of his life.

★

I woke at six in the morning and turned on the local news. Primary reds and yellows and blues bounced out of the ageing television screen and off the dingy brown carpet and walls, an assault of color after the endless gray of the day before. It seemed I'd left havoc in my trail. The storm had closed interstates and airports in the Chicago area, bringing everything to a standstill. Here in Iowa it wasn't so bad. The snow had stopped, and no more was forecast. There was only one small problem: "Our high this Thursday in central Iowa will be zero degrees Fahrenheit. The low, with wind chill, about minus forty."

The precise chilly emptiness of that zero was what hit me. The only rational response to such an absurd forecast seemed to be to get out quick. I could hear the big semis running on the interstate, so I knew it was passable. Just stay in their tracks. Drive in the slush made by the friction of their tires on the roadway. Head west for warmth. Maybe even make it as far as Salt Lake City.

I set off in the predawn dark, bundled in parka over Polartec vest, boots over double socks, a wool scarf wrapped around my head and a hat clamped over the scarf. And the heater on. The sun was up by the time I reached the Missouri. Like the Mississippi behind me, the river was an icy mass, all but indistinguishable from the whited-out landscape around it. The sky turned to a blue so pale it was a painful glare, and I added sunglasses to my get-up.

Exit 454, said the first sign for Omaha. My heart went heavy. Four hundred and fifty-four miles to be gone over, to be ticked off, one by one, on the odometer and under the wheels, sign by sign, exit by exit.

Most of Nebraska was a white blank to Rand and McNally; so was the next state, Wyoming. White on the map, and white in reality, the vast high plains snowed in under that cold pale sky as I followed the line of the Platte River past Lincoln, Grand Island, Kearney, North Platte. There was nothing for the eye to distinguish but the occasional green of a road sign. And then the radio began to give me another set of numbers to dial into my computations of time, speed, and distance. With each weather update on the radio, each new station's broadcast area entered as the previous one dissolved into static, the mercury was rising.

Nine degrees, twelve, sixteen . . . As the temperatures rose, so too did my spirits. Sixteen Fahrenheit seemed like springtime after zero. I could see the Rockies in the distance, low ridges from this far away but at least visible, and if visible, reachable. I passed the sign announcing the beginning of the Mountain Time zone—an extra hour of daylight driving, a gift from the gods of the clock—and counted down the towns on the Nebraska map. Hardly towns at all, but hamlets of five thousand people or fewer, made significant purely by the white emptiness in which they were placed: Ogallala, Sidney, Kimball . . .

Kimball? A town of some twenty-five hundred souls that was only in the road atlas because there was nothing else for miles in any direction. Kimball it would be, then: my goal for an hour as I checked clock against speedometer against odometer against exit signs, cross-checking and cross-referencing the inevitable and immutable as though by doing so, I could bring the town closer. Then I was there—a sole exit, a truck stop, a moment of puzzlement at where twenty-four hundred of those twenty-five hundred souls could be—only to forget the town ever existed as I flashed on by and it was swallowed into the past of miles already traveled. All that existed was the future, miles still to be traveled, towns and cities still to be attained, then flashed past, and in turn forgotten.

My new goal was Cheyenne, Wyoming, coming near as Nebraska rolled to a close beneath my wheels. There was the pathetic excitement of seeing the exit numbers drop into the double digits, then the single ones. And then I'd made it, over the border into Wyoming, celebrating like a fugitive fleeing the grasp of the state police, only to be faced with the appalling vision of a sign saying Exit 401.

But the sky was a clear blue now, and the mountains shining jaggedly in front of me, and I was headed for Cheyenne and then Laramie, mythical names from a childhood mesmerized by Westerns. Beethoven's Sixth came on the radio, the Pastoral Symphony out of Cheyenne, and if pastoral wasn't quite the word for this high ranching country, it made no difference after what I'd driven through to get here. I swayed along with the music, conducted the orchestra, opened my mouth wide and sang out the violin sections, serenaded the mountains as I climbed up through the first hills.

The concert ended, and there was a weather flash—high winds on the east slopes of the Rockies—but I'd been through worse than a bit of wind already. The words "forty miles an hour" only registered somewhere past Cheyenne, as the air began to blast from my left. Two and a half tons of metal veered to the right under the force of it. I began to drive with a permanent correction set into the wheel, steering slightly into the wind to keep in a straight line, like a pilot crabbing in to land against a crosswind. Forty-mile-an-hour air found every chink in the truck and came whistling through, icy bullets piercing my leggings and stinging my knees. No ballistic protection here. Metal that had seemed so solid was suddenly as thin and ineffectual as a hand-me-down cloth coat. I gazed out at the slopes, vast whitenesses interrupted by stark black buttes swept clean of snow by the blasting wind. How long would I last outside the truck? Twenty minutes, maybe? Ten?

The wind whipped curling wisps of powdery snow across the road. They looked like long white snakes writhing over the asphalt, so many of them that they all but covered it. I fought the illusion that the road itself was writhing beneath my wheels, but it only got stronger as the snow snakes multiplied, piling one on top of another. Then the surface of the road disappeared as the snakes covered it entirely, and kept rising, dozens and then hundreds of them forming and falling apart and forming again, wriggling higher and higher, a foot deep, then two, then waist high. The whole road was alive now, in sinuous motion, and the only way to tell I was still on the asphalt was by searching for the tips of the guideposts along the side, finding my way from one amber reflector to the next. A powdery mist rose up either side of the truck, while all the time, directly above me, the sky was a clear blue.

I was simultaneously awed and entranced, terrified and exhilarated. Stopping was out of the question: I could see nothing beyond the next amber reflector. If I tried to pull off the road, I risked going headlong down a mountainside. If I stayed on the asphalt and stopped, I'd be rear-ended by the next fool driving this stretch. There was no choice but to keep going, in the blind, dumb faith that the snow snakes wouldn't rise higher still and wipe out all vision.

And then, abruptly, it ended. Just short of Laramie, the wind eased, the snow snakes disappeared, the road was clear, and I was through. Three thirty in the afternoon and no chance of making Salt Lake City with my eyes open, but at least if I could make it over the Continental Divide . . .

Speeding now, racing oncoming darkness, the mountains turning pink and orange and purple in the dying sun, and by five it was dark and I was just past Rawlins, the east fork of the Divide at 6,755 feet. I drove on over the great high plateau at the top of the Rockies, no stopping me now, following the clear tracks made by semis through the compact snow and ice, going seventy through the luminous darkness, the moon picking out silhouettes of peaks, shining silver on the snow, night driving easy with so much ambient light around me and few headlights in my eyes. I was riding high on top of the world now, over the west fork of the Divide at Table Rock, until the exhaustion finally hit and I knew for certain I'd never make Salt Lake that night. I turned in at Rock Springs, still in Wyoming. I'd driven 755 miles since the morning, and was still a thousand miles from home.

I ate supper at a restaurant with walls covered in hunting trophies, one of each: bison, elk, moose, deer, jack rabbit, cougar, bear . . . Took a table with a phone on the wall beside it, truck-stop style, and started calling, trying to shake off the feeling of being under siege, assaulted by numbers, by miles and minutes. Trying to assure myself that I was still here, still connected to normal life, even if only by long-distance wires.

I called New York, Seattle, Los Angeles, telling friends about snakes on the road and heads on the walls. They sounded worried. "Drive carefully," they all said.

"Don't worry, I'll be fine," I replied each time. "I'm well past the worst of it. I'll get a good night's sleep here and make it a four-day trip, I promise."

Not all believed me. "Beware of get-homeitis," said a flying friend in Seattle, using the pilot's term for the illusion of metallic invulnerability. You persuade yourself you can handle low clouds and icing conditions, that it's not as bad as it looks and the forecasters have got it all wrong and you can be home when you said you would. The power of the engine helps foster this illusion, and it's a self-fulfilling one. The more you fly without mishap, the more you convince yourself that you can handle anything that might happen. Until suddenly you can't.

"It's not get-homeitis," I assured him. "I'll stop when I get too tired. I know enough by now to be sensible."

Knowing the lie even as I spoke it.

The road was inside me. It was imprinted on my eyelids as I closed my eyes. In my blood, thrumming, as I lay waiting for sleep. My body was attuned to motion. My mind focused on that thousand miles to home.

I slept badly, woke at six thirty on Friday morning, and was on the road again by seven. I knew it was too much to hope for, but maybe, just maybe, if the weather was good and the road was clear and the gods of caffeine were on my side, I could make Seattle that night. Impossible, stupid, ridiculous . . . Yes, yes, I knew all that. But I'd taken on the road-warrior status conferred by long spells of nonstop driving. Dream the impossible dream. No pain, no gain. Go, girl. Just do it.

Down from Rock Springs I went, down the western slopes of the Rockies and into Utah and on down toward the Great Salt Lake. A moment's hesitation—the Sundance Film Festival was on in Park City, not much farther down I-80, and a neighbor had a movie showing there. But I'd never find him, let alone a room, and in any case I didn't really want to stop. I turned north on I-84. A quick breakfast in Ogden, then I skirted the lake, hidden as always in haze, and went on up toward Twin Falls, Idaho, the point where I'd turned south five months before, heading for Bonneville. From here on in, it was familiar territory. A road driven twice in five months: what could be easier?

I listened, amazed, as the temperature rose with each newscast: twenty-nine, thirty . . . I felt like cheering out loud when it reached thirty-two. Then thirty-four, thirty-five, thirty-seven . . . I stopped outside Boise for a late lunch and danced around in the parking lot of the diner: shed scarf and gloves, unzipped parka and vest, spread my arms wide in amazement at how mild it was—all of three degrees above freezing.

It would all be easy going now, the storm outrun and the mercury rising and the snow and ice dissolving to clear pavement. Plus, as I crossed into Oregon, the gift of an extra hour of daylight with the start of the Pacific Time zone. I was in the next-door state to home and my mouth almost watered at the thought of it. I could practically feel the texture of the broadloom carpet under my bare feet, the silky luxury of the Persian rug in the bathroom, the firm softness of my own bed. I could smell the scent of rosemary and lavender out on the deck. Hear the splashes of ducks and cormorants diving for food. See light refracted from the water playing on the wooden ceiling.

The road rose into the Wallowa Range—easy now, snow up here—and I drove warily over Ladd Pass, at four thousand feet. But the snow had turned to slush, and the going was relatively easy. Maybe I really could make Seattle by the end of the day.

Down in La Grande, nestled between two passes, I stopped for coffee and another bite to eat. The diner was full of truckers working the phones, checking with their dispatchers, swapping information about road conditions. "Bad over Ladd Pass," my neighbor at the counter said.

"I just came over Ladd. It was fine."

"Yeah? Where you heading?"

"Seattle."

"When you aim to get there by?"

"Maybe this evening."

"Might be pushing your luck. Next pass on, Meacham, they're slipping and sliding all over the place."

"You just came over?"

"No, but that's what I hear. And freezing rain over the Cascades."

His face gaunt and lined, the face of a man to whom the worst always happens. His fingers tapped nervously on the counter. His cheek twitched. Too much speed, it looked like. The kind that comes in pills. Bad for the nerves.

It was four in the afternoon and I'd been on the road nine hours. Make that ten, including the time change. I really should stop soon. Maybe over the next pass.

On top of Meacham, a little snow was falling, but nothing serious. I came down the long, steep, switchback descent toward the Umatilla Indian Reservation in low gear, with not a slip or a slide. The big trucks, all chained up, seemed to be doing fine too. After that pilled-up trucker back in La Grande, I'd expected to see them belly-up by the side of the road or jackknifed across it. "The wimp," I thought. "The whiner."

Only some three hundred miles to home now. I ran through them in my mind: across the Columbia River and up through Yakima to Ellensburg, then over the Cascades on I-90 and the quick, final run downhill into Seattle. A four-hour drive. Okay, five. Maximum.

I could be home by ten, maybe eleven. Just time to dump everything inside the door and drift off into a long sleep in my own bed, secure in the knowledge that I'd have no driving to do when I woke up, no more road ahead of me. And come the morning I'd ignore the bags and boxes strewn around me on the floor, make myself anything I wanted to eat or drink, stretch out on the green leather sofa with my head on one arm, my feet up on the other, and call friends and say the words I'd been longing to say for the past three days: "I'm back."

And suddenly the very idea of one more night in a motel room was unbearable. The weary brown carpet, the towels thin and grayed with use, the bottle stains on the table, the yellow sodium lights piercing the edges of the drapes, televisions blaring and toilets flushing either side of me while I tossed around trying to sleep despite the road inside in my head, knowing that at that very moment I could have been pulling up outside home . . .

No, pointless. I was so close, it would be foolish not to continue. Not so hard to keep going another four or five hours, not after three days. Load up with a triple espresso at Pendleton. Grab a couple of sandwiches. Order another triple to go. Turn the radio up loud, country music foot-tapping twanging. Open the window a couple of inches. All set to go.

Over the Columbia and into Washington State. Home territory. The temperature thirty-six, safely above freezing. Rain falling as I wound upward into the hills above the river on I-82, two lanes either side of a concrete median divider. Just me and the big semis in the dark and the wet, going the distance. I picked up a public radio station relaying out of Yakima. Coming up, said the announcer, the next in a rebroadcast of Terry Gross's *Fresh Air* interviews with the members of Monty Python. This evening, John Cleese.

I smiled in anticipation. What more could I want after thirteen thousand miles? Only another three hours to go, my favorite Python on the radio, the comforting knowledge that I'd sleep that night in my own bed.

I moved into the outside lane to overtake yet another big semi. The rain pattered on the windshield, familiar and reassuring. The asphalt glistened in the headlights. John Cleese laughed. I was as good as home . . .

ACKNOWLEDGMENTS

My deepest thanks to the many people who made this book possible, starting with Norah Vincent, the commissioning editor, and William Zinsser, who suggested I write it. Judith Muhlberg, director of Ford Automotive Operations Public Affairs, kindly arranged for the loan of the Ford Expedition, which was indeed an excellent narrative vehicle; I just wish I could have returned it in better shape. Former motorcycle land-speed record-holder Dennis Manning brought me up to speed on his sport with humor and frankness, and Louise-Ann Noeth, aka Land-speed Louise, kept me up to date on new developments. Keith Martin shepherded me through the intricacies of the collector-car world at Pebble Beach with balletic expertise, while Chrysler and Mercedes-Benz were splendidly hospitable. I've never had such a good time with a film crew as I did with Talking Turkey Pictures director Ned Judge, cameraman Dale Sonnenberg, production manager Margaret Ersheler, and soundman Scott Carrier. Sue Mead gave generous moral support and technical know-how on off-roading, and in Ojai, George Walczak and Liz Norris-Walczak were the best company a wandering soul could ask for. Special thanks to Jonathan Mark for his support in extremis in Houston, to British Airways for their willingness to go out of their way to help me in an emergency, and to my Good Samaritan, Ed Gantz. In Detroit, Christine Anderson and Paul Eisenstein were generous hosts, while Mike Sante, business editor of the *Detroit Free Press,* gave both support and understanding.

In Seattle, I am immensely grateful to my friends and neighbors

Ann Bassetti and Gene Nutt, without whose logistical support I could never have taken off for as long as I did. Also to the reference staff of the Seattle Public Library, who fielded queries with unerring goodwill and efficiency.

"Will we be in your book?" asked the members of Nancy Cole's third-grade class at Sierra House Elementary School in South Lake Tahoe, California, when I finally met them at the end of the school year. "All of us? Our full names?" But of course. I could not have asked for better virtual companions than Christopher Aguilar, Billy Beal, Colton Becker, Kristen Dore, Chad Hawkes, David Hunt, Daniel Jolley, Niles Kallenbach, Bianca Lopez, Mireya Lopez, Alberto Marin, Jessica Mariscal, Karla Mendoza, Diana Meza, Heather Newman, Jorge Orozco Jr., Ricky Paradzinski, Allyson Ritchie, Martin Rubio, Hans Van Housen, Kameron Vindiola, Rogelio Vivas, and Joey Walker. My heartfelt thanks to them, and very best wishes for their futures.

Finally, special thanks to Free Press editorial director Liz Maguire, to her assistant Chad Conway, to Aaron Hamburger of Watkins-Loomis, and as always, to my good friend Gloria Loomis, agent nonpareil.